Consumer Culture and Postmodernism

Theory, Culture & Society

Theory, Culture & Society caters for the resurgence of interest in culture within contemporary social science and the humanities. Building on the heritage of classical social theory, the book series examines ways in which this tradition has been reshaped by a new generation of theorists. It also publishes theoretically informed analyses of everyday life, popular culture and new intellectual movements.

EDITOR: Mike Featherstone, *Nottingham Trent University*

SERIES EDITORIAL BOARD
Roy Boyne, *University of Durham*
Mike Hepworth, *University of Aberdeen*
Scott Lash, *Goldsmiths College, University of London*
Roland Robertson, *University of Aberdeen*
Bryan S. Turner, *National University of Singapore*

THE TCS CENTRE
The Theory, Culture & Society book series, the journals *Theory, Culture & Society* and *Body & Society*, and related conference, seminar and postgraduate programmes operate from the TCS Centre at Nottingham Trent University. For further details of the TCS Centre's activities please contact:

The TCS Centre
School of Arts and Humanities
Nottingham Trent University
Clifton Lane, Nottingham NG11 8NS, UK
email: tcs@ntu.ac.uk
web: http://sagepub.net/tcs/

Recent volumes include:

Informalization: Manners and Emotions Since 1890
Cas Wouters

The Culture of Speed: The Coming of Immediacy
John Tomlinson

The Dressed Society: Clothing, the Body and Some Meanings of the World
Peter Corrigan

Advertising in Modern and Postmodern Times
Pamela Odih

Consumer Culture and Postmodernism

2nd edition

Mike Featherstone

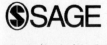

Los Angeles | London | New Delhi
Singapore | Washington DC

First published 2007
Reprinted 2009, 2010, 2011

SAGE Publications Ltd
1 Oliver's Yard
55 City Road
London EC1Y 1SP

SAGE Publications Inc.
2455 Teller Road
Thousand Oaks, California 91320

SAGE Publications India Pvt Ltd
B 1/I 1 Mohan Cooperative Industrial Area
Mathura Road
New Delhi 110 044

SAGE Publications Asia-Pacific Pte Ltd
33 Pekin Street #02-01
Far East Square
Singapore 048763

Library of Congress Control Number: 2007922932

British Library Cataloguing in Publication data

A catalogue record for this book is available from the British Library

ISBN 978-1-4129-1013-2
ISBN 978-1-4129-1014-9 (pbk)

Typeset by C&M Digital (P) Ltd., Chennai, India
Printed in Great Britain by Ashford Colour Press Ltd, Gosport, Hampshire

For Edna, Claire and John

Contents

Preface to the First Edition

I first became interested in consumer culture in the late 1970s. The stimulus was the writings of members of the Frankfurt School and other proponents of Critical Theory which were featured and discussed so well in journals like *Telos* and *New German Critique*. The theories of the culture industry, reification, commodity fetishism and the instrumental rationalization of the world directed attention away from a focus on production towards consumption and processes of cultural change. These various conceptualizations were particularly helpful to me in understanding an area which has long been undertheorized – at least in terms of attention directed at it by social and cultural theorists – the study of ageing. Despite the important theoretical problems it raises in terms of the intersection of lived time and historical time, the generational experience, the relationship of body and self, etc., it was clear that few attempts had been made to explore these problems in relation to substantive processes of cultural change. The writing of critical theorists and others (especially Ewen, 1976) seemed to provide a useful bridge by directing attention to the role of the media, advertising, images, the Hollywood ideal etc., and raised the question of their effects on identity formation and everyday practices. At this time I was writing a book with Mike Hepworth (Hepworth and Featherstone, 1982) on the redefinition of middle age as a more active phase of 'middle youth', and an explanation which pointed to the development of new markets and the extension of active consumer-culture lifestyles with their emphasis upon youth, fitness and beauty to this group seemed plausible. This became explicitly formulated in a paper entitled 'Ageing and Inequality: Consumer Culture and the Redefinition of Middle Age' presented at the 1981 British Sociological Association Conference (Featherstone and Hepworth, 1982). It was followed by a more theoretical piece 'The Body in Consumer Culture' (Featherstone, 1982) and subsequently a special issue of the journal *Theory, Culture & Society* on Consumer Culture in 1983.

Today while there has been a steady growth of interest in, and use of the term, 'consumer culture', the theories of Adorno, Horkheimer, Marcuse and other critical theorists are no longer accorded great significance. Their approach is often presented as an elitist critique of mass culture which draws upon what are now regarded as dubious distinctions between real and pseudo individuality and true and false needs. They are generally regarded as looking down on the debased mass culture and as having little sympathy for the integrity of the popular classes' pleasures. The latter position has been strongly endorsed by the swing to postmodernism. Yet despite the populist turn in analyses of consumer culture some of the questions raised by the critical theorists such as 'how to discriminate between cultural values', 'how to make aesthetic judgements', and their relation to the practical questions of 'how we should live', it can be argued have not actually been superseded but have merely been put aside.

Of interest here is the reflexive point which emerges most strongly in the chapters on postmodernism: the question of relevance: how and why we choose a particular frame of reference and evaluative perspective. If the study of consumption and concepts such as consumer culture manage to push their way into the mainstream of social science and cultural studies conceptual apparatus, what does this mean? How is it that the study of consumption and culture – both incidentally until recently previously designated as derivative, peripheral' and feminine, as against the centrality which was accorded to the more masculine sphere of production and the economy – are granted a more important place in the analysis of social relations and cultural representations? Is it that we have moved to a new stage of intra- or inter-societal organization in which both culture and consumption play a more crucial role? Variants of this thesis can be found in the writings of Bell, Baudrillard and Jameson which are discussed in this volume. Yet in addition to this plausible assumption that we have moved into a stage of 'capitalism' (consumer capitalism), 'industrialization' (post-industrial or information society) or 'modernity' (high modernity or postmodernity) which is sufficiently new and distinctive to warrant a new concept to redirect our attention, we must also face the possibility that it is not the 'reality' which has changed, but our perception of it. This latter viewpoint is captured in the epigram by Max Weber which heads the final chapter 'Each sees what is in his own heart'. We therefore need to investigate the processes of concept-formation and de-formation among cultural specialists (artists, intellectuals. academics and intermediaries), This directs our attention towards the particular processes which take place within the specialist cultural field and its various subfields: the struggles between established and outsider groups to monopolize and stabilize symbolic hierarchies. It is only by attempting to understand the changing practices interdependencies and power balances of culture specialists which influence the production of specialist culture, in the restricted sense of cultural models, interpretations, conceptual apparatuses, pedagogies and commentaries, that we can better understand our modes of perception and evaluation of culture 'out there'. This problem, that of the interrelationship between the changing nature of the various specialist formulations of culture and the various regimes of signification and practices which make up the fabric of everyday lived culture is not only important in understanding the swing towards positive and negative evaluations of mass, popular and consumer cultures. but also, I would argue, is central to the understanding of postmodernism. In my case, my interest in postmodernism was the outgrowth of the problems encountered in attempting to understand consumer culture, and the need to explore the direct links made between consumer culture and postmodernism by Bell, Jameson, Baudrillard, Bauman and others.

A number of the chapters in this volume therefore also illustrate my concern to come to terms with the perplexing set of problems posed by the rise of the postmodern. They attempt to investigate the postmodern not only as a cultural movement (postmodernism) produced by artists, intellectuals and other cultural specialists, but also inquire into how this restricted sense of postmodernism relates to alleged broader cultural shifts in everyday experiences and practices which can be deemed postmodern. This relationship cannot merely be assumed to be one in which cultural specialists play a passive role as particularly well-attuned receivers, articulators and interpreters of signs and traces of cultural change. Their active role and interest in educating and forming audiences which become sensitized to interpreting particular sets of experiences and artefacts via the label postmodern, must also be investigated. This also points to the salience of the changing interdependencies and power struggles between cultural specialists and other groups of specialists (economic, political, administrative and cultural intermediaries) which influence their capacity to monopolize and de-monopolize knowledge, means of orientation and cultural goods. In short we need to ask not only the question 'what is the postmodern?' but why and how we are concerned with this particular question. We need, therefore, to inquire into the conditions of possibility for the positive reception of the concept of the postmodern and its emergence as a powerful cultural image, irrespective of the actual cultural changes and social processes which some would wish to foreground as evidence of the postmodern: the alleged shift beyond the modern.

While it may be quite legitimate to work from a high level of abstraction and label a particular large slice of Western history as 'modernity', defined in terms of a specific set of characteristics, and then assume that we have moved away from this core towards something else, as yet ill-defined, there is the danger that, the more the opposite set of features initially formulated as the negativity of modernity is considered, the more it begins to take on a tantalizing life of its own and seems to be made real. Those whose gaze was formerly directed by images and figures of order, coherence and systematic unity, now learn to look through new cognitive frameworks emphasizing disorder, ambiguity and difference. It is then not a large step towards 'postmodernity': a term which carries the weight of a fundamental epochal shift which becomes accorded credibility with a set of deductions from equally speculative terminology such as post-industrial or information society listed to support it. There is nothing wrong with high level speculative theory except if it becomes presented and legitimated as having surpassed, or succeeded in discrediting the need for, empirical research. Unfortunately this would sometimes seem to have happened with the term 'postmodern' and its family of associates. In effect some would argue that the implications of postmodernism are that we must seek to discredit and abandon the old methodologies and not attempt to account for the postmodern, rather we should practise postmodernism and formulate a postmodern sociology.

A central intention then in this volume is to understand how postmodernism has arisen and become such a powerful and influential cultural image. This is not to assume that postmodernism is merely a deliberate 'artificial' construct of disaffected intellectuals out to increase their own power potential. Far from it. Rather it is to raise questions about the production, transmission and dissemination of knowledge and culture. The various chapters also take the experiences and practices designated as postmodernism seriously and seek to investigate and comprehend the range of phenomena associated with this category. Yet, once we focus on actual experiences and practices, it is clear that there are similarities between these alleged postmodern experiences and practices and many of those designated as modern (in the sense of *modernité*), and even premodern. This should therefore direct us away from some of the simple dichotomies and trichotomies suggested by the terms 'tradition', 'modern' and 'postmodern' and also lead us to consider similarities and continuities in experiences and practices which can effectively be regarded as trans-modern (and its associated category: *transmodernité*). It is such theoretical issues, the problems of conceptualization and definition necessary to comprehend the alleged salience or expansion of the role of culture within contemporary societies which make the question of the postmodern so intriguing.

Such theoretical questions about the relationship of culture to society, which imply that we have too long operated with an overtly social conception of social structures and suggest that our general conception of culture is in need of major revision. have emerged in the 1980s. Indeed it is difficult to separate the question of the postmodern from the noticeable rise of interest in theorizing culture, which has propelled it from a peripheral status towards the centre of the various academic fields. This has also been reflected in the attention we have given to postmodernism in *Theory, Culture & Society* in a number of special issues. Our attention in the first place was directed towards the 'debates' between Habermas and Foucault which prompted me to construct a special issue of *TCS* around the question of 'The Fate of Modernity' (1985, 2(3)). It became clear in the planning of this issue and the subsequent response that the question of postmodernism needed a much broader and fuller treatment. This occurred in the double special issue on 'Postmodernism' (1988, 5(2–3)). I recall a good deal of scepticism at the time about whether postmodernism was merely a passing fad or fashionable theme of short duration. Postmodernism has surely now outlived the duration of a fad, and shows signs of remaining a powerful cultural image for some time yet. This is a very good reason for social scientists and others to be interested in it. Yet whether from this impulse there emerge useful social scientific conceptualizations of the postmodern which can be integrated into the current conceptual armoury, or even surpass it and point to the emergence of, or need for, new modes of conceptualization and cognitive frameworks, remains to be seen. As it stands, we cannot but welcome the emergence of the postmodern for the range of social and cultural theoretical problems it has thrown up.

I would like to thank all my colleagues and friends involved in *Theory, Culture & Society* for their help and encouragement in putting together this book. In particular I have discussed many of the ideas at length with Mike Hepworth, Roland Robertson and Bryan S. Turner and I much appreciate their support. I would also like to acknowledge the encouragement and help of Stephen Barr, Zygmunt Bauman, Steve Best, Josef Bleicher, Roy Boyne, David Chaney, Norman Denzin, the late Norbert Elias, Jonathan Friedman, the late Hans Haferkamp, Doug Kellner, Richard Kilminster, Arthur Kroker, Scott Lash, Hans Mommaas, Stephen Mennell, Carlo Mongardini, Georg Stauth, the late Friedrich Tenbruck, Willem van Reijen, Andy Wernick, Cas Wouters and the late Derek Wynne, with whom I've discussed many of the issues raised in this volume. In addition I must mention the generous support given by my colleagues in the Department of Administrative and Social Studies at Teesside Polytechnic and in particular the role of Laurence Tasker and Oliver Coulthard who provided the institutional support and encouragement which has helped to make *Theory, Culture & Society* a viable journal, and has been so crucial in nourishing and sustaining my interest in the postmodern. I would also like to thank Jean Connell, Marlene Melber and the Data Preparation Section for so patiently keying in the many versions of the various chapters.

The chapters have appeared in the following previous versions:

1 'Modern and Postmodern: Definitions and Interpretations' was given at seminars at Goldsmiths College, London University in February 1988, Trent University, Peterborough, Ontario in March 1988 and at the Amalfi European Prize for Sociology Conference in Amalfi, Italy in May 1988. A further version was given at the Centro de Investigacao y Estudos de Sociologia, Lisbon, June 1989. A version of it appeared as 'In Pursuit of the Postmodern', *Theory, Culture & Society* 5(2–3), 1988.

2 'Theories of Consumer Culture' is a revised version of the paper 'Perspectives on Consumer Culture' which first appeared in *Sociology*, 24(1), 1990.

3 'Towards a Sociology of Postmodern Culture' was presented at a seminar at Leeds University in May 1987 and at the European Sociological Theories Group Conference on Social Structure and Culture in Bremen in June 1987. It has appeared in H. Haferkamp (ed.), *Social Structure and Culture*, Berlin: de Gruyter, 1989 and in H. Haferkamp (ed.), *Sozial Struktur und Kultur*, Berlin: de Gruyter, 1990.

4 'Cultural Change and Social Practice' was given at a workshop on the work of Fredric Jameson organized by Doug Kellner at the International Association for Literature and Philosophy Conference,, Lawrence,

Kansas in May 1987. It was revised for publication in D. Kellner (ed.), *Postmodernism/Jameson/Critique*, Washington: Maisonneuve Press, 1989.

5 'The Aestheticization of Everyday Life' was first given at the Popular Culture Association Conference, New Orleans in April 1988. It was also given at the Conference on Modernity as History, Copenhagen in September 1988 and at a seminar at Lund University, Sweden in October 1988. A version of it appeared in S. Lash and J. Friedman (eds) (1992), *Modernity and Identity*, Oxford: Basil Blackwell.

6 'Lifestyle and Consumer Culture' was first presented at the Conference on Everyday Life, Leisure and Culture at the University of Tilburg in December 1985. It appeared in Ernst Meijer (ed.), *Everyday Life: Leisure and Culture*, Tilburg: Dutch Centre for Leisure Studies, 1987 and in *Theory, Culture & Society*, 4(1), 1987.

7 'City Cultures and Postmodern Lifestyles' was presented at the 7th European Leisure and Recreational Association Congress on Cities for the Future, Rotterdam in June 1989. It has appeared in the post-congress volume *Cities for the Future*, ed. L.J. Meiresonne, The Hague: Stichting Recreatic, 1989.

8 'Consumer Culture and Global Disorder' was presented at the Conference on Religion and the Quest for Global Order, St Martin's, West Indies in October 1987. It appeared in W.R. Garrett and R. Robertson (eds), *Religion and the Global Order*, New York: Paragon House.

9 'Common Culture or Uncommon Cultures?' was first given at the Higher Education Foundation Conference on the Value of Higher Education, St Anne's College, Oxford in March 1989. A revised version has appeared in *Reflections on Higher Education*, 4 (Dec.), 1989.

Preface to the Second Edition

Consumer culture

It is now some fifteen years since *Consumer Culture and Postmodernism* was published in 1991, with many of the original versions of the various chapters in the book having been written in the period 1983 to 1990. In the intervening period the stock of consumer culture has risen and that of postmodernism has fallen. Interest in consumer culture has gathered pace with the appearance of journals, book series, study groups, conferences, research programmes devoted to scrutinizing every aspect of the topic. At the same time postmodernism has dropped out of sight and is no longer a fashionable term, indeed for many it is decidedly *demodé*. The rise of consumer culture is perhaps surprising, given the lack of critical purchase the term had in sociology and cultural studies in the 1980s. For some the term needed to be treated with suspicion as it was linked to mass society theory. For those in British cultural studies it was associated with the culture industry analyses of Adorno and the Frankfurt School, or even worse the theories of reification and fetishism of commodities of Lukács, who was seen as discredited with the rise of interest in Althusser in the 1970s. Books like Stuart Ewen's *Captains of Consciousness: Social Roots of the Consumer Culture* (1976) which was one of the first usages of the term consumer culture and Daniel Bell's *The Cultural Contradictions of Capitalism* (1976) made little impact.

It was the conjunction of consumer culture with postmodernism that sparked a good deal of interest in investigating the actuality of the post-modern. The work of Fredric Jameson (1979, 1984a, 1984b) was particularly influential here. Postmodernism was seen as the cultural logic of late capitalism, the third stage of capitalism, that of the consumer society in the post-World War II era. In effect a consumer society was seen as a culturally saturated society, in which production was geared to consumption with the circulation of a 'surfeit of signs and images' giving rise to both a Disneyland simulational culture and 'a stylish promiscuity' which overloaded the traditional cultural sphere of literary and artistic production. Whereas for Jameson it was the new mass consumer culture which was destroying intellectual culture, for Bell (1976) it was the a section of the intellectual and artistic elite, those associated with the development of modernism in the 1920s, who he saw as legitimating the transgressive and hedonistic tendencies in the nascent consumer culture, turning people away from the 'puritan ethic'. Postmodernism came later, in the 1960s and was regarded as a more dangerous intensification of these transgressive tendencies. In both cases postmodernism became associated with a consumer culture which was viewed negatively, the superficial hedonistic culture which either eroded the development of ethical, responsible active citizens needed to sustain democratic politics, or impeded the potential for people to imagine the alternative of a socialist future. Yet by the 1990s consumer culture ceased to be viewed negatively by many people in sociology and cultural studies. The numbers of textbooks proliferates, suggesting that consumer culture has become an increasingly popular undergraduate course. By the end of the decade we get the emergence of journals such as *Consumption, Markets and Culture* (1998–) followed by the *Journal of Consumer Culture* (2001–). Consumer culture also became legitimated as a research topic in the United Kingdom with the co-funded Economic and Social Research Council and the Arts and Humanities Research Council's *Cultures of Consumption* programme of research initiated in 2002, which further spawned a series of seminars, exhibitions and publications.

Here we can identify a number of issues arising out of this new wave of researching and writing on consumer culture. First, there has been a laudable expansion of scope and interdisciplinary focus. New histories and geographies of consumption provide an expanded sense of the multiple origins and trajectories of consumer culture around the world. There are, therefore now a growing number of detailed historical and contemporary studies of consumption outside the West (see the discussion of the rise of consumer culture in China and Japan material in the new additional chapter in this book, on 'Modernity and the Cultural Question').

Second, the question of the limits of consumer culture has been given sharper focus through the awareness of the finite resource base of consumption and the persistence and sharpening of global inequalities. It can be argued that the vision of abundance has been central to consumer culture in modernity. Increasingly since the eighteenth century in the West, science and technology have been seen as factors of production which along with the capacity for invention, have enabled the productive exploitation of nature and the expansion of the range of goods. Visions of abundance became associated with free of movement and social mobility and attached to particular symbolic and actual places, with 'America' becoming the key example from the final decades of the nineteenth century onwards and throughout much of the twentieth century (see Ewen and Ewen, 1982; Leach, 1993; McGovern, 1998). The right to consumption became increasingly seen as the reward for industrial expansion. Modern living became associated with the endless supply of new goods, to furnish more efficient homes filled with 'labour-saving' devices, along with the access to new styles and fashions, coupled with a greater emphasis upon 'personality' and the presentation of self via techniques of grooming and body maintenance. This vision of consumer culture as involving active lifestyle construction and bodily renewal became linked to mobility: the promise of social mobility and personal transformation, along with the freedom of physical mobility, the capacity to move in search of employment, leisure or new significant others. In the United States this coalesced around a particular form of mobility: automobility (Featherstone, 2004). Something which in the course of the twentieth century restructured the pattern of urban development with new dispersed locations for the expanding service and tertiary sector; manifest in workplace (the industrial estate and business park, home (the suburbs), and consumption and leisure spaces (shopping centres and malls, holiday resorts, theme parks). The first cracks in this model of the postwar consumer society began to occur in the discussions of the limits to growth in the wake of the 1973 oil crisis, with successive events, especially global warming in the 1990s increasingly reinforcing this view.

It became clear that the consumer society has limits: it is also a risk society, not only accumulating new goods, but also new 'bads' (Beck, 1993, 1996). Not only global warming, but also BSE (mad cow disease), genetically modified food, new viruses and superbugs. Yet despite the intermittent media scares over the generation of new risks and continuing concerns over global warming, the notion of a limited consumer society, or the transformation into a 'conserver society' has hardly fired the public imagination or brought forth new political strategies. While some politicians acknowledged the need to tackle the carbon dioxide emissions problem in the 1997 'Kyoto Protocol to the United Nations Framework Convention on Climate Change', others have been reluctant to sign up to ecological policies if they risk jeopardizing the sustained economic growth which ensures their continued re-election. In addition there have been those in various parts of the world who followed President Bush and have disputed the grounds of the problem, despite compelling evidence from the scientific community and high profile publicity campaigns, such as that mounted by Al Gore with his global warming movie and book *An Inconvenient Truth* (2006). The movie was headlined on the US Fox News Channel in May 2006 with the question 'Al Gore's Global Warming Movie: Could it Destroy Our Economy?' with a discussion in which some participants dismissed it in terms of 'hysteria' and 'socialist regulation'. Consumer culture and questions of sustainable consumption are clearly public sphere issues, yet we have to ask questions about the nature of the public sphere as it is a undoubtedly a mediatized and affective public sphere, an arena of segmentation and massification, of not just potential 'rational argument', but of expression, invention and creation (Terranova, 2007).

Global problems of consumer culture

The promise of consumer culture is central to the expansion of the new Asian economies, in particular China and India, which have staved off the possibility of a severe global recession over the last decade. Yet, this expansion of consumer culture means more goods, more air travel, more waste, pollution and carbon dioxide emissions. This dimension of the politics of consumption pushes consumer culture onto the international political agenda, with various national politicians seeking to engage in a tit-for-tat blame-game, or to deny the problem exists. Consumer culture, then is difficult to relinquish or scale down as it has becomes both a major source of industrial production and employment. In addition it is a key mode of legitimation, a visible sign of the economic success and standing of a nation-state. Curbing consumption is not a popular option which means politicians, seek out 'technological fix' solutions which will allow the economy to proceed at full speed, but somehow clean up or recycle pollution and waste. Hence, the interest in the development of nanotechnology and other new technologies which will allegedly produce waste-eating organisms, along with the interest in more efficient forms of power such as the hydrogen engine, or nuclear fusion energy (Cooper, 2006). If consumer culture is central to the contemporary neo-liberal increasingly globally integrated economies of nationstates, and politicians' electoral success depends upon economic growth, to seek to constrain consumption becomes the unpopular and potentially unelectable option.

As consumer culture globalizes, there is also the sense, then, of the planetary limits to consumption: that we are literally consuming the planet and our human future at an unsustainable rate (an argument made forcefully by James Lovelock (2006) in *The Revenge of Gaia*). There has, of course, been a long history of attempts to shackle and regulate consumption and develop a more ethical and morally responsible attitude, at every stage of the expansion of consumer culture (Sassatelli, 2006; McGovern, 1998). There have been various forms of religious asceticism and Puritanism and secular forms of regulation. Over the last decade a clearer notion of the consumer-citizen has emerged with the citizen defined as having rights to be a consumer, and the consumer defined as having responsibilities to ask questions about the consequences, risks and planetary costs of consumption. For example, it was reported recently that there are calls to extend the energy efficiency labelling of 'white goods', such as fridges, to other goods, not just in terms of output (energy running costs) but also in terms of 'carbon costs,' the actual input of energy expended in their manufacture (Finch and Vidal, 2007). The comparison of different goods will provide interesting evidence and make for many difficult ethical judgements.

As has been emphasized in this book, consumption cannot be regarded as merely hedonistic, expressive and impulsive, however much this features in the advertising and lifestyle imagery. It clearly involves consumers in calculation, comparisons and research: in short consumer culture involves knowledge. Not just knowledge of cost-efficient goods and bargains, or that of the connoisseur or taste-maker who know their wine, décor, restaurants and travel destinations, but also (especially in the new middle class) knowledge of the ethical background of goods. Consumer movements not only seek to regulate the safety and advertising claims of goods, but also to circulate information about the ethical practices of companies (companies with good work practices outside the West, those which avoid cruelty to animals, etc.) and where to buy 'fair trade' goods which support local producers. This is not to say that the ethical gesture on the part of the consumer, is merely a cost, for it can also be displayed as a sign of virtue, of a particular form of ethically consistent conduct (see Featherstone, 1995), which is not immune from being classified by others as only another clever move in the unavoidable round of distinction games. Likewise 'good citizen' actions by retailers and manufactures, as we find in the announcements of 'carbon cost' labelling and emission controls by British supermarket and retail chains such as Tesco and Marks & Spencer in January 2007.

The success in Britain and Europe in the late 1990s of consumer campaigns to persuade supermarkets to label the genetically-modified content of food and other goods, is an important episode in the politics of consumption, but by no means the final chapter. In addition, the intensification of circulation of information through the internet, email lists, blogs etc., means that there is also greater knowledge about the manufacture of goods in the sweatshops of the Global South. The working conditions, low pay and lack of employment rights and protection of those who are subjected to the new forms of compound and indented labour, casts a shadow over the lifestyle advertising and brand images of everyday consumer culture goods such as trainers and jeans, turning hidden conditions of production into an ethical and political issue (Bender and Greenwald, 2003; Brecher and Costello, 1994; Klein, 2001). The highly publicized protests against the World Trade Organization new rounds of global deregulation which occurred in Seattle, Cancún and other places, has also further politicized the act of consumption. These tendencies make people more aware of the network of dependencies, by which consumption is tied to global inequalities. This was one of the driving forces behind the World Social Forum, with its vision that 'another world is possible,' a viable alternative to neo-liberal corporate globalization. The WSF has sought to develop networks and dialogue between a motley array of labour, feminist, new social movements, charity and religious groups largely from the south to explore new forms of global public sphere and civil society participation and democratization (Fisher and Ponniah, 2003; Santos, 2006; Patomäki, 2006; Patomäki and Teivainen, 2004).

In short, consumption can no longer be seen as an innocent act, but as part of the chains of interdependencies and networks which bind people together across the world in terms of production, consumption and also the accumulation of risks. Yet, however much there is a perceived political dimension to consumption and cosmopolitan potential to unite people together through their common human condition in the face of global risks and planetary dangers, consumer culture has become too firmly established as part of the taken-for-granted value assumptions of the contemporary age for it to be easily modified, or discarded altogether. If there is an emergent global culture, consumer culture has to be seen as a central part of this field. An additional problem with cosmopolitan virtue, is that it can be seen as merely the advocacy of a particular version of cosmopolitanism, such as that associated with market trader cultures, or the European Kantian ideal, which doesn't sufficiently take into account Chinese, Indian, Islamic and other cosmopolitanism traditions (Featherstone, 2002; Cheah, 2007). There is no guarantee that the current international discussions about global warming and the need to regulate consumption will produce a consensus and concerted action.

Diminishing expectations do not sit easily with consumer culture values. If, as in the current phase, the real income of workers in various parts of the Western world, in particular the United States, is threatened by the movement of jobs to Asia, notably Indian and China, then the right to consumption, to be a consumer-citizen becomes a political issue of another order. It is in this context that people start to speak about 'The End of the American Dream?' (Schifferes, 2006), at a time when the United States economy fails to sustain growth in real income levels despite major productivity increases by workers. Certainly the international context is one in which the Washington Consensus, the world economic order which underpins the economic globalization which fuels consumer culture, is under threat. There has even been talk of a new Beijing Consensus, premised on the rise of China which could steer the global economy in a different direction (*The Economist*, 16 September 2006). This suggests that in the longer term, the capacity of the United States to sustain its global military dominance in the face of the rise of Asia and 'the long war against terrorism' becomes more problematic. The difficulties of continuing to hold onto its 'state of exception' status (Malik, 2006), to continue to seek to steer the world in line with US political, economic and cultural objectives in this new context, has the danger of producing within the United States a strong nationalism with civilizational and Christian religious overtones – what William Connolly (2007) refers to as 'The Christo-Capitalist Assemblage'.

The above mentioned threat to the capacity to sustain income levels in the working classes in the West in face of the relocation and migration of jobs to cheaper labour markets is driven by the dynamic of neo-Liberal economic globalization (Featherstone, 2001b, 2006a). The neo-Liberal pact which became established in the 1980s initially in the United States and Britain, which has subsequently become globalized, provided a package of welfare state cuts, governmental deregulation of financial markets and other bodies, introduction of measurable assessment, competition and league tables for government funded bodies such as universities, hospitals etc., along with low rates of income tax and the promise of economic growth. One consequence has been the widening of the gap between the rich and the poor within Western societies, but also globally too. According to a global study from the World Institute for Development Economics Research of the United Nations the richest 1 per cent of the world's population owns 40 per cent of the planet's wealth. The richest 10 per cent own over 85 per cent of the world's assets, with over half the world's population owning barely 1 per cent of the global wealth. This is a world in which over

800 million people go to bed hungry every night (Randerson, 2006). That those at the top end of the scale are able to increase their wealth more rapidly than people at the bottom is confirmed by *Forbes Magazine*, which mentions that there were 140 (dollar) billionaires in the world in 1986, 476 in 2003 and 793 in 2006. Their combined wealth amounts to $2.6 trillion in December 2006 – up 18 per cent since March 2006. They not only have a greater capacity to increase their capital accumulation, but to retain a level of invisibility in national surveys, and of course national income tax payments (see Parenti, 2002; Venn, 2006).

This is the world given over to 'liquid modernity' (Bauman, 2000) and 'the new capitalism' (Sennett, 1999, 2006), in which capital and capitalists are mobile and have a much weaker sense of attachment to place and responsibility for local others. This diminished sense of local attachment has been referred to as 'the revolt of the elites' (Lasch, 1996). At the bottom end, there are not only those who go hungry already mentioned above, but the dwellers in the expanding array of shantytowns in the urban areas and megacities of the global South. According to Mike Davis (2006: 2) the 2006 urban population of 3.2 billion will expand to 10 billion by 2050. Over 95 per cent of this growth will occur in the urban areas of developing counties. This slum growth in the South, is most marked in Africa (Simone, 2004). The explosion of megacities outside the West, not only problematizes many of our assumptions about urban development, the 'slumification of the world' provides important challenges for consumer cultural analysis to understand different circuits of consumption.

The other point to note about the growth in the number of billionaires is the example they set for consumer culture lifestyles. The *Forbes* website has a section on lifestyle with details of luxury homes (you can take a photographic tour of the homes of fifteen of the world's richest people), most expensive cars, megayachts, most expensive private islands, and how to travel like a billionaire (private jet, helicopter etc.). Luxury, is of course no stranger to consumer culture and, indeed, the visibility of luxury outside court societies, in the merchant groups in Asia as well as Europe, can be seen as an important dynamic in developing the concern for new goods and a fashion system which drew in other groups (see discussion in chapter 11 'Modernity and the Cultural Question' in this new edition; also Burke, 1993; Berry, 1994; Berg and Clifford, 1999). It has been argued that today, as the pull of place and local status hierarchies diminish, the visibility of luxury in the media becomes a more potent reference point for people. Certainly the lifestyles of the rich and upper-middle classes attract attention with television providing endless programmes which revolve around the improvement and furnishing of a stylish home, purchase of a second home, holiday planning, cars, fashion, celebrity events etc. The programmes endeavour to strike a balance between the interest in the lifestyles of celebrities, the new rich and the upper-middle class, and the endeavours of 'ordinary people', who seek improvement and transformation on a tight budget.

The concept of transformation is still central to consumer culture, with magazines, advertising and television presenting an endless range of material on the transformation of lifestyle, living space, relationships, identities and of course, bodies (Featherstone, 1998, 1999). The body is presented as the central vehicle to the consumer culture good life: the source of pleasurable sensations which must be 'looked after' (maintained, repaired and improved). Yet the body is also understood in terms of its image, as the visible indicator of the self, hence the attention given to 'the look' (presentation, grooming, style). Celebrities, the new rich and middle class are presented as enjoying access to a whole array of personal body services. In the television transformation programmes 'ordinary' young adults and middle-aged people are guided through rigorous fitness regimes, cosmetic surgery, learning make-up and body grooming, clothing sense and deportment to fit them out as a new person able to 'look ten years younger' (Featherstone, 1982, 2007). Yet for the vast majority of the less affluent in countries like the United States and the United Kingdom, with obesity levels hitting the 20–30 per cent band, to engage successfully in such transformation regimes can seem impossibly distant goals. At the same time it is possible to point to World Health Organization data which shows that obesity levels in France are less than 7 percent, and in Japan they are much smaller still. Clearly, we cannot assume there is a common global consumer culture with uniform effects.

At the same time, if the tendencies noted by Reich (2006) with reference to the United States continue, then we can expect a further expansion of wealth in the top layers of the social structure and a shrinking of the middle layers, as well as shifts within the working class from manufacturing jobs to services. Specifically, he notes that symbol analysts (university-educated knowledge professionals such as lawyers, engineers, accountants, journalists) have expanded to make up 20 per cent of the workforce. But this group is suffering a decline in relation to what he refers to as the global symbol analysts (CEOs and CFOs of global corporations, and partners and executives in global investment banks, law firms and consultancies). The current tendency is a relative decline in income levels of the national as against the global symbol analysts, with those in the West facing greater competition from the expanding numbers of English-speaking graduates in China, India and other parts of the world. Most global symbolic analysts have been educated at elite universities and can work in English (unlike their national counterparts), as well as being at home moving around the circuit of global cities. They also help fuel the army of migrating service workers (cleaners, cooks, nannies and sex workers, many of them women) at the bottom end of the workforce. This latter group expands as a result of the outsourcing of service work from those in the middle and upper levels and includes the legions of maids who are on short-term contracts with very limited employment rights (Cheah, 2007; Ehrenreich and Hochschild, 2003).

These tendencies are producing a more complex global consumer culture. New levels of luxury are evident at the top end of the social structure with a good deal of celebration of the lifestyles and consumption patterns of the rich. But for those below, who watch the celebrity and elite consumption in the media, their consumption is more the consumption of dreams, plus the occasional purchases of cheaper scaled-down luxuries. Financial institutions constantly bombard consumers in the United States, Britain and other countries, to sign up for easily accessible credit. Debt has long ceased to have the pejorative overtones it carried in nineteenth century moral tale novels. Asceticism, rationing and self-control do not fit well with consumer culture imagery of the good life. Credit became more readily available from the 1920s onwards in the United States as advertisers strove to overcome Puritan restraint and saving (Ewen, 1976). In the 1950s William Whyte in his best-selling *The Organization Man* (1956) reminded readers that 'thrift is now un-American' (Belk, 2004: 80). Today, both national governments and individual consumers are encouraged to borrow excessively. Yet it would be a mistake to assume that this is a universal tendency on the one hand, or that economies or the planet can sustain an overall American-style consumer culture in the long run, on the other. Certainly if we look at consumer culture in Japan it reveals a very different pattern, having a long history of sustained urban consumption and leisure with department stores, cinemas, dance halls, cafés, magazines and advertising developing in the 1920s (Tamari, 2006). Thrift and saving have always been central to modern Japanese consumer culture and it has proved exceedingly difficult to stimulate the economy with cheap credit, as attempted on a regular basis in the aftermath of the collapse of the 1980s bubble economy. This lack of enthusiasm for American-style consumption based on consumer debt and credit-card spending not only is evident in Japan and other parts of Asia, but also in France, Germany, Italy and other European countries (Garon and MacLachlan, 2006).

There is, then, a greater awareness today of the costs of consumer culture, of the unsustainable implications of the generalization of the United States model to the rest of the world. The expansion of the Chinese and Indian economies are already bringing home the prospect of the growing ecological footprint of this third of humanity (see WWF Living Planet Report, 2000 for discussion of ecological footprints and the 3.5 planets needed if everyone in the world consumed like Americans). Yet as we have already mentioned above, the 'crisis' is by no means guaranteed to be recognised as such by all, or agreement reached, or solutions proffered. Few people are willing to contemplate reining-in their own consumption, to sacrifice for others, either on a personal or nation-state level. Western economies may well be obsessed with a 'growth fetish', yet it is hard to imagine a return to a 'stationary state' or move to a 'post-growth society' as advocated in the past by John Stuart Mill, Maynard Keynes and others (Hamilton, 2003). Certainly it means abandoning the obsession with realising the 'dreams of abundance', which was central to twentieth-century American society as it sought to leave behind forever the 'era of scarcity' (Lears, 1998: 453). Yet rather than abandon the notion of abundance, Lears argues that we should consider the cultivation of 'psychic abundance' and 'seek to abolish time famine and to create genuine leisure by abandoning obsessions with productivity' (1998: 466). This takes us into the debates about the 'art of living' and the various modes of care of the self, ethical conduct and 'sociality with things', which could provide alternatives to our high material consumption, mobility and travel way of life (Featherstone, 1992, 1995).

Yet not all consumption needs to involve the consumption of material goods, and not all fascination with new sensations and invention needs to be fed through the commodity market process. The internet and new forms of communications technology have started to open up the potential for greater immaterial consumption (this is based on the notion of immaterial labour developed by Tarde and others; see discussion in Lazzarato, 2007; Terranova, 2007; Toscano 2007). When we read a book, we use, or 'consume' something which is still available for others and involves little additional energy or cost. Public libraries are institutions based upon this model, as are the various forms of free and commercial downloads of information, images, movies and data from the internet. Consumer culture necessarily promotes ambivalence, it offers a world beyond scarcity and hardship, the dream of abundance, yet its modus operandi is through the commodity form, the calculus of monetary value. It encourages a calculating hedonism, a cost-benefit analysis of pleasure, time and other people. Yet it also encourages a calculus of public policies, the consequences of growth, along with the costs to other forms of life and the planet, of our actions.

Life after postmodernism …

Postmodernism has fared less well over the last twenty years than consumer culture in the social sciences and humanities. This is hardly unexpected, as the opening chapter on 'Modern and Postmodern: Definitions and Interpretations' indicates, from the very start there were many who proclaimed it to be a short-run fad and were already talking about 'post-postmodernism'. Yet there continues to be an interest in postmodernity. As this book firmly suggests there is a need to distinguish carefully between the different filiation lines of the various members of the family of terms which spring from the postmodern. The key influential terms was of course postmodernism, an intellectual and artistic movement with clear social roots. To scale up the attribution of the characteristics associated with postmodernism to an epochal shift has always seemed problematic. The discovery of the dynamics, the 'where, when, who and how many', of the postmodern, when defined as a mode of experience or set of practices that can be attributed to specific groups of people and pinned down in time and space, has always been challenging. Nevertheless, various definitions of postmodernity have been made and some researchers see it is having been clearly established through empirical research which provides evidence that the advanced societies are going through a process of 'postmodernization', through the spread of post-scarcity values (Ingelhardt, 1997). Like many variations of modernization theory, there is often the implicit assumption that researchers have discovered cutting edge cultural changes in 'advanced societies', which will be replicated elswhere around the world.

There are, then, dangers that the postmodern will be read as an extension of the modernization theory problematic. Johann Arnason (2001: 131), for example, writing in favour of 'multiple modernities,' notes that the 'idea of an ongoing and innovative pluralization of modernity is obviously incompatible with postmodernist positions, and it gives a specific twist to the critique of postmodernism: those who consigned modernity to the past based their claims on misguided notions of a uniform pattern embodied in a whole historical epoch' (the topic of multiple and alternative modernities is addressed in the new chapter in this book on 'Modernity and the Cultural Question'). Arnason's attempt to pluralize modernity and step down from the authority of higher level concepts and Eurocentric models of history is to be applauded. He goes on to tell us that the ideal of multiple modernities rules out the notion of globality as a general condition characteristic of a new epoch, and then outlines a number of criticisms of modernization theory and, by implication, postmodernization theory. These include: the move away from uniform structures to the recognition of greater diversity; the caution against the building of northwest European 'vanguard' societies into basic concepts in favour of more historical exploration; the doubt that there can be a unifying project of modernity; that civilizational differences provide key differentiating factors among modernities. It is interesting to note that all these factors, bar perhaps the last one, would not be at all difficult to incorporate into many of the positions which thrived in the opening developed by postmodernism. Certainly those who work in social and cultural theory who draw upon the writings of Foucault, Derrida, Lyotard, the postcolonial-inspired writings of Chakrabarty, Mbembe, Said, Sakai, Spivak and others, would not find these positions problematic. Rather, the question would, I suspect, tend to revolve around the issue of what is at stake in the move from the conception of a singular modernity to multiple modernities or postmodernity/postmodernism. However much there has been an understandable reaction to 'anything goes' variants of postmodernism, it is important to recognize the productive side of the declassificatory orientation ushered in by the postmodern.

A key aspect of the unstable conceptual field opened up by the postmodern, then, is to question linear metanarratives and assumption of ordered historical development. There are clearly many genealogies of the postmodern and when one looks into its use in different societies around the world, the term fulfils different needs within particular local contexts (for a history of the postmodern see Bertens, 1995). To take the example of Japan, the postmodern became a short-lived fashionable term in the 1980s at the time of Japanese economic growth (the bubble economy) in which Japan threatened to outpace the United States and Japanese intellectuals and academics were delving into history to discover Japanese difference and distance Japan from the West: the 'always already' postmodern of Tokugawa Japan (Gluck, 1998; see discussion in chapter 11 of this book). In China, postmodernism was introduced from the West through interest in the writings of Derrida, Foucault, Barthes and others in the 1980s. It was taken up as a strong critique of both the state modernization project and modernism, which was also seen as legitimate.

After 1989 postmodernism could be discussed more openly and after 1992, with the economic reforms and the development of consumer culture, post-modernism had a new space to develop in. The rapid expansion of the Chinese economy in the 1990s, the urbanization of Shanghai and Beijing, offered new postmodern architecture, the expansion of television and advertising media and consumer culture in general led to a new sense of experience which could not be recovered into the traditional Communist Party vision of moderniza-tion (see Chen, 2006; also Dirlik and Zhang, 2000). The different use of post-modernism in both China and Japan, points to the importance of understanding the local context to get the sense of what is at stake in the term postmodernism, which although given global impetus, clearly has a wide range of local inflections around the world.

The Chinese example suggests an interesting sociology of knowledge account of the reception of postmodern. A process, which was incidentally furthered in its earlier phase by the regular visits of Fredric Jameson to Beijing which helped stimulate a new generation of Chinese intellectuals to read his works and influential ideas on postmodernism (Dirlik and Zhang, 2000: 1). It is also worth adding that the Chinese translation of this book, *Consumer Culture and Postmodernism*, which was published in 2000, also proved timely not only in terms of its references to Western debates on postmodernism, which were useful background to the discussions in China, but also in terms of the chapters on consumer culture. The dramatic growth of the Chinese economy since the 1990s has encouraged the development of consumer culture within China and opened up many questions for intel-lectuals and academics about the direction Chinese society should take and both the critical potential and social limitations of consumer culture. The globalization process is making us more aware of the reception of works around the world and the changing structure of the global knowledge econ-omy. If, as Naoki Sakai (2001) argues, theoretical knowledge can be seen as flowing out from Western centres with data flowing back from the rest of the world, this process is becoming more complex. Not only through the continuing expansion of Western knowledge institutions such as universi-ties, publishing houses and media conglomerates to set up branches and franchises in the rest of the world, to cater for the growing global market for English-speaking symbol analysts that Reich (2006) speaks about. But there are also signs of the emergence of other centres of knowledge pro-duction and formation around in the world, China being the most promi-nent example. The contemporary rise of China certainly poses interesting questions for Western-centred genealogies of modernity and threatens to declassify some of the disciplinary conceptual hierarchies.

A new sociology of knowledge

This question of the various interests and power balances which structure the processes of global knowledge formation has been one which has been taken up in recent years in *Theory, Culture & Society*, with the first volume of the *Theory, Culture & Society New Encyclopaedia Project* on Problematizing Global Knowledge published in 2006, as a *TCS* special issue. This is the first of a number of planned special issues which include megacities, media, food, religion, consumer culture. The aim of the project is to use the encyclopaedia form to rethink the formation of knowledge under the impact of globalization and digitization. These processes not only increase the storage, scope and speed of access to knowledge, making more content available. They also provide new opportunities to problematize existing disciplinary classifications by providing new spaces for counterexamples, dialogue and critical reflection. In effect they can encourage declassification moves and challenges to the authority of existing knowledge (see Featherstone, 2006b, Featherstone and Venn, 2006). The Problematizing Global Knowledge volume is interesting not only through the use of supplements, which deconstruct the authority of entries and provide additional content from different parts of the world, but for its theoretical reflection on knowledge. Many things have happened since postmodernism initiated a new wave of critical reflection on the formation of knowledge and culture in the 1980s. Postcolonialism in particular has deepened the critique of Eurocentric knowledge and has sought to provide alternative genealogies of national and global histories (Chakrabarty, 2000; Houtondji, 2002; Mbembe, 2001; Venn, 2006). Other important theoretical tendencies which have been addressed within *Theory, Culture & Society*, include complexity theory (Urry, 2005), Derridian deconstruction (Turner, 2005; Venn, 2005); posthumanism (Gane, 2006; Braidotti, 2006); the new vitalism, inspired by Deleuze, Negri and others which has led to a revival of interest in Henri Bergson (Fraser *et al.*, 2005; Lash, 2005, Lazaratto, 2007; Olma, 2007; the recent attempt to develop a new Deleuzian-inspired philosophy of the social science by De Landa, 2006, also deserves mentioning). A number of pieces in the Problematizing Global Knowledge volume, notably those which deal with assemblage, event, the unclassifiable, translation, the knowledge apparatus, method, media theory, life, experience, global assemblage, global sovereignty and archive, favour a more processual and contingent theory of knowledge formation. Postmodernism, then, may have been eclipsed in significance, yet the theoretical impulse it provided has encouraged the search for alternative modes of critical knowledge formation.

******

Given the period of time which has elapsed since the publication of *Consumer Culture and Postmodernism*, it was a pleasant surprise to be asked by Sage Publications to bring out a second edition. The book has sold well and has been translated into more than ten languages, which suggests that a good number of people have found it useful. My involvement in the journal *Theory, Culture & Society*, which was started in 1982, has been central to the development of my ideas on postmodernism and the book clearly shows the influence of that heady 'adventure of ideas' in the first decade of the journal's life. As editor I was able to indulge some of my own interests and the special issues on *Consumer Culture* (1983) and *The Fate of Modernity* (1985) were direct outcomes of my interest in critical theory in the 1970s, albeit given a new inflection through the rise of postmodernism (double special issue 1988). Also significant influences was the interest in the body which developed specifically through my work with Mike Hepworth (Hepworth and Featherstone, 1982; Featherstone and Hepworth, 1982, 1991) and Bryan Turner (Featherstone, Hepworth and Turner, 1991) with regular papers featured on this topic in *Theory, Culture & Society*; this led to the development of the journal *Body & Society* in 1995. Globalization was also an important influence in my writings in this book, which was brought into *Theory, Culture & Society* by Roland Robertson in the 1980s and featured in a number of articles prior to the influential special issue on *Global Culture* that I edited in 1990 (Featherstone, 1990).

My ideas have been formed in the process of many discussions with the tremendous group of people, working in and around the journal *Theory, Culture & Society*. Especially those on the editorial board: Vikki Bell, Ryan Bishop, Josef Bleicher, Roy Boyne, Norman Denzin, Nicholas Gane, Mike Hepworth, Scott Lash, John Phillips, Roland Robertson, Rob Shields, Bryan S. Turner and Couze Venn. I have benefited a great deal from their intellectual generosity and willingness to tackle new ideas. In addition, I have a special debt to my colleagues in the *Theory, Culture & Society* Centre at Nottingham Trent University who have provided great support for the journal along with all the other schemes we have developed over the last decade since *Theory, Culture & Society* moved to Nottingham. In particular I would like to mention: Roger Bromley, Neal Curtis, Nigel Edley, Sandra Harris, Richard Johnson, Joost van Loon, Susan Manthorpe, John Marks, Ali Mohammadi, Chris Rojek, Tomoko Tamari, John Tomlinson, Neil Turnbull, Patrick Williams, Patrick Wright, David Woods and Couze Venn. I would also like to thank Antonio A. Arantes, Roger Burrows, Takaaki Chikamori, Chua Beng Huat, Susantha Goonatilake, John Hutnyk, Huimin Jin, Celia Lury, Kenichi Kawasaki, Tetsuo Nishiyama, Bruce Mazlish, Makio Morikawa, Tetsuo Maruyama, Volker Schmidt, Kuniharu Tokiasu, Wiljan van den Akker, Andy Wernick, Kathleen Woodward and Shunya Yoshimi, for their intellectual encouragement and support. The new edition has a special debt to Mike Hepworth, Huimin Jin and Couze Venn who made excellent suggestions to improve the additional chapter and preface to the second edition. At Sage Publications in London, Stephen Barr, Cheryl Merritt, Robert Rojek, Katie Sayers, Mila Steele have provided great encouragement and support for *Theory, Culture & Society* and the *Theory, Culture & Society* Book Series, as well as being wonderful people to work with. As the new edition is in press we have learned of the death of my close friend and long-standing *TCS* colleague, Mike Hepworth. We worked together on many projects from the 1960s onwards. This second edition is dedicated to Mike's memory.

1

Modern and Postmodern: Definitions and Interpretations

Any reference to the term 'postmodernism' immediately exposes one to the risk of being accused of jumping on a bandwagon, of perpetuating a rather shallow and meaningless intellectual fad. One of the problems is that the term is at once fashionable yet irritatingly elusive to define. As the 'Modern-day Dictionary of Received Ideas' confirms, 'This word has no meaning. Use it as often as possible' (*Independent*, 24 December 1987). Over a decade earlier, in August 1975, another newspaper announced that 'postmodernism is dead', and that 'post-post-modernism is now the thing' (Palmer, 1977: 364). If postmodernism is an ephemeral fashion then some critics are clear as to who are responsible for its prominence:

> today's paid theorists surveying the field from their booklined studies in polytechnics and universities are obliged to invent movements because their careers – no less than those of miners and fishermen – depend on it. The more movements they can give names to, the more successful they will be. (Pawley, 1986)

For other critics these strategies are not just internal moves within the intellectual and academic fields; they are clear indicators and barometers of the 'malaise at the heart of contemporary culture'. Hence 'It is not difficult to comprehend this cultural and aesthetic trend now known as Postmodernism – in art and architecture, music and film, drama and fiction – as a reflection of ... the present wave of political reaction sweeping the Western world' (Gott, 1986). But it is all to easy to see postmodernism as a reactionary, mechanical reflection of social changes and to blame the academics and intellectuals for coining the term as part of their distinction games. Even though certain newspaper critics and para-intellectuals use the term in a cynical or dismissive manner, they confirm that postmodernism has sufficient appeal to interest a larger middle-class audience. Few other recent academic terms can claim to have enjoyed such popularity. Yet it is not merely an academic term, for it has gained impetus from artistic 'movements' and is also attracting wider public interest through its capacity to speak to some of the cultural changes we are currently going through.

Before we can look at the means of transmission and dissemination of the concept, we need a clearer notion of the range of phenomena which are generally included under the umbrella concept postmodernism. We therefore need to take account of the great interest and even excitement that it has generated, both inside and outside the academy, and to ask questions about the range of cultural objects, experiences and practices which theorists are adducing and labelling postmodern, before we can decide on its political pedigree or dismiss it as merely a short swing of the pendulum.

In the first place the broad range of artistic, intellectual and academic fields in which the term 'postmodernism' has been used, is striking. We have music (Cage, Stockhausen, Briers, Holloway, Tredici, Laurie Anderson); art (Rauschenberg, Baselitz, Mach, Schnabel, Kiefer; some would also include Warhol and 1960s pop art, and others Bacon); fiction (Vonnegut's *Slaughterhouse Five*, and the novels of Barth, Barthelme. Pynchon, Burroughs, Ballard, Doctorow); film *(Body Heat, The Wedding, Blue Velvet, Wetherby);* drama (the theatre of Artaud); photography (Sherman, Levine, Prince); architecture (Jencks, Venturi, Bolin); literary theory and criticism (Spanos, Hassan, Sontag, Fiedler); philosophy (Lyotard, Derrida, Baudrillard, Vattimo, Rorty); anthropology (Clifford, Tyler, Marcus); sociology (Denzin); geography (Soja). The very names of those included and excluded in the list will doubtless strike some as controversial. To take the example of fiction, as Linda Hutcheon (1984: 2) argues, some would wish to include the novels of García Márquez and even Cervantes under the heading of postmodernism and others would want to refer to them as neobaroque and baroque. Scott Lash would want to regard Dada as postmodernism *avant la lettre* (Lash, 1988). There are those who work and write unaware of the term's existence and others who seek to thematize and actively promote it. Yet it can be argued that one of the functions of the interest in postmodernism on the part of critics, para-intellectuals, cultural intermediaries and academics has been to diffuse the term to wider audiences in different national and international contexts (this is one of the senses in which one can talk about the globalization of culture); and to increase the speed of interchange and circulation of the term between the various fields in the academy and the arts, which now want to, and have to, pay more attention to developments among their neighbours. In this sense it is possible that some greater agreement on the meaning of the term might eventually emerge as commentators in each particular field find it necessary to recapitulate and explain the multiplex history and usages of the term in order to educate new, academic audiences.

To work towards some preliminary sense of the meaning of postmodernism it is useful to identify the family of terms derived from 'the postmodern' and these can best be understood by contrasting them to those which derive from 'the modern'.

modern	postmodern
modernity	postmodernity
modernité	*postmodernité*
modernization	postmodernization
modernism	postmodernism

If 'the modern' and 'the postmodern' are the generic terms it is immediately apparent that the prefix 'post' signifies that which comes after, a break or rupture with the modern which is defined in counterdistinction to it. Yet the term 'postmodernism' is more strongly based on a negation of the modern, a perceived abandonment, break with or shift away from the definitive features of the modern, with the emphasis firmly on the sense of the relational move away. This would make the postmodern a relatively ill-defined term as we are only on the threshold of the alleged shift, and not in a position to regard the postmodern as a fully fledged positivity which can be defined comprehensively in its own right. Bearing this in mind we can take a closer look at the pairings.

Modernity–postmodernity

This suggests the epochal meaning of the terms. Modernity is generally held to have come into being with the Renaissance and was defined in relation to Antiquity, as in the debate between the Ancients and the Moderns. From the point of view of late nineteenth- and early twentieth-century German sociological theory, from which we derive much of our current sense of the term, modernity is contrasted to the traditional order and implies the progressive economic and administrative rationalization and differentiation of the social world (Weber, Tönnies, Simmel): processes which brought into being the modern capitalist-industrial state and which were often viewed from a distinctly antimodern perspective.

Consequently, to speak of postmodernity is to suggest an epochal shift or break from modernity involving the emergence of a new social totality with its own distinct organizing principles. It is this order of change that has been detected in the writing of Baudrillard, Lyotard and, to some extent, Jameson (Kellner, 1988). Both Baudrillard and Lyotard assume a movement towards a post-industrial age. Baudrillard (1983a) stresses that new forms of technology and information become central to the shift from a productive to a reproductive social order in which simulations and models increasingly constitute the world so that the distinction between the real and appearance becomes erased. Lyotard (1984) talks about the postmodern society, or postmodern age, which is premised on the move to a post-industrial order. His specific interest is in the effects of the 'computerization of society' on knowledge and he argues that the loss of meaning in postmodernity should not be mourned, as it points to a replacement of narrative knowledge by a plurality of language games, and universalism by localism. Yet Lyotard, like many users of the family of terms, sometimes changes register from one term to the next and switches usages. preferring more recently to emphasize that the postmodern is to be regarded as part of the modern. for example, in 'Rules and Paradoxes and Svelte Appendix' he writes ' "postmodern" is probably a very bad term because it conveys the idea of a historical "periodization". "Periodizing", however, is still a "classic" or "modern" ideal. "Postmodern" simply indicates a mood, or better a state of mind' (Lyotard, 1986–7: 209). The other interesting point to note about Lyotard's use of postmodernity in *The Postmodern Condition* is that where he talks about the changes in knowledge accompanying the move to the post-industrial society he still conceives this as occurring within capitalism, adding weight to the argument of critics that the move to the postmodern society is undertheorized in Lyotard's work (see Kellner, 1988). Although the move is assumed at some points, it is easier to avoid the accusations of providing a grand narrative account of the move to postmodernity and the eclipse of grand narratives, by insisting on a more diffuse notion of 'mood' or 'state of mind'. Fredric Jameson (1984a) has a more definite periodizing concept of the postmodern. Yet he is reluctant to conceive of it as an epochal shift; rather postmodernism is the cultural dominant, or cultural logic, of the third great stage of capitalism, late capitalism which originates in the post-World War II era.

Lyotard's invocation of a postmodern mood or state of mind points us towards a second meaning of modernity–postmodernity. The French use of *modernité* points to the experience of modernity in which modernity is viewed as a quality of modern life inducing a sense of the discontinuity of time, the break with tradition, the feeling of novelty and sensitivity to the ephemeral, fleeting and contingent nature of the present (see Frisby, 1985a). This is the sense of being modern associated with Baudelaire which, as Foucault (1986: 40) argues, entails an ironical heroicization of the present: the modern man is the man who constantly tries to invent himself. It is this attempt to make sense of the experience of life in the new urban spaces and nascent consumer culture, which developed in the second half of the nineteenth century, which provided the impetus for the theories of modern everyday life in the work of Simmel, Kracauer and Benjamin discussed by David Frisby (1985b) in his *Fragments of Modernity*. The experience of modernity also forms the subject matter of Marshall Berman's (1982) book *All That Is Solid Melts into Air* in which he looks at the visions and idioms accompanying the modernization process which he pulls together under the term 'modernism'. Berman discusses the modern sensibility that is manifest in a wide range of literary and intellectual figures from Rousseau and Goethe in the eighteenth century to Marx, Baudelaire, Pushkin and Dostoevsky in the nineteenth.

Apart from the confusing use of modernism to take in the whole of the experience and the culture that accompanied the modernization process, Berman and many of those who are currently trying to delineate the equivalent experience of postmodernity focus upon a particularly restrictive notion of experience: that which appears in literary sources and is so designated by intellectuals. But we have to raise the sociological objection against the literary intellectual's licence in interpreting the everyday, or in providing evidence about the everyday lives of ordinary people. Of course, some intellectuals may have articulated well the experience of the shocks and jolts of modernity. Yet we need to make the jump from modernity or

4

postmodernity as a (relatively restricted) subjective experience to outlining the actual practices and activities which take place in the everyday lives of various groups. Certainly the descriptions of subjective experience may make sense within intellectual practices, and within aspects of the practices of particular audiences educated to interpret these sensibilities, but the assumption that one can make wider claims needs careful substantiation.

To take an example of the alleged experience of postmodernity (or *postmodernité*), we can refer to Jameson's (1984a) account of the Bonaventura Hotel in Los Angeles. Jameson gives a fascinating interpretation of the experience of the new hyperspace of postmodern architecture, which, he argues, forces us to expand our sensorium and body. Yet we get little idea how individuals from different backgrounds actually experience the hotel, or better still, how they incorporate the experience into their day-to-day practices. Perhaps for them to interpret the experience as postmodern they need guidelines to make sense of things they may not fully notice, or view through inappropriate codes. Hence, if we want to understand the social generation and interpretation of the experience of postmodernity we need to have a place for the role of cultural entrepreneurs and intermediaries who have an interest in creating postmodern pedagogies to educate publics. The same can be said for two other features of postmodern culture identified by Jameson: the transformation of reality into images and the fragmentation of time into a series of perpetual presents. Here we can take an example which encompasses both features: the media, which tends to be central to many discussions of the postmodern sensibility (one thinks for example of Baudrillard's simulational world, where 'TV is the world'). Yet for all the alleged pluralism and sensitivity to the Other talked about by some theorists one finds little discussion of the actual experience and practice of watching television by different groups in different settings. On the contrary, theorists of the postmodern often talk of an ideal-type channel-hopping MTV (music television) viewer who flips through different images at such speed that she/he is unable to chain the signifiers together into a meaningful narrative, he/she merely enjoys the multiphrenic intensities and sensations of the surface of the images. Evidence of the extent of such practices, and how they are integrated into, or influence, the day-to-day encounters between embodied persons is markedly lacking. Thus while learned references to the characteristic experiences of postmodernity are important we need to work from more systematic data and should not rely on the readings of intellectuals. In effect we should focus upon the actual cultural practices and changing power balances of those groups engaged in the production, classification, circulation and consumption of postmodern cultural goods, something which will be central to our discussion of postmodernism below.

Modernization–postmodernization

On the face of it, both terms seem to sit unhappily amid discussion of modernity-postmodernity, modernism–postmodernism. Modernization has been regularly used in the sociology of development to point to the effects of economic development on traditional social structures and values. Modernization theory is also used to refer to the stages of social development which are based upon industrialization, she growth of science and technology, the modern nation state, the capitalist world market, urbanization and other infrastructural elements. (In this usage it has strong affinities with the first sense of modernity we discussed above.) It is generally assumed, via a loose base-superstructure model, that certain cultural changes (secularization and the emergence of a modern identity which centres around self-development) will result from the modernization process. If we turn to postmodernization it is clear that a concomitant detailed outline of specific social processes and institutional changes has yet to be theorized. All we have is the possibility of deriving the term from those usages of postmodernity which refer to a new social order and epochal shift mentioned above. For example, Baudrillard's (1983a) depiction of a postmodern simulational world is based upon the assumption that the development of commodity production coupled with information technology have led to the 'triumph of signifying culture' which then reverses the direction of determinism, so that social relations become saturated with shifting cultural signs to the extent that we can no longer speak of class or normativity and are faced by 'the end of the social'. Baudrillard, however, does not use the term 'postmodernization'.

Yet the term does have the merit of suggesting a process with degrees of implementation, rather than a fully fledged new social order or totality. One significant context for the utilization of the term 'postmodernization' is the field of urban studies and here we can point to the writings of Philip Cooke (1988) and Sharon Zukin (1988a). For Cooke, postmodernization is an ideology and set of practices with spatial effects which have been notable in the British economy since 1976. Zukin also wants to use postmodernization to focus on the restructuring of socio-spatial relations by new patterns of investment and production in industry, services, labour markets and telecommunications. Yet, while Zukin sees postmodernization as a dynamic process comparable to modernization, both she and Cooke are reluctant to regard it as pointing to a new stage of society, for both see it as taking place within capitalism. This has the merit of focusing on processes of production as well as consumption and the spatial dimension of particular cultural practices (the redevelopment of downtowns and waterfronts, development of urban artistic and cultural centres. and the growth of the service class and gentrification) which accompany them.

Modernism–postmodernism

As with the pairing modernity–postmodernity, we are again faced with a range of meanings. Common to them all is the centrality of culture. In the most restricted sense, modernism points to the styles we associate with the artistic movements which originated around the turn of the century and which have dominated the various arts until recently. Figures frequently cited are: Joyce, Yeats, Gide, Proust, Rilke, Kafka, Mann, Musil, Lawrence, Virginia Woolf and Faulkner in literature; Rilke, Pound, Eliot, Lorca, Valery in poetry; Strindberg and Pirandello in drama; Matisse, Picasso, Braque, Cézanne and the Futurist, Expressionist, Dada and Surrealist movements in painting; Stravinsky, Schoenberg and Berg in music (see Bradbury and McFarlane, 1976). There is a good deal of debate about how far back into the nineteenth century modernism should be taken (some would want to go back to the bohemian avant-garde of the 1830s). The basic features of modernism can be summarized as: an aesthetic self-consciousness and reflexiveness; a rejection of narrative structure in favour of simultaneity and montage; an exploration of the paradoxical, ambiguous and uncertain open-ended nature of reality; and a rejection of the notion of an integrated personality in favour of an emphasis upon the de-structured, de-humanized subject (see Lunn, 1985: 34 ff.). One of the problems with trying to understand postmodernism in the arts is that many of these features are appropriated into various definitions of postmodernism. The problem with the term, as with the other related terms we have discussed, revolves around the question of when does a term defined oppositionally to, and feeding off, an established term start to signify something substantially different?

According to Kohler (1977) and Hassan (1985) the term 'postmodernism' was first used by Federico de Onis in the 1930s to indicate a minor reaction to modernism. The term became popular in the 1960s in New York when it was used by young artists, writers and critics such as Rauschenberg, Cage, Burroughs, Barthelme, Fielder, Hassan and Sontag to refer to a movement beyond the 'exhausted' high modernism which was rejected because of its institutionalization in the museum and the academy. It gained wider usage in architecture, the visual and performing arts, and music in the 1970s and 1980s and then was rapidly transmitted back and forth between Europe and the United States as the search for theoretical explanations and justifications of artistic postmodernism shifted to include wider discussions of postmodernity and drew in, and generated an interest in, theorists such as Bell, Kristeva, Lyotard, Vattimo, Derrida, Foucault, Habermas, Baudrillard and Jameson (see Huyssen 1984). Among the central features associated with postmodernism in the arts are: the effacement of the boundary between art and everyday life; the collapse of the hierarchal distinction between high and mass/popular culture; a stylistic promiscuity favouring eclecticism and the mixing of codes; parody, pastiche, irony, playfulness and the celebration of the surface 'depthlessness' of culture; the decline of the originality/genius of the artistic producer; and the assumption that art can only be repetition.

There is also a wider usage of the terms 'modernism' and 'postmodernism' which refers to broader cultural complexes: that is, modernism as the culture of modernity, and postmodernism as the emergent culture of postmodernity. Daniel Bell (1976) takes up this position in which he sees the fundamental cultural assumption of modernity, the ideal of the autonomous self-determining individual, as giving rise to the bourgeois entrepreneur in the economic realm and the artistic search for the untrammelled self (which finds its expression in modernism) in the cultural realm. For Bell modernism is a corrosive force, unleashing an adversarial culture which in conjunction with the hedonistic culture of mass consumption subverts traditional bourgeois values and the Puritan ethic. Bell's analysis is based on the notion of the disjunction of the three realms, the polity, culture and economy, so there is no sense in looking for a base-superstructural model in his work in which a shift in the economy or socioeconomic order such as to the post-industrial society would give rise to a new culture of postmodernism. Rather, postmodernism is perceived as a heightening of the antinomian tendencies of modernism with desire, the instinctual, and pleasure unleashed to carry the logic of modernism to its furthest reaches exacerbating the structural tensions of society and disjunction of the realms (Bell, 1980). Jameson (1984a) too uses postmodernism to refer to culture in the broader sense and talks about postmodernism as a cultural logic, or cultural dominant, which leads to the transformation of the cultural sphere in contemporary society. While Jameson shows some reluctance in adopting the view of periodization which assumes a sudden shift and transformation of all aspects of culture, he follows Mandel (1975) and links the stages of modernism to monopoly capitalism and postmodernism to post-World War II late capitalism. This suggests that he uses a form of the base-superstructural model. Yet he also goes part of the way along the same route as Baudrillard, without referring to him, to argue that postmodernism is based upon the central role of reproduction in the 'de-centred global network' of present-day multinational capitalism which leads to a 'prodigious expansion of culture throughout the social realm, to the point at which everything in our social life ... can be said to have become "cultural"' (Jameson, 1984a: 85–7).

There is one further point that needs to be taken up from the work of Bell and Jameson before going on to look at the use of postmodernism as a cipher for fundamental cultural changes as well as the possible expansion of the significance of culture in contemporary Western societies. John O'Neill (1988) has argued that both Bell and Jameson adopt a nostalgic reaction to postmodernism, and are united against postmodernism in their 'will to order', their desire to renew the threatened social bond via religion (Bell) or the Marxist utopia (Jameson). Both have the merit or flaw, depending on where you stand, of wanting to totalize: to depict postmodernism in its degrees of connectedness and disjunction to the contemporary social order. They also want to judge postmodernism as negative; they have a distaste for it, a response which has not passed unnoticed on the part of those critics who welcome the playfulness and pluralistic, 'democratic' spirit of postmodernism, and would see Jameson (and by association, Bell) as nostalgically bemoaning the loss of authority of the intellectual aristocracy over the population (see Hutcheon, 1986–7; During, 1987).

For those who welcome postmodernism as a mode of critical analysis which opens up ironies, intertextuality and paradoxes, attempts to devise a theory of postmodern society or postmodernity, or delineate the role of postmodernism within the social order, are essentially flawed efforts to totalize or systematize. In effect they are authoritarian grand narratives which are ripe for playful deconstruction. Critics are, for example, quick to point out this apparent inconsistency in Lyotard's *Postmodern Condition*. Kellner (1988), for example, argues that Lyotard's notion of postmodernity itself entails a master narrative, that we can't have a theory of the post-modern without one. It should be added that Lyotard (1988) has recently emphasized the need to move away from what he sees as the misunder-standing of his book as an example of totalizing reason. For those who take seriously the implications of postmodernism as a mode of critical theoriz-ing or cultural analysis, the attempt to produce a sociological understand-ing must necessarily fail as it cannot avoid totalizations, systematizations and legitimation via the flawed grand narratives of modernity: science, humanism, Marxism, feminism etc. Sociological synthesis must be aban-doned for playful deconstruction and the privileging of the aesthetic mode. A postmodern sociology so conceived would abandon its generalizing social science ambitions and instead parasitically play off the ironies, incoher-ences, inconsistencies and intertextuality of sociological writings. There are, of course, lessons to be learned from a postmodern sociology: it focuses attention on the ways in which theories are built up, their hidden assump-tions, and questions the theorist's authority to speak for 'the Other', who as many researchers are finding out, is now often actively disputing both the account and the authority of the academic theorist. Yet if we are to attempt to make sense of the emergence of postmodernism and the changes taking place in the culture of contemporary Western societies we need to move beyond the false oppositions of foundationalism and relativism, of single epistemology and plural ontology, and investigate specific social and cul-tural processes and the dynamics of the production of particular funds of knowledge. In effect we must relinquish the attractions of a postmodern sociology and work towards a sociological account of postmodernism (see chapter 3).

To follow such an approach would entail focusing on the interrelationship between three aspects or meanings of the culture of postmodernism. In the first place we can consider postmodernism in the arts and in the academic and intellectual fields. Here we could usefully employ the field approach of Bourdieu (1971, 1979) and focus upon the economy of symbolic goods: the conditions of supply and demand for such goods, the processes of competi-tion and monopolization, and the struggles between established and out-siders. We could, for example, direct attention to the act of *naming* as an important strategy of groups engaged in struggles with other groups; the use of new terms by outsider groups who have an interest in destabilizing existing symbolic hierarchies to produce a reclassification of the field more in line with their own interests: the conditions which are breaking down the barriers between sub-fields of the arts and academic subjects; the conditions which dictate changes in the demand for particular types of cultural goods by various state agencies, consumers, audiences and publics.

To adequately deal with the last areas, indeed to adequately conceptualize all the above areas, would take us outside the specific analysis of particular artistic and intellectual fields and their interrelationship. Here we would need to consider postmodernism in terms of a second 'level' of culture, what is often called the cultural sphere, and consider the means of transmission, and circulation to audiences and publics and the feedback effect of the audience response in generating further interest amongst intellectuals. To focus on this second area we need to look at artists, intellectuals and academics as specialists in symbolic production and consider their relationship to other symbolic specialists in the media, and those engaged in consumer culture, popular culture and fashion occupations. Here we need to focus on the emergence of what Bourdieu (1984) calls the 'new cultural intermediaries', who rapidly circulate information between formerly sealed-off areas of culture, and the emergence of new communication channels under conditions of intensified competition (Crane, 1987). We also need to consider the competition, changing balances of power and interdependences between specialists in symbolic production and economic specialists (cf. Elias, 1987b) within conditions of a growth in the former group's power potential as producers and consumers accompanying the growth of mass and higher education in Western nations in the postwar era. We need to examine some of the processes of de-monopolization and de-hierarchization of previously established and legitimate cultural enclaves which has brought about a phase of cultural declassification in the Western world (DiMaggio, 1987). Finally, in addition to considering these changes on an intrasocietal level we need also to consider the processes of intensified competition on an intersocietal level which is shifting the balance of power away from Western intellectuals and artists and their right to speak for humanity, as well as the emergence of genuine global cultural questions through what Roland Robertson (1990) has called 'globalization'. These processes point to changes within the broader cultural sphere which are worthy of investigation in their own right; processes which, it can be argued, the concept of postmodernism has served to sensitize us to.

The concept of postmodernism is not, however, merely an empty sign which can be manipulated by artists, intellectuals and academics as part of the power struggles and interdependencies within their particular fields. Part of its appeal is that it speaks to the above changes and also purports to illuminate changes in the day-to-day experiences and cultural practices of broader groups in society. It is here that the evidence is weakest and the possibility of simply relabelling experiences as postmodern which were formerly granted little significance, is most obvious. It is here that we face the problem of an adequate definition of postmodernism and find a good deal of loose conceptual confusion with notions of 'the loss of a sense of historical past', 'schizoid culture', 'excremental culture', 'the replacement of reality by images', 'simulations', 'unchained signifiers' etc., multiplying. Scott Lash (1988) has endeavoured to move to a tighter definition of postmodernism as involving de-differentiation and the figural which are held to be central to postmodern regimes of signification; yet here too we possess little systematic evidence about day-to-day practices, and we need information in terms of the stock sociological questions 'who? when? where? how many?' if we are to impress colleagues that postmodernism is more than a fad. Yet there is also a sense in which postmodernism proceeds under its own steam, with the changes in the cultural sphere we have hinted at above, leading to the formation of new audiences and publics interested in postmodernism. Such audiences and publics may eventually adopt postmodern practices and become attuned to postmodern experiences under the guidance of pedagogues produced by cultural intermediaries and paraintellectuals. Such 'feedback' could lead to postmodernism becoming translated into reality.

To summarize, there is, as yet, no agreed meaning to the term 'postmodern' – its derivatives, the family of terms which include postmodernity, *postmodernité*, postmodernization and postmodernism are often used in confusing and interchangeable ways. I have attempted to outline and discuss some of these meanings. Postmodernism is of interest to a wide range of artistic practices and social science and humanities disciplines because it directs our attention to changes taking place in contemporary culture. These can be understood in terms of (1) the artistic, intellectual and academic fields (changes in modes of theorization, presentation and dissemination of work which cannot be detached from changes in specific competitive struggles occurring in particular fields): (2) changes in the broader cultural sphere involving the modes of production, consumption and circulation of symbolic goods which can be related to broader shifts in the balance of power and interdependencies between groups and class fractions on both inter and intrasocietal levels; (3) changes in the everyday practices and experiences of different groups, who as a result of some of the processes referred to above, may be using regimes of signification in different ways and developing new means of orientation and identity structures. It is apparent that in recent years we have witnessed a dramatic upsurge of interest in the issue of culture. Culture. once on the periphery of social science disciplines, particularly in sociology. has now been thrust increasingly towards the centre of the field and some of the barriers between the social sciences and humanities are in the process of being dismantled (Featherstone, 1988). We can understand this in terms of two processes which must be interrelated: first, the way in which culture has shifted in the arsenal of social science concepts from something which is essentially explicable in terms of other factors to broader metacultural questions concerning the cultural underpinning, or 'deep' cultural coding, of the social (see Robertson, 1988); second, the way in which the culture of contemporary Western societies seems to be undergoing a series of major transformations which must be investigated in terms of intrasocietal, intersocietal and global processes. It should be apparent that this is one reason for the rise of interest in postmodernism, and a further reason why as cultural theorists and researchers we should be interested in it.

2

Theories of Consumer Culture

This chapter identifies three main perspectives on consumer culture. First is the view that consumer culture is premised upon the expansion of capitalist commodity production which has given rise to a vast accumulation of material culture in the form of consumer goods and sites for purchase and consumption. This has resulted in the growing salience of leisure and consumption activities in contemporary Western societies which, although greeted as leading to greater egalitarianism and individual freedom by some, is regarded by others as increasing the capacity for ideological manipulation and 'seductive' containment of the population from some alternative set of 'better' social relations. Second, there is the more strictly sociological view, that the satisfaction derived from goods relates to their socially structured access in a zero-sum game in which satisfaction and status depend upon displaying and sustaining differences within conditions of inflation. The focus here is upon the different ways in which people use goods in order to create social bonds or distinctions. Third, there is the question of the emotional pleasures of consumption, the dreams and desires which become celebrated in consumer cultural imagery and particular sites of consumption which variously generate direct bodily excitement and aesthetic pleasures.

This chapter argues that it is important to focus on the question of the growing prominence of the *culture* of consumption and not merely regard consumption as derived unproblematically from production. The current phase of over-supply of symbolic goods in contemporary Western societies and the tendencies towards cultural disorder and de-classification (which some label as postmodernism) is therefore bringing cultural questions to the fore and has wider implications for our conceptualization of the relationship between culture, economy and society. This has also led to an increasing interest in conceptualizing questions of desire and pleasure, the emotional and aesthetic satisfactions derived from consumer experiences, not merely in terms of some logic of psychological manipulation. Rather sociology should seek to move beyond the negative evaluation of consumer pleasures inherited from mass culture theory. We should endeavour to account for these emergent tendencies in a more detached sociological manner, which should not merely entail a reverse populist celebration of mass pleasures and cultural disorder.

The production of consumption

If from the perspectives of classical economics the object of all production is consumption, with individuals maximizing their satisfactions through purchasing from an ever-expanding range of goods, then from the perspective of some twentieth-century neo-Marxists this development is regarded as producing greater opportunities for controlled arid manipulated consumption. The expansion of capitalist production, especially after the boost received from scientific management and 'Fordism' around the turn of the century, it is held, necessitated the construction of new markets and the 'education' of publics to become consumers through advertising and other media (Ewen, 1976). This approach, traceable back to Lukács's (1971) Marx–Weber synthesis with his theory of reification, has been developed most prominently in the writings of Horkheimer and Adorno (1972), Marcuse (1964) and Lefebvre (1971). Horkheimer and Adorno, for example, argue that the same commodity logic and instrumental rationality manifest in the sphere of production is noticeable in the sphere of consumption. Leisure time pursuits, the arts and culture in general become filtered through the culture industry; reception becomes dictated by exchange value as the higher purposes and values of culture succumb to the logic of the production process and the market. Traditional forms of association in the family and private life as well as the promise of happiness and fulfilment, the 'yearning for a totally different other' which the best products of high culture strove for, are presented as yielding to an atomized, manipulated mass who participate in an *ersatz* mass-produced commodity culture targeted at the lowest common denominator.

From this perspective it could, for example, be argued that the accumulation of goods has resulted in the triumph of exchange-value, that the instrumental rational calculation of all aspects of life becomes possible in which all essential differences, cultural traditions and qualities become transformed into quantities. Yet while this utilization of capital logic can account for the progressive calculability and destruction of residues of traditional culture and high culture – in the sense that the logic of capitalist modernization is such to make 'all that is solid melt into air' – there is the problem of the 'new' culture, the culture of capitalist modernity. Is it to be merely a culture of exchange value and instrumental rational calculation – something which might be referred to as a 'non-culture' or a 'post-culture'?[1] This is one tendency within the work of the Frankfurt School, but there is another. Adorno, for example, speaks of how, once the dominance of exchange-value has managed to obliterate the memory of the original use-value of goods, the commodity becomes free to take up a secondary or *ersatz* use-value (Rose, l978: 25). Commodities hence become free to take on a wide range of cultural associations and illusions. Advertising in particular is able to exploit this and attach images of romance, exotica, desire, beauty, fulfilment, communality, scientific progress and the good life to mundane consumer goods such as soap, washing machines, motor cars and alcoholic drinks.

A similar emphasis upon the relentless logic of the commodity is to be found in the work of Jean Baudrillard who also draws upon the commodification theory of Lukács (1971) and Lefebvre (1971) to reach similar conclusions to Adorno. The major addition to Baudrillard's (1970) theory is to draw on semiology to argue that consumption entails the active manipulation of signs. This becomes central to late capitalist society where sign and commodity have come together to produce the 'commodity-sign'. The autonomy of the signifier, through, for example, the manipulation of signs in the media and advertising, means that signs are able to float free from objects and are available for use in a multiplicity of associative relations. Baudrillard's semiological development of commodity logic, entails for some an idealistic deflection of Marx's theory and movement from a materialist emphasis to a cultural emphasis (Preteceille and Terrail, 1985). This becomes more noticeable in Baudrillard's (1983a, 1983b) later writings where the emphasis shifts from production to reproduction, to the endless reduplication of signs, images and simulations through the media which effaces the distinction between the image and reality. Hence the consumer society becomes essentially cultural as social life becomes deregulated and social relationships become more variable and less structured by stable norms. The overproduction of signs and reproduction of images and simulations leads to a loss of stable meaning, and an aestheticization of reality in which the masses become fascinated by the endless flow of bizarre juxtapositions which takes the viewer beyond stable sense.

This is the postmodern, 'depthless culture' of which Jameson (1984a, 1984b) speaks. Jameson's conception of postmodern culture is strongly influenced by Baudrillard's work (see Jameson, 1979). He also sees postmodern culture as the culture of the consumer society, the post-World War II stage of late capitalism. In this society culture is given a new significance through the saturation of signs and messages to the extent that 'everything in social life can be said to have become cultural' (Jameson, 1984a: 87). This 'liquefaction of signs and images' is also held to entail an effacement of the distinction between high and mass culture (Jameson, 1984b: 112): an acceptance of the equal validity of Las Vegas Strip pop culture, alongside 'serious' high culture. At this point we should note the assumption that the immanent logic of the consumer capitalist society leads towards postmodernism. We will return to this question later to discuss images, desires and the aesthetic dimension of consumer culture.

It is clear that the production of consumption approach has difficulty in addressing the actual practices and experiences of consumption. The Frankfurt School's tendency to regard the culture industries as producing a homogeneous mass culture which threatens individuality and creativity[2] has been criticized for its elitism and inability to examine actual processes of consumption which reveal complex differentiated audience responses and uses of goods (Swingewood, 1977; Bennett et al., 1977; Gellner, 1979; B.S. Turner, 1988; Stauth and Turner, 1988).

Modes of consumption

If it is possible to claim the operation of a 'capital logic' deriving from production, it may also be possible to claim a 'consumption logic' which points to the socially structured ways in which goods are used to demarcate social relationships. To speak of the consumption of goods immediately hides the wide range of goods which are consumed or purchased when more and more aspects of free time (which includes everyday routine maintenance activities as well as leisure) are mediated by the purchase of commodities. It also hides the need to differentiate between consumer durables (goods we use in maintenance and leisure, for example refrigerators, cars, hi-fis, cameras) and consumer non-durables (food, drink, clothing, body-care products) and the shift over time in the proportion of income spent on each sector (Hirshman, 1982: ch. 2; Leiss, Kline and Jhally, 1986: 260). We also need to pay attention to the ways in which some goods can move in and out of commodity status and the different length of life enjoyed by commodities as they move from production to consumption. Food and drink usually have a short life, although this is not always the case; for example a bottle of vintage port may enjoy a prestige and exclusivity which means that it is never actually consumed (opened and drunk), although it may be consumed symbolically (gazed at, dreamt about, talked about, photographed and handled) in various ways which produce a great deal of satisfaction. It is in this sense that we can refer to the *doubly* symbolic aspect of goods in contemporary Western societies: symbolism is not only evident in the design and imagery of the production and marketing processes, the symbolic associations of goods may be utilized and renegotiated to emphasize differences in lifestyle which demarcate social relationships (Leiss, 1978: 19).

In some cases the object of purchasing may be to gain prestige through high exchange value (the price of the bottle of port is constantly mentioned), especially the case within societies where the aristocracy and old rich have been forced to yield power to the new rich (for example Veblen's 'conspicuous consumption'). The opposite situation can also be envisaged in which a former commodity becomes stripped of its commodity status. Hence gifts and inherited objects may become de-commodified on reception and become literally 'priceless' (in the sense that it is extreme bad taste to consider selling them or to attempt to fix a price upon them) in their ability to symbolize intense personal relationships and their capacity to invoke memories of loved ones (Rochberg-Halton, 1986: 176). Art objects, or objects produced for ritual, and hence given a particular symbolic charge, tend often to be ones excluded from exchange, or not permitted to remain in the commodity status for long. At the same time their professed sacred status and denial of the profane market and commodity exchange may paradoxically raise their value. Their lack of availability and 'pricelessness' raises their price and desirability. For example, Willis's (1978) description of the way bike boys make sacred the original '78 records of Buddy

Holly and Elvis Presley and refuse to use compilation albums which may have better reproduction, illustrates this process of the de-commodification of a mass object.

Hence while there is the capacity for commodities to break down social barriers, to dissolve the long-established links between persons and things, there is also the countertendency, the movement towards de-commodification, to restrict, control and channel the exchange of goods. In some societies stable status systems are protected and reproduced by restricting possibilities for exchange, or for the supply of new goods. In other societies there is an ever-changing supply of commodities which gives the illusion of complete changeability of goods and unrestricted access to them; yet here, legitimate *taste*, knowledge of the principles of classification, hierarchy and appropriateness is restricted, as is the case in fashion systems. An intermediate stage would be *sumptuary* laws, which act as consumption-regulating devices, prescribing which groups can consume which goods and wear types of clothing in a context where a previous stable status system is under strong threat from a major upsurge in the number and availability of commodities – the case in late premodern Europe (Appadurai, 1986: 25).

In contemporary Western societies the tendency is towards the second case mentioned, with an ever-changing flow of commodities making the problem of reading the status or rank of the bearer of the commodities more complex. It is in this context that taste, the discriminatory judgement, the knowledge or culture capital, which enables particular groups or categories of people to understand and classify new goods appropriately and how to use them, becomes important. Here we can turn to the work of Bourdieu (1984) and Douglas and Isherwood (1980) who examine the ways goods are used to mark social differences and act as communicators.

Douglas and Isherwood's (1980) work is particularly important in this respect because of their emphasis on the way in which goods are used to draw the lines of social relationships. Our enjoyment of goods, they argue, is only partly related to their physical consumption, being also crucially linked to their use as markers; we enjoy, for example, sharing the names of goods with others (the sports fan or the wine connoisseur). In addition the mastery of the cultural person entails a seemingly 'natural' mastery not only of information (the autodidact 'memory man') but also of how to use and consume appropriately and with natural ease in every situation. In this sense the consumption of high cultural goods (art, novels, opera, philosophy) must be related to the ways in which other more mundane cultural goods (clothing, food, drink, leisure pursuits) are handled and consumed, and high culture must be inscribed into the same social space as everyday cultural consumption. In Douglas and Isherwood's (1980: 176 ff.) discussion consumption classes are defined in relation to the consumption of three sets of goods: a staple set corresponding to the primary production sector (for example food); a technology set corresponding to the secondary production sector (travel and consumer's capital equipment); and an information set corresponding to tertiary production (information, goods, education, arts, cultural and leisure pursuits). At the lower end of the social structure the poor are restricted to the staple set and have more time on their hands, while those in the top consumption class not only require a higher level of earnings, but also a competence in judging information goods and services in order to provide the feedback necessary from consumption to employment, which becomes itself a qualification for employment. This entails a lifelong investment in cultural and symbolic capital and in time invested in maintaining consumption activities. Douglas and Isherwood (1980: 180) also remind us that ethnographic evidence suggests that the competition to acquire goods in the information class generates high admission barriers and effective techniques of exclusion.

The phasing, duration and intensity of time invested in acquiring competences for handling information, goods and services as well as the day-to-day practice, conservation and maintenance of these competences, is, as Halbwachs reminds us, a useful criterion of social class. Our use of time in consumption practices conforms to our class habitus and therefore conveys an accurate idea of our class status (see the discussion of Halbwachs in Preteceille and Terrail, 1985: 23). This points us towards the need for detailed time-budget research (see for example Gershuny and Jones, 1987). Such research, however, rarely incorporates, or is incorporated into, a theoretical framework drawing attention to patterns of investment over the life course which make such class-related differentiation of time use possible. The chances, for example, of encountering and making sense (that is, knowing how to enjoy and/or use the information in conversational practices) of a Godard film, the pile of bricks in the Tate Gallery, a book by Pynchon or Derrida, reflect different long-term investments in informational acquisition and cultural capital.

Such research has, however, been carried out in detail by Pierre Bourdieu and his associates (Bourdieu et al., 1965; Bourdieu and Passeron, 1990; Bourdieu, 1984). For Bourdieu (1984) 'taste classifies and classifies the classifier'. Consumption and lifestyle preferences involve discriminatory judgements which at the same time identify and render classifiable our own particular judgement of taste to others. Particular constellations of taste, consumption preferences and lifestyle practices are associated with specific occupation and class fractions, making it possible to map out the universe of taste and lifestyle with its structured oppositions and finely graded distinctions which operate within a particular society at a particular point in history. One important factor influencing the use of marker goods within capitalist societies is that the rate of production of new goods means that the struggle to obtain 'positional goods' (Hirsch, 1976), goods which define social status in the upper reaches of society, is a relative one. The constant supply of new, fashionably desirable goods, or the usurpation of existing marker goods by lower groups, produces a paperchase effect in which those above will have to invest in new (informational) goods in order to reestablish the original social distance.

In this context knowledge becomes important: knowledge of new goods, their social and cultural value, and how to use them appropriately. This is particularly the case with aspiring groups who adopt a learning mode towards consumption and the cultivation of a lifestyle. It is for groups such as the new middle class, the new working class and the new rich or upper class, that the consumer-culture magazines, newspapers, books, television and radio programmes which stress self-improvement, self-development, personal transformation, how to manage property, relationships and ambition, how to construct a fulfilling lifestyle, are most relevant. Here one may find most frequently the self-consciousness of the autodidact who is concerned to convey the appropriate and legitimate signals through his/her consumption activities. This may be particularly the case with the group Bourdieu (1984) refers to as 'the new cultural intermediaries', those in media, design, fashion, advertising and 'para' intellectual information occupations, whose jobs entail performing services and the production, marketing and dissemination of symbolic goods. Given conditions of an increasing supply of symbolic goods (Touraine, 1985), demand grows for cultural specialists and intermediaries who have the capacity to ransack various traditions and cultures in order to produce new symbolic goods, and in addition provide the necessary interpretations on their use. Their habitus, dispositions and lifestyle preferences are such that they identify with artists and intellectuals, yet under conditions of the de-monopolization of artistic and intellectual commodity enclaves they have the apparent contradictory interests of sustaining the prestige and cultural capital of these enclaves, while at the same time popularizing and making them more accessible to wider audiences.

It should be apparent that the problems of inflation produced by an over-supply and rapid circulation of symbolic goods and consumer commodities have the danger of threatening the readability of goods used as signs of social status. Within the context of the erosion of the bounded state-society as part of a process of the globalization of markets and culture, it may be more difficult to stabilize appropriate marker goods. This would threaten the cultural logic of differences in which taste in cultural and consumer goods and lifestyle activities are held to be oppositionally structured (see the chart in which they are mapped out in Bourdieu, 1984: 128–9). This threat of disorder to the field or system would exist even if one accepted the premise derived from structuralism that culture itself is subject to a differential logic of opposition. To detect and establish such structured oppositions that enable groups to use symbolic goods to establish differences, would thus work best in relatively stable, closed and integrated societies, in which the leakages and potential disorder from reading goods through inappropriate codes is restricted. There is the further question of whether there are relatively stable sets of classificatory principles and dispositions, that is, the habitus, which are socially recognizable and operate to establish the boundaries between groups. The examples of cultural disorder, the overwhelming flood of signs and images which Baudrillard (1983a) argues is pushing us beyond the social, are usually taken from the media with television, rock videos and MTV (music television) cited as examples of pastiche, eclectic mixing of codes, bizarre juxtapositions and unchained signifiers which defy meaning and readability.

On the other hand if one 'descends' to the everyday practices of embodied persons held together in webs of interdependencies and power balances with other people, it can be argued that the need to glean clues and information about the other's power potential, status and social standing by reading the other person's demeanour will continue. The different styles and labels of fashionable clothing and goods, however much they are subject to change, imitation and copying, are one such set of clues which are used in the act of classifying others. Yet as Bourdieu (1984) reminds us with his concept of symbolic capital, the signs of the dispositions and classificatory schemes which betray one's origins and trajectory through life are also manifest in body shape, size, weight, stance, walk, demeanour, tone of voice, style of speaking. sense of ease or discomfort with one's body, etc. Hence culture is incorporated, and it is not just a question of what clothes are worn, but how they are worn. Advice books on manners, taste and etiquette from Erasmus down to Nancy Mitford's 'U' and 'non-U', only impress their subjects with the need to naturalize dispositions and manners, to be completely at home with them as second nature, and also make clear that this entails the capacity to spot imposters. In this sense the newly arrived, the autodidact, will unavoidably give away signs of the burden of attainment and incompleteness of his/her cultural competence. Hence the new rich who may adopt conspicuous consumption strategies are recognizable and assigned their place in the social space. Their cultural practices are always in danger of being dismissed as vulgar and tasteless by the established upper class, aristocracy and those 'rich in cultural capital'.

We therefore need to consider the pressures which threaten to produce an oversupply of cultural and consumer goods and relate this to more general processes of cultural declassification (DiMaggio, 1987). We also need to consider those pressures which could act towards the deformation of habitus, the locus of taste and classificatory choices. It may be that there are different modes of identity. and habitus formation and deformation emerging which make the significance of taste and lifestyle choice more blurred – if not throughout the social structure, at least within certain sectors, for instance the young and fractions of the middle class. We have also to consider that the much-talked-about cultural ferment and disorder, often labelled postmodernism, may not be the result of a total absence of controls, a genuine disorder, but merely point to a more deeply embedded integrative principle. Hence there may be 'rules of disorder' which act to permit more easily controlled swings – between order and disorder, status consciousness and the play of fantasy and desire, emotional control and de-control, instrumental calculation and hedonism – which were formerly threatening to the imperative to uphold a consistent identity structure and deny transgressions.

Consuming dreams, images and pleasure

As Raymond Williams (1976: 68) points out, one of the earliest uses of the term consume meant 'to destroy, to use up, to waste, to exhaust'. In this sense, consumption as waste, excess and spending represents a paradoxical presence within the productionist emphasis of capitalist and state socialist societies which must somehow be controlled and channelled. The notion of economic value as linked to scarcity, and the promise that the discipline and sacrifices necessitated by the drive to accumulate within the production process will lead to the eventual overcoming of scarcity, as consumer needs and pleasures are met, has been a strong cultural image and motivating force within capitalist and socialist societies alike. At the same time within the middle class, and especially among traditional economic specialists, we have the persistence of the notion of disciplined hard work, the 'inner worldly ascetic conduct' celebrated in nineteenth-century 'self-help' individualism and later twentieth-century Thatcherism. Here consumption is an auxiliary to work, and retains many of the displaced orientations from production. It is presented as orderly, respectable and conserving: old or traditional petit-bourgeois values which sit uneasily alongside new petit-bourgeois notions of leisure as creative play, 'narcissistic' emotional exploration and relationship building (cf. Bell's 1976 discussion of the paradox of modern consumer societies: to be a 'Puritan by day and a playboy by night'). This fraction within the new middle class, the cultural specialists and intermediaries we have already referred to (which also includes those from the counterculture who have survived from the 1960s and those who have taken up elements of their cultural imagery in different contexts), represents a disturbing group to the old petit-bourgeois virtues and the cultural mission of Thatcherism. This is because they have the capacity to broaden and question the prevalent notions of consumption, to circulate images of consumption suggesting alternative pleasures and desires, consumption as excess, waste and disorder.[3] This occurs within a society where, as we have emphasized, a good deal of production is targeted at consumption, leisure and services and where there is the increasing salience of the production of symbolic goods, images and information. It is therefore more difficult to harness the productive efforts of this expanding group of cultural specialists and intermediaries to the production of a particularly narrow message of traditional petit-bourgeois virtues and cultural order.

From this perspective we should pay attention to the persistence, displacements and transformation of the notion of culture as waste, squandering and excess. According to Bataille's (1988; Millot, 1988: 681 ff.) notion of general economy, economic production should not be linked to scarcity, but to *excess*. In effect the aim of production becomes destruction, and the key problem becomes what to do with *la part maudite*, the accursed share, the excess of energy translated into an excess of product and goods, a process of growth which reaches its limits in entropy and anomie. To control growth effectively and manage the surplus the only solution is to destroy or squander the excess in the form of games, religion, art, wars, death. This is carried out through gifts, potlatch, consumption tournaments, carnivals and conspicuous consumption. According to Bataille, capitalist societies attempt to channel the *part maudite* into full economic growth, to produce growth without end. Yet it can be argued that on a number of levels there are losses and leakages which persist, and, in terms of the argument just mentioned, capitalism also produces (one is tempted to follow the postmodernist rhetoric and say 'overproduces') images and sites of consumption which endorse the pleasures of excess. Those images and sites also favour blurring of the boundary between art and everyday life. Hence we need to investigate: (1) the persistence within consumer culture of elements of the pre-industrial carnivalesque tradition; (2) the transformation and displacement of the carnivalesque. into media images. design. advertising, rock videos, the cinema; (3) the persistence and transformation of elements of the carnivalesque within certain sites of consumption: holiday resorts, sports stadia. theme parks, department stores and shopping centres; (4) its displacement and incorporation into conspicuous consumption by states and corporations. either in the form of 'prestige' spectacles for wider publics, and/or privileged upper management and officialdom.

In contrast to those, largely late-nineteenth-century theories, inspired by notions of the rationalization, commodification and modernization of culture, which exhibit a nostalgic *Kulturpessimismus*, it is important to emphasize the tradition within popular culture of transgression, protest, the carnivalesque and liminal excesses (Easton et al., 1988). The popular tradition of carnivals, fairs and festivals provided symbolic inversions and transgressions of the official 'civilized' culture and favoured excitement, uncontrolled emotions and the direct and vulgar grotesque bodily pleasures of fattening food, intoxicating drink and sexual promiscuity (Bakhtin, 1968; Stallybrass and White, 1986). These were *liminal* spaces, in which the everyday world was turned upside down and in which the tabooed and fantastic were possible, in which impossible dreams could be expressed. The liminal, according to Victor Turner (1969; see also Martin, 1981: ch. 3), points to the emphasis within these essentially delimited transitional or threshold phases upon *anti-structure* and *communitas*, the generation of a sense of unmediated community, emotional fusion and ecstatic oneness. It should be apparent that these enclaved liminal moments of ordered disorder were not completely integrated by the state or the emerging consumer culture industries and 'civilizing processes' in eighteenth- and nineteenth-century Britain.

To take the example of fairs: fairs have long held a dual role as local markets and as sites of pleasure. They were not only sites where commodities were exchanged; they entailed the display of exotic and strange commodities from various parts of the world in a festive atmosphere (see Stallybrass and White, 1986 and also the discussion in chapter 5 below). Like the experience of the city, fairs offered spectacular imagery, bizarre juxtapositions, confusions of boundaries and an immersion in a *mêlée* of strange sounds, motions, images, people, animals and things. For those people, especially in the middle classes, who were developing bodily and emotional controls as part of civilizing processes (Elias, 1978b, 1982), sites of cultural disorder such as fairs, the city, the slum, the seaside resort, become the source of fascination, longing and nostalgia (Mercer, 1983; Shields, 1990). In a displaced form this became a central theme in art, literature and popular entertainment such as the music hall (Bailey, 1986a). It can also be argued that those institutions which came to dominate the urban marketplace, the department stores (Chaney, 1983; R.H. Williams, 1982) plus the new national and international exhibitions (Bennett, 1988), both developed in the second half of the nineteenth century, and other twentieth-century sites such as theme parks (Urry, 1988), provided sites of ordered disorder which summoned up elements of the carnivalesque tradition in their displays, imagery and simulations of exotic locations and lavish spectacles.

For Walter Benjamin (1982b) the new department stores and arcades, which emerged in Paris and subsequently other large cities from the mid-nineteenth century onwards, were effectively 'dream worlds'. The vast phantasmagoria of commodities on display, constantly renewed as part of the capitalist and modernist drive for novelty, was the source of dream images which summoned up associations and half-forgotten illusions – Benjamin referred to them as *allegories*. Here Benjamin uses the term allegory not to point to the unity or coherence of the doubly-coded message which is occluded, as in traditional allegories such as *Pilgrim's Progress*, but to the way a stable hierarchically ordered meaning is dissolved and the allegory points only to kaleidoscopic fragments which resist any coherent notion of what it stands for (see Wolin, 1982: Spencer, 1985). In this aestheticized commodity world the department stores, arcades, trams, trains, streets and fabric of buildings and the goods on display, as well as the people who stroll through these spaces summon up half-forgotten dreams, as the curiosity and memory of the stroller is fed by the ever-changing landscape in which objects appear divorced from their context and subject to mysterious connections which are read on the surface of things. The everyday life of the big cities becomes aestheticized. The new industrial processes provided the opportunity for art to shift into industry, which saw an expansion of occupations in advertising, marketing, industrial design and commercial display to produce the new aestheticized urban landscape (Buck-Morss, 1983). The growth of the mass media in the twentieth century with the proliferation of photographic images heightened the tendencies of which Benjamin talks. Indeed the unacknowledged impact of Benjamin's theory can be detected in some of the theorizations of postmodernism, such as those by Baudrillard (1983a) and Jameson (1984a, 1984b). Here the emphasis is on immediacies, intensities, sensory overload, disorientation, the *mêlée* or liquefaction of signs and images, the mixing of codes, the unchained or floating signifiers of the postmodern 'depthless' consumer culture where art and reality have switched places in an 'aesthetic hallucination of the real'. Clearly these qualities cannot be claimed to be unique to postmodernism and have a much longer genealogy, suggesting continuities between the modern and postmodern, and indeed, the premodern (see chapters 4 and 5).

There is a strong populist strand in the writings of Benjamin which is usually contrasted to the alleged elitism of Horkheimer and Adorno. Benjamin emphasized the utopian, or positive moment in the mass-produced consumer commodities which liberated creativity from art and allowed it to migrate into the multiplicity of mass-produced everyday objects (the influence of surrealism on Benjamin's theoretical framework is evident here). This celebration of the aesthetic potential of mass culture and the aestheticized perceptions of the people who stroll through the urban spaces of the large cities has been taken up by commentators who emphasize the transgressive and playful potential of postmodernism (Hebdige, 1988: Chambers, 1986, 1987). Here the perceptions of Benjamin and Baudrillard are accepted to point to the enhanced role of culture in contemporary Western cities, increasingly centres not only of everyday consumption but also of a wider range of symbolic goods and experiences produced by the culture industries (the arts, entertainment, tourism, heritage sectors). Within these 'postmodern cities' (Harvey, 1988) people are held to engage in a complex sign play which resonates with the proliferation of signs in the built environment and urban fabric. The contemporary urban *flâneurs*, or strollers, play with and celebrate the artificiality, randomness and superficiality of the fantastic *mélange* of fictions and strange values which are to be found in the fashions and popular cultures of cities (Chambers, 1987: Calefato, 1988). It is also argued that this represents a movement beyond individualism with a heightened emphasis upon the affectual and empathy, a new 'aesthetic paradigm' in which masses of people come together temporarily in fluid 'postmodern tribes' (Maffesoli, 1988a).

While there is a strong emphasis in such writings upon the sensory overload, the aesthetic immersion, dreamlike perceptions of decentred subjects, in which people open themselves up to a wider range of sensations and emotional experiences, it is important to stress that this does not represent the eclipse of controls. It needs discipline and control to stroll through goods on display, to look and not snatch, to move casually without interrupting the flow, to gaze with controlled enthusiasm and a blasé outlook, to observe others without being seen, to tolerate the close proximity of bodies without feeling threatened. It also requires the capacity to manage swings between intense involvement and more distanced aesthetic detachment. In short to move through urban spaces, or to experience the spectacles of the theme park and heritage museums, demands a 'controlled de-control of the emotions' (Wouters, 1986). The imagery may summon up pleasure, excitement, the carnivalesque and disorder, yet to experience them requires self-control and for those who lack such control there lurks in the background surveillance by security guards and remote-control cameras.

These tendencies towards the aestheticization of everyday life relate to the distinction between high and mass culture. A dual movement has suggested the collapse of some of the boundaries between art and everyday life and the erosion of the special protected status of art as an enclaved commodity. In the first place there is the migration of art into industrial design, advertising, and associated symbolic and image production industries we have mentioned. Second, there has been the internal *avant-gardiste* dynamic within the arts which, in the form of Dada and surrealism in the 1920s (Bürger, 1984) and in the form of postmodernism in the 1960s, sought to show that any everyday object could be aestheticized (see discussion in chapters 3 and 4 below). The 1960s Pop Art and postmodernism entail a focus upon everyday commodities as art (Warhol's Campbell's soup cans), an ironic playing back of consumer culture on itself, and an anti-museum and -academy stance in performance and body art. The expansion of the art market and increase in working artists and ancillary occupations, especially in metropolitan centres, plus the use of art as a vehicle for public relations by large corporations and the state, have resulted in significant changes in the artist's role (see Zukin, 1982a).

It has been argued that it is no longer useful to speak of an artistic *avant-garde* in the sense of a group of artists who reject both popular culture and the middle-class lifestyle (Crane, 1987). While the artist's lifestyle may still have an attractive romantic ambience for those engaged in the gentrification of inner-city areas and for members of the middle class in general who increasingly value the role of culture in lifestyle construction (Zukin, 1988b), many artists have relinquished their commitment to high culture and *avant-gardisme* and have adopted an increasingly open attitude towards consumer culture and now show a willingness to truck with other cultural intermediaries, image-makers, audiences and publics. Hence, with the parallel processes of the expansion of the role of art within consumer culture and the deformation of enclaved art with its separate prestige structure and lifestyle, a blurring of *genres* and the tendencies towards the deconstruction of symbolic hierarchies has occurred. This entails a pluralistic stance towards the variability of taste, a process of cultural declassification which has undermined the basis of high culture–mass culture distinctions. It is in this context that we get not just scepticism towards advertising's effectiveness, in that its capacity to persuade people to purchase new products – or indoctrinate – is questioned (Schudson, 1986) but a celebration of its aesthetic pedigree. Design and advertising thus not only become confused with art, but are celebrated and museumified as art. As Stephen Bayley (1979: 10) remarks: 'industrial design is the art of the twentieth century' (also quoted in Forty 1986: 7).

The attractions of the romantic-bohemian lifestyle with the artist presented as an expressive rebel and stylistic hero has been a strong theme, particularly with respect to popular and rock music, in Britain in the postwar era. Frith and Horne (1987) document this particular injection of art into popular culture which also helped to deconstruct the distinction between high and popular culture. In addition it can be seen as furthering the process of a controlled de-control of the emotions we have spoken of, with jazz, blues, rock and black music presented as forms of direct emotional expression which were regarded as both more pleasurable, involved and authentic by predominantly young audiences, and as dangerously threatening, uncontrolled, 'devil's music' to predominantly older, adult audiences used to more controlled and formal patterns of public behaviour and emotional restraint (Stratton, 1989). Yet there is also a sense in which, despite the popularity of artistic lifestyles and the various neo-dandyist transformations of making life a work of art, this project implies a degree of integration and unity of purpose which is becoming increasingly obsolete, despite the compelling nature of some of the symbols of these lifestyles. There is less interest in constructing a coherent style than in playing with, and expanding, the range of familiar styles. The term style suggests coherence and hierarchical ordering of elements, some inner form and expressiveness (Schapiro, 1961). It has often been argued by twentieth-century commentators that our age lacks a distinctive style. Simmel (1978), for example, refers to the age of 'no style' and Malraux (1967) remarked that our culture is a museum without walls' (see Roberts, 1988), perceptions which become heightened in postmodernism with its emphasis upon pastiche, 'retro', the collapse of symbolic hierarchies, and the playback of cultures.

A similar argument can be made with reference to the term 'lifestyle', that the tendency within consumer culture is to present lifestyles as no longer requiring inner coherence. The new cultural intermediaries, an expanding faction within the new middle class, therefore, while well disposed to the lifestyle of artists and cultural specialists, do not seek to promote a single lifestyle, but rather to cater for and expand the range of styles and lifestyles available to audiences and consumers (see the discussion in chapter 6 below).

Conclusion

In his book *All Consuming Images*, Stuart Ewen (1988) discusses an advertisement for Neiman Marcus, a fashionable US department store, which seemingly combines a unity of opposites. It juxtaposes two photographs of the same woman. The first presents an image of an upper-class woman dressed in Parisian *haute couture;* the text beneath the image stresses that *attitude* is 'disposition with regard to people', 'wearing the correct thing at the correct hour', 'exactly sized', 'a mode', 'dressing to please someone else', 'evaluation', 'strolling the avenue'. The second photograph is of a brooding Semitic woman dressed in a Palestinian scarf and desert kaftan. In graffiti-style typeface the text emphasizes that *latitude* is 'freedom from narrow restrictions', 'changing the structure of a garment when the mood hits', 'whatever feels comfortable', 'a mood', 'dressing to please yourself', 'evolution', 'loving the street life'. Within contemporary culture women and men are asked not to choose, but to incorporate both options. To regard their dress and consumer goods as communicators, as 'symbols of class status' (Goffman, 1951), demands appropriate conduct and demeanour on the part of the wearer/user in order to further the visible classification of the social world into categories of persons. In this sense, within consumer culture there still persist prestige economies, with scarce goods demanding considerable investment in time, money and knowledge to attain and handle appropriately. Such goods can be read and used to classify the status of their bearer. At the same time consumer culture uses images, signs and symbolic goods which summon up dreams, desires and fantasies which suggest romantic authenticity and emotional fulfilment in narcissistically pleasing oneself, instead of others. Contemporary consumer culture seems to be widening the range of contexts and situations in which such behaviour is deemed appropriate and acceptable. It is, therefore, not a question of a choice between these two options presented as alternatives; rather it is *both*. Today's consumer culture represents neither a lapse of control nor the institution of more rigid controls, but rather their underpinning by a flexible underlying generative structure which can both handle formal control and de-control and facilitate an easy change of gears between them.

Notes

1 This approach is one which has a long history within German sociology and reveals a distaste for rationalized *Gesellschaft* and a nostalgia for *Gemeinschaft* (see Liebersohn, 1988; B.S. Turner, 1987; Stauth and Turner, 1988). It also has been sustained in critical theory down to the work of Habermas (1984, 1987) in his distinction between system and lifeworld in which the commodification and instrumental rationalization imperatives of the techno-economic-administrative system threaten the uncoerced communicative actions of the lifeworld, and hence impoverish the cultural sphere.

2 Not all the Frankfurt School followed this position. Lowenthal (1961) stressed the democratic potential of mass marketed books in the eighteenth century. Swingewood (1977) has developed this argument into a strong critique of mass culture theory.

3 It is noticeable in the books with titles such as *Objects of Desire* (Forty, 1986), *Channels of Desire* (Ewen and Ewen, 1982), *Consuming Passions* (Williamson, 1986), *Dream Worlds* (R.H. Williams, 1982). Campbell (1987) also deals extensively with the historical genesis of desire for consumer goods. For a critique of the psychological as opposed to sociological grounding of his approach see the discussion in chapter 8 below. It should be added that the recent upsurge of interest in the sociology of the emotions (see Denzin, 1984; Hochschild, 1983: Elias, 1987d: Wouters, 1989), would suggest that we are at last moving towards a sociological framework for understanding the emotions.

3

Towards a Sociology of Postmodern Culture

Postmodernism in sociology

In *Social Theory and Modern Sociology* Anthony Giddens outlines 'Nine Theses on the Future of Sociology, in which the first thesis suggests that 'Sociology will increasingly shed the residue of nineteenth-and early twentieth-century social thought' (1987a: 26). Here Giddens develops the currently popular argument that sociology is and will continue to be bound up with the 'project of modernity'. He does so to point away from the economic reductionism that he sees as a pervasive legacy of nineteenth-century thought, to focus on three other major parameters of modernity: the development of administrative power, the development of military power, and warfare. Finally, he states:

> There is the cultural dimension of modernity – something obviously highly complex in its own right. In some guises. the analysis of this dimension has long been a preoccupation of sociology. Sociologists have understood the emergence of their own discipline against the background of the rise of 'rationalism' and the 'disenchantment of the world' attendant upon secularization. But once more it would probably be true to say that the culture of modernity has been understood largely as the reflex of capitalism or industrialism. Even Max Weber's famous attempt to claim an independent role for 'ideas' concentrated upon the conditions that initially gave rise to capitalism, rather than proposing a continuing role for a particular autonomous modern culture. Current controversies about what many have labelled 'post-modernity' should perhaps rather be seen as the first real initiatives in the ambitious task of charting the cultural universe resulting from the ever-more complete disintegration of the traditional world. At a minimum they surely express the strong sense that pre-established models of cultural analysis were radically defective. (Giddens, 1987a: 28–9)

Although there are many interesting issues in this quotation, only two brief points will be made here. First, Giddens highlights the potential of post-modernity, or perhaps we should say postmodernism, as a superior model for charting contemporary culture. Unfortunately, this point is not developed and in Giddens's only previous reference to postmodernism in a paper entitled 'Modernism and Post-Modernism', commenting on Habermas (1981a), he does not, to my knowledge, refer to postmodernism in the text (Giddens, 1981a). Giddens's emphasis on the potential of postmodern cultural analysis could perhaps be connected to his preference for a 'middle strategy that seeks to go beyond the duality of objectivism and relativism through the development of an 'ontology of potentials' as part of his structuration theory (see Cohen, 1986, 1987). Second, the quotation is one of his few direct references to culture as a substantive dimension of modernity or of society. That Giddens (1987b) is now at last turning toward the development of a theory of a cultural production, which might underpin his discussion of the culture of modernity and postmodernity, is evident in his essay 'Structuralism, Post-structuralism and the Production of Culture'.

In more general terms, one cannot but be aware of the way in which the conference on 'Social Structure and Culture' in Bremen in 1988, that brought together representatives of various Sociological Theory Groups from a number of European nations, was merely another symptom of the general elevation of culture to the centre of theorizing within sociology in recent years. One could also point to the inclusion of a major symposium on culture with five sessions at the international Sociological Association Congress in New Delhi in 1986 and the recent formation of a Culture Section by the American Sociological Association which held its first sessions in 1987. It has been suggested by Donaldson Langer (1984: 9) that this recent upsurge of interest in broader cultural questions and perception of the sociology of culture as a legitimate field of inquiry represents a major shift within sociology. Up until the mid-1970s sociological interest in culture and the arts was often considered eccentric, dilettantish and, at best, marginal. In this tradition the discipline boundaries between those sociologists who had some interest in the arts, and literary critics and art historians, who saw sociology as irrelevant to understanding the sacred domain of culture, were relatively strong. One symptom of the breakdown of the barriers between the fields has been the emergence of a range of journals in the English-speaking world since the 1970s which have become open to theorizations of culture which draw their audiences from a wide range of disciplines. Some deal exclusively with culture. Here we can think of *Working Papers in Cultural Studies; Ideology and Consciousness; Oxford Literary Review; Block; Semiotext(e); Tabloid; Substance; New German Critique; Diacritics; Theory and Society; Humanities in Society; Telos; Thesis Eleven; Praxis International; Canadian Journal of Political and Social Theory; Philosophy and Social Criticism; Media, Culture and Society; Politics, Culture and Society; Social Text; Theory, Culture & Society; Representations; Discourse; Cultural Anthropology; Critique of Anthropology; Culture and History; New Formations; Cultural Studies* and *Textual Practice.* The rise of interest in feminism, Marxism, structuralism, poststructuralism, semiology, critical theory and psychoanalysis also helped to raise the profile of cultural questions. In addition, those interested in theorizations of culture – the relationship between culture and society and questions of ideology, language, knowledge, discourse, subjectivity and agency, which have become intertwined with the explanations of changes in the arts and the cultural sphere – might well now expect to have to sift through a range of journals outside sociology and not only in cultural studies and the arts but also in politics, history, geography, art, architecture, philosophy, and planning. (For a brief discussion of these changes in relation to French social theory see Featherstone, 1986.)

These changes require careful documentation and explanation in terms of the dynamic of the academic and intellectual fields as well as their capacity to respond to and thematize sociocultural changes. They should not be taken just on the level of a paradigm shift or the victory of a superior set of methodologies. which is often how they have been presented to academic audiences, who could be forgiven a degree of bewilderment at the dazzling array of cultural theorists served up. The sociological theorists who had until recently some sense of a firm set of central issues and debates, which in their most ambitious form could aspire to provide a foundation for sociology to ground the other subjects in the social sciences, now had to take a step backward as deconstruction, poststructuralism and postmodernism appeared on the agenda or even threatened to render the existing agendas obsolete. Foucault, Lyotard, Deleuze, Derrida and Baudrillard have all recently been discussed in papers at the British Sociological Association's Theory Group meetings which now examines wider ranging topics with a cultural emphasis such as 'Modernity and Postmodernity' and 'the Body' as well as establishing stronger links with other European Sociological Theory Groups to accelerate the interchange of information.

For many sociologists the terms 'postmodernity' and 'postmodernism' may well have come first to the fore in the early 1980s with the 'debate' between Habermas and Foucault. Both terms do, of course, have a much longer history: the first use of 'postmodernism' was described as a minor reaction to modernism by Federico de Onis in 1934; 'postmodernity' was first coined to designate a new cycle in Western civilization by Toynbee in 1947 (see Hassan, 1985). The artistic use of the term 'postmodernism' gained priority over the epochal use as the term became popular in the 1960s, when it was used in the United States by young artists such as Rauschenberg, Cage, Burroughs and Barthelme and critics such as Fiedler, Hassan and Sontag to refer to a movement beyond the 'exhausted' high modernism which was regarded as having become institutionalized in the museum and in the academy. The term gained wider usage in architecture, the visual and performing arts, and music in the 1970s and then underwent a rapid series of mutations as it was exported to France in the late 1970s and adopted by critics such as Kristeva and Lyotard. It was then exported back to the United States largely in the form of Derrida's poststructuralist deconstructionism. The term was also exported to Germany in the late 1970s and assumed by Habermas (1981a) and his 1980 Adorno prize essay in the context of a discussion of modernity as an uncompleted project in which he called Foucault and Derrida 'young conservatives' (see Huyssen, 1984). The debates between Habermas and Foucault and Lyotard and Habermas and the formulations of them in terms of critical theory versus postmodernity have been largely conducted by third parties (see Bernstein, 1985; Hoy, 1986). There are many dimensions to the debate of which would like to make two salient points. First, Habermas's (1981a) dissatisfaction with Foucault and Derrida (and by association with Deleuze and Lyotard) was for endorsing a decentred boundless subjectivity, content to experience expressive intensities that were effectively derived from the postmodernist avant-garde which had sought to break down the boundaries between art and everyday life and hence gave primacy to aestheic experiences and gestures over morality and communicative modes of truth. Habermas, from earlier essays such as 'Technology, Science and Ideology' (1971) onward, had sought to theorize and find ways to reverse the perceived invasion of the communicative structures of the sociocultural life-world by instrumental and strategic rationality. From this perspective to have to deal with a new threat to the sociocultural life-world's communicative potential arising from the aesthetic sphere presents a further unwelcomed complication. Second, Habermas's (1985a: 203) own attempt to harness the critical potential of aesthetic experience to illuminate communicative truths should, one would expect, have only limited success given the difficulty of translating across two different cultural modalities.

The growth of interest in poststructuralism, deconstruction and postmodernism, coupled with Habermas's (1984) work on the trajectory of and relationship between the different sectors of cultural modernity, science, morality and art, therefore needs to be understood on a number of levels within the context of a more general emergence of interest in wider cultural questions. These point both to the metatheoretical foundations of modes of knowledge, as well as to the type of cultural complex that could best provide some version of the good, meaningful or satisfactory life. Postmodernism effectively thrusts aesthetic questions toward the centre of sociological theory: it offers aesthetic models and justifications for the reading and critique of texts (the pleasure of the text, intertextuality, writerly texts) and aesthetic models for life (the expressive aestheticization of life, art as the good of life).

This oversimplified narrative, then, may help us to point toward the recent growth of interest in culture within sociology, one recent manifestation of which is Giddens's (1987a) acknowledgement of culture as a fourth dimension of modernity and his suggestion that postmodernism may potentially offer a superior mode of analysis with which to chart the modern cultural universe. Yet before we can unpack and try to assess the conceptual and anticonceptual apparatus within the postmodern arsenal – the emphasis upon discontinuities, writerly texts, paradoxes. ironies, its playful reflexivity, celebration of difference, and critique of universalizations and totalizations, including the end of metanarratives and the end of history – we must return briefly to Giddens. His sixth thesis on the future of sociology states that 'Sociologists will redevelop a concern with large-scale, long-term processes of social transformation' (Giddens, 1987a: 41). A claim that, on the face of it, seems to run directly counter to the assumption that postmodern modes of analysis are superior. It also, and Giddens is aware of this, runs counter to his previous endorsement in the first thesis of the need to break free from the tradition of nineteenth-century thought. Giddens argues that we need to focus on long-term processes to capture the large-scale social changes that are accelerating in the twentieth century.

Large-scale, long-term process sociology has undergone a revival in recent years. Here one thinks of the work of Wallerstein (1974, 1980), Habermas (1984), Giddens (1985) himself, and, more recently, Mann (1986) and Hall (1985). Yet the major exponent who springs most immediately to mind is Elias with his theory of civilizing processes (Elias, 1978b, 1982), the sociogenesis of sociology (Elias, 1984a), and the changing balance of power between the sexes (Elias, 1987a). Elias (1971) argued that sociologists should go beyond a common view of history held in sociology and history that tends to assume social changes are unstructured. Rather than see history as a ceaseless pilgrimage of groups that come and go. whose knowledge seems equally valid, we 'have to investigate ... the structure of long-term changes in the intergenerational groupings of human producers and carriers of ... knowledge' (Elias, 1972: 125). We have to be aware that there are instances of knowledge produced by specialist groups gaining a momentum of its own, and that specialist groups of knowledge producers may gain a limited and relative autonomy in relation to other interdependent groups (Elias, 1971: 250). Hence according to Elias we can escape the quagmire of absolute relativism with its forced equalities and overstated polarities that occurs when we refuse to see the dynamics of knowledge. Rather we can investigate developments in particular funds of knowledge that bring about relative autonomy, in contrast to the emphasis upon breaks and discontinuities in the theories of knowledge of, for example, Kuhn and Bachelard (Elias, 1972).[1]

The discussion of long-term processes hence raises the question of whether we should aim to provide a sociology of postmodernism rather than advocate a postmodern sociology. If we seek to understand postmodernism should we forgo sociological methodologies and use postmodern models of analysis to produce a postmodern account of postmodernism? This would effectively point to a sublation of sociology and a new postmodern sociology or antisociology. Let us speculatively examine some of the possibilities that might result. A postmodern account of postmodernism would resist the examination of developments in knowledge and the interrelation between specialists in symbolic production and other groups to provide a parasitical account – a parasite of a parasite – which would use postmodern strategies to play on the unities and differences within postmodernism, its paradoxes, ironies, incoherences, intertextuality and multiphrenic qualities. Alternatively, it might follow the strategy of smuggling in a coherent metanarrative, a tale telling a version of the fall, to announce the end of metanarratives (Hutcheon (1987) and others have accused Lyotard of this strategy). Yet a further possibility would be to assume that certain developments, long-term processes, have built up cumulatively to a final rupture that has rent the historical process to produce a new postsocietal configuration: postmodern culture. As this perspective argues that we are already within a postmodern culture any attempt to theorize postmodernism using the old techniques and methodologies would necessarily fail. The account of the postmodern simulational world developed by Baudrillard (1983a, 1983b) is of this type with its emphasis on the cultural overload produced by an overproduction of information via the media which leads to an implosion of meaning and a simulational world, a hyperspace in which we live beyond normativity and classification in an aesthetic hallucination of reality. Baudrillard is certainly one of the most extreme of the academic writers on postmodernism in pushing the logic of postmodernism as far as it will go, revelling in the postmodern linguistic tropes and images of a postsociety – the end of the social – beyond the reach of sociological explanation (for a North American account of postmodern 'excremental culture' that draws much from Baudrillard, see Kroker and Cook, 1987). For Baudrillard, any attempt to discuss the glutinous masses in terms of normativity, or class analysis in the manner of Bourdieu, is doomed to failure as it is a form of analysis belonging to the previous stage of the system now superseded.

A further implication of a postmodern sociology would be to emphasize not only the end of the social but also the end of history. The account of postmodernism presented by Vattimo (1985) emphasizes that postmodern is not just to be conceived as signifying a historical break that points to a move beyond modernity. Postmodernism involves the notions of a post-metaphysical and postmodern epoch, with the rejection of the modernist idea of historical development, or a unifying point of view that can be imposed upon history. In effect there has always already been the end of history; it is only now that we can recognize and accept it. Postmodernism's critique and rejection of the metanarratives of modernity (science, religion, philosophy, humanism, socialism, feminism etc.), all of which seek to impose some sense of coherence and cogency onto history, direct us away from universalizations toward the particularity of local knowledge. This is a shift that is advocated on a theoretical level via arguments that build on the work of Nietzsche, Heidegger and Derrida; yet this advocated theoretical shift itself may well have come to the fore at a particular moment in time and therefore should be symbiotically related to what is regarded as a more general de-historicization of experience that is taking place within contemporary consumer culture, which also undercuts universalizations and the sense of ordered narrativity on the everyday level through its accentuation of a multifaceted and ever-changing present.

The questions we face in trying to understand postmodern culture sociologically, therefore, revolve around understanding how these two aspects: the production and circulation of postmodern theories (many of which have a sense of end of history, albeit a non-tragic finality, about them), and the wider production and circulation of everyday postmodern cultural experiences and practices, are related. Here we need not be for or against postmodernism, rather we have to explain sociologically how postmodernism is possible, and how an interest in the loose family of notions associated with it have come into being. This is despite the obvious accusation of advocates of postmodernism that this very enterprise is fatally flawed and represents an outmoded attachment to modernist metatheory. In brief, then, we seek to understand and point towards the need for an investigation of the relationship between the two aspects: the theoretical and everyday, of the claimed movement towards the postmodern. In this way *postmodernism*, which is theorized and expressed in intellectual and artistic practices, could be seen as an index or harbinger of a broader *postmodern culture*, a wider set of changes in the production, consumption and circulation of cultural goods and practices. Eventually it may be the case that these tendencies assume epochal proportions and hence signify a move toward *postmodernity*.

If we reject the notion of a postmodern sociology in favour of a sociological account of postmodernism and regard it as part of a large-scale long-term process we face a daunting task beyond the scope of this chapter. All that this chapter seeks to do is sketch the outlines such an approach might follow. *First*, we wish to contest some of the closures that occur if we follow postmodernism's claims (albeit often implicit) to be a superior methodology and to have detected a significant break in the historical process that puts us into or on the edge of a postmodern culture and eventual epoch or antiepoch of postmodernity. *Second*, the intention is to suggest tentatively that postmodernism should be understood in terms of processes taking place within the dynamic of intergroup relations.[2] More specifically, we need to ask who are the producers and carriers of postmodern symbolic goods. We need to examine the actual practices of postmodernism to discover the dynamics and processes that are at work within various fields – art, architecture, music, literature – and among intellectuals and academics, as well as examining ways in which new conditions emerge that increase the circulation and interchange between producers and disseminators in these fields. Here we can think of strategies of outsiders against the established, of monopolization and usurpation processes, the effects of inflation etc. These changes themselves should be related to the long-term processes that have led to a general rise in the numbers of specialists in symbolic production, dissemination and reproduction, and changed their relationship to other groups in society and raised both their general valorization by society and their own capacity to argue for and demonstrate their social effectiveness. This is not to argue that the emergence, numerical rise and increased power-potential of these groups within the middle class and, more recently, what has been termed the new middle class, amounts to anything like the rise of a new class based on cultural capital that can challenge the old bourgeois class with its assumed increasingly obsolete power base in economic capital. The intellectuals and specialists in symbolic production are far from becoming the type of new hegemonic class that Gouldner (1979) argued. Yet having said this we should not underestimate the changes in the interdependencies and balance between economic specialists and symbolic specialists that have occurred. The emergence and expansion of sectors of the new middle class, or what has been termed the service class (Lash and Urry, 1987), creates not only specialists in symbolic production and dissemination but also a potential audience that may be more sensitive and attuned to the range of cultural and symbolic goods and experiences that have been labelled postmodern.

More specifically in relation to the emergence of postmodernism in the arts in the 1960s and in certain academic and intellectual fields in the 1970s we should focus attention on the emergence of a particularly large generational cohort, 'the 1960s generation', which entered higher education in larger numbers than ever before, and which developed orientations, tastes and dispositions that are carried with them as they move through adult life. It can also be argued that artists and intellectuals detect, crystallize and disseminate particular definitions of a generational consciousness to various publics and markets. In this sense the sensibilities of 'the 1960s generation' that they articulated underrepresent the more stable and traditional orientations of members from business, industrial, scientific backgrounds or aspirations and play up the aestheticization of life, the emotional decontrol and informalization. It has often been observed that there are continuities between 'the 1960s generation' and a whole range of countercultural movements going back as far as the Romantics (Abrams and McCulloch, 1975; Martin, 1981; Weiss, 1986; Sayre and Löwy, 1984).

What is of interest here is that this project of the aestheticization of life with its celebration of the artist as hero and the stylization of life into a work of art – both the expressivity of the artist's project and the lifestyle – found resonances in a larger audience beyond intellectual and artistic circles through the expansion of particular occupational groups specializing in symbolic goods who acted as both producers/disseminators and consumers/audiences for cultural goods. The expansion of the 'new cultural intermediaries', as Bourdieu (1984) calls them, has involved a widening of the range of legitimate cultural goods and the breaking down of some of the old symbolic hierarchies. The new tastemakers, constantly on the lookout for new cultural goods and experiences, are also engaged in the production of popular pedagogies and guides to living and lifestyle. They encourage an inflation in cultural goods, constantly draw upon artistic and intellectual trends for inspiration. and help to create new conditions of artistic and intellectual production by working alongside them. The new cultural intermediaries can be found in market-oriented consumer cultural occupations – the media, advertising, design, fashion etc. – and in state-funded and private helping professions counselling, educational and therapy occupations. To understand the receptivity to postmodern goods and practices we therefore need to investigate the processes within society that have brought into greater prominence specialists in symbolic production and, specifically, the changing relations between artists, intellectuals, academics, and cultural intermediaries and their shifting interdependencies in a wider figuration containing businessmen, politicians and administrators. Of course the struggle between what has been called the new petite bourgeoisie (Bourdieu, 1984) and the old petite bourgeoisie, with Thatcherism in Britain mounting strong attacks on artists and intellectuals in the name of Victorian values, still continues. Yet it is interesting to note the resilience of the specialists in symbolic production and dissemination and their capacity to adopt new tactics in unfavourable situations. Rather, perhaps, we should see this process in the Eliasian metaphor of a balance, with swings towards the centres of symbolic production in the 1960s and 1970s and swings away towards the greater dominance of centres of economic production in the 1980s (Wouters, 1987). The notion of a struggle between symbolic and economic specialists should also not blind us to their basic interdependencies and ways in which excess finance capital in the 1980s may be used to finance postmodern architecture or inflate art markets, or the ways in which cities encourage symbolic specialists to move into renewal areas (for example, SoHo in New York described by Zukin, 1982a, 1982b) to speed up gentrification and a general rise in the prestige and symbolic capital of the city. Hence there may be particular sites where what has been referred to as the process of 'postmodernization' (Cooke, 1988) is taking place.

The development of postmodernism within the cultural and intellectual fields

If we examine some of these changes in more detail it would be useful to first focus on the place of postmodernism within specific artistic, intellectual and academic fields. First, there is not yet a unified view of postmodernism evident across the fields of architecture, literature, music, art, photography, the performing arts, philosophy and criticism. Jameson (1984c: 62), for example, distinguishes between the promodernist postmodernism of Lyotard and the antimodernist postmodernism of Jencks. Recalling his first use of the concept in his book, *The Language of Postmodern Architecture*, Jencks (1984: 6) tells us that

> When I first wrote the book in 1975 and 1976 the word and concept of Post-Modernism had only been used with any frequency in literary criticism. Most perturbing, as I later realized it had been used to mean 'Ultra-Modern', referring to the extremist novels of William Burroughs and a philosophy of nihilism and anti-convention. While I was aware of these writings of Ihab Hassan and others, I used the term to mean the opposite of all this: the end of avant-garde extremism, the partial return to tradition and the central role of communicating with the public – and architecture is *the* public art.

In the field of literary criticism the term postmodern had been used a few years earlier by Spanos, possibly ignorant of its previous use by other literary critics such as Hassan in the 1960s. Spanos (1987: 2), like Jencks, recalled his first use of the term in setting up the journal *boundary 2*.

> In the fall of 1970 ... I persuaded my colleague the novelist Robert Kroetsch that the time or, as I would put it now, the occasion called for the inauguration of *boundary 2* the 'journal of postmodern literature' we had corresponded about ... In subtitling *boundary 2* 'a journal of postmodern literature' we were, it turns out, introducing a term that has become fundamental to the critical discourse of contemporary American literary history. At that time, however, I was not at all sure what we intended by the word *postmodern*. What prompted its use was my strong sense that literary modernism, especially as a critical discourse, had come to its end, that the differential space opened up by the boundary it had crossed in the late decades of the nineteenth century and early

decades of the twentieth had been sealed off and thoroughly colonized by and within another boundary.

What the two examples seem to suggest is a preoccupation with the issues of their own particular field and the coining of a term that they wished to use to detect, indicate, establish and legitimate a break and promote a new mode of analysis that was distanced from that of the established, especially the established modernism in their field: hence *postmodernism*. Since the mid-1970s there has been a greater circulation of information by commentators, artists and academics who have latched onto and sought to explore the meanings of the term, which has furthered the possibility of a more generally accepted range of meaning for postmodernism.

The art of *naming* itself is an important strategy on the part of groups engaged in struggles with other groups. The use of a new term like postmodernism by outsiders or newcomers to the field may occur when their chances to move upward through the existing legitimate hierarchical structures are restricted. These avant-garde tactics are designed to create a space ahead of the established, which will ultimately lead to a reclassification of the field that redesignates the established as the outmoded.

It is tempting to see postmodernism as an avant-garde strategy, arising initially in the artistic field, and place it within a long history of avant-garde movements that go back to not only the 1850s and 1870s in Paris, but also to the Futurist, Dada and Surrealist Movements and left avant-garde in Russia and Germany in the 1920s. The problem with this approach is that it tends to focus on the similarities of outsider strategies, the periodic break out of antagonism and conflict in the uneasy interdependence that the specialists in symbolic production find themselves engaged in with economic specialists, or the construction of an 'eternal' cycle of activism, antagonism, militarism and agonism which all such movements are meant to go through (Poggioli, 1973). It fails to sufficiently differentiate between the *general* conditions for the emergence of avant-gardes since the 1850s in metropolitan centres, with their access to publicity and communications, and the necessity of a professional and leisure class audience and the *particular* conditions of specific movements (Tagg, 1985/6). In the case of postmodernism we can think of the need to examine the specific relationship between artists, critics, intellectuals, dealers and the art institutions that occurred in the 1960s in New York when postmodern art emerged. We need to do this in the awareness that those active in the production and designation of postmodern texts/objects, antitexts/antiobjects may resist all attempts to draw similarities between their mode of work and previous avant-gardes, and indeed that circumstances may pertain that may make it unlikely for them to cohere into an avant-garde movement, despite efforts on the part of critics, dealers, and those active in art institutions to promote a distinct break and new avant-garde.

Indeed one of the characteristics of postmodern art in the 1960s was its attack on institutionalized art: on the museums and galleries, the critical academic hierarchies of taste, and the consecration of works of art as clearly demarcated objects of display. This attack on autonomous, institutionalized art was itself not new: as Peter Bürger (1984) demonstrates it occurred with the historical avant-garde of the 1920s with its rejection of Aestheticism. In this context it is interesting to dote that in the 1960s there was a revival of interest in the Dada and Surrealist Movements and in particular the work of Marcel Duchamp (Huyssen 1984). It has also been argued that postmodernism first occurred with the 1920s historical avant-garde who effectively practised postmodernism *avant la lettre* (Lash and Urry, 1987). In the 1960s we have similar and perhaps more extreme attempts to break down the barriers between art and everyday life, to resist art becoming a museum commodity-object. Here we think of the 'happenings' and landscape art devised by Christo, the Bulgarian-American artist, whose 'events' included wrapping part of the Australian coast and draping an enormous curtain over a Colorado valley. Yet even this attempt at antiart, to deny a permanent art object by emphasizing a transitory experience that could not be objectified and commodified, soon found its way back into the art institutions via photographers, films, books and exhibitions of Christo's work (Martin, 1981: 110).

One of the leading postmodern critics in the 1960s, Susan Sontag (1967), argued in this vein that the art object should not be a text, but another sensory object in the world. This new sensibility favoured music, dance, painting, sculpture and architecture over the novel. This emphasis upon sensation, on the primary immediacy of the figural as opposed to the discursive, has led the postmodern aesthetics to be characterized as an aesthetics of the body (Lash and Urry, 1987). Two brief examples can be given to illustrate this. The first is the body art of Oppenheim. A videotape entitled 'I'm Failing' shows Oppenheim trying to drown himself in a tank of water (a parody, perhaps, of Salvador Dali's earlier 'Inverted Submarine' in which he nearly drowned himself: a description appears in his autobiography). Another video shows in slow motion rocks being dropped on Oppenheim's stomach. The videotape of his multimedia presentation 'Disturbational Art' is interesting in that it shows Oppenheim eating ten gingerbread men and then microscopic colour slides of the excreta containing the gingerbread men, which are projected in galleries (open to misreading as merely abstract painting), alongside a running loop videotape of the whole ingestion and excremental process (Wall, 1987). The second example is that of the Australian body artist, Stelarc, who uses medical instruments to film the insides of his own body – blood flows, muscles, heartbeats – his own interiority and 'acoustical landscape' which shows the body as something both repulsive and fascinating (Kroker and Kroker, 1987: vi).

It is clearly difficult to conceive how such body art, happenings or art that plays on repetition and chance (in music we can think of Briers' 'Sinking of the Titanic', which attempts to mimic music played under water and can be played in any number of ways to achieve a similar openness to some visual works or art, or Laurie Anderson's music in which all the instruments are synthesized bits of her own voice and the lyrics random chaining of cut-up vocal phrases) can be recuperated into established hierarchies of taste and aesthetic systems. This, of course, is the point: to collapse the old distinctions between high culture and mass culture, to challenge the notion of the autonomous creative artist and artisanal definition of art that modernism perpetuated, to show that art is everywhere, not only in the body, but also in the degraded landscape of mass culture. Hence the rise of pop art in the 1960s and its characterization as a cultural break linked to the rise of the counterculture (see Hebdige, 1983; Huyssen, 1981; Martin, 1981).

There is an important sense in which the artists' own self-understanding of their project in producing postmodern works/antiworks of art only becomes articulated through their relationship to the critics and intellectuals. It is often remarked that in the case of postmodernism the critics have played a more powerful role than ever before, and that 'Postmodernism has in some ways become a critics' term without ever quite becoming an artistic movement' (Bradbury, 1983: 325). While there has been a growth in the numbers of artists-theoreticians since the end of the 1960s (along with a general expansion of art institutions, publishing of books and journals dealing with art theory and culture criticism, and the various audiences that will be discussed later), we should not overlook the way in which this is related to a long-term process of expansion in the numbers and the power-potential of the specialists in symbolic production since the eighteenth century. From the eighteenth century onwards we have had the growth of independent disciplines of aesthetics and art history, the growth of periodical literature, the emergence of the critic as an independent profession, and the growth of academies, exhibitions and specific sites of artisic production and dissemination – studios, galleries, art schools, universities, museums etc. (Burglin, 1985/6). If the critic or philosopher is seen today as intervening more actively in not only articulating artistic practices but in promoting particular theories that the artist then tries to articulate, then it should be emphasized that this situation is by no means unique. Members of the Dada movement, which sprang up toward the end of World War I, as we have already mentioned, were concerned with the desecration of all art, with highlighting the absurdity of 'art for art's sake' aestheticism, and with dismantling all codes, not least what they saw as the absurd war culture. The penchant for montage and the attack on the illusory unity of each text to reveal its polysemy shows the influence of Nietzsche's philosophy, and it is interesting to note that one of the founders of Dada, Hugo Ball, had previously written a thesis on Nietzsche (Kuenzli, 1987).

In the 1970s in the United States one detects a similar process with Derrida and deconstruction replacing Nietzsche to become appropriated as one of the central reference points for postmodern theory which was disseminated through a much denser network of secondary texts, journals and journalistic commentaries. To take one example, in the field of photography deconstruction theory was promoted by New York critics such as Douglas Crimp to argue that photography could no longer aim to produce originality as photographs were always repetitions or 'already-seen'. Hence photographs should simulate and represent common images (Cindy herman), rephotograph unaltered images of recognized high-art photographers (Levine) or rephotograph advertising images (Andre, 1984).

It can of course be argued that postmodernism does not so much represent a break or crisis in the larger social process but is a symptom of a more specific crisis within the intellectuals' own field. In effect postmodernism represents a loss of confidence on the part of the intellectuals in the universal potential of their project. A self-devaluation of the currency of intellectual goods that occurs at the same time is a more general social devaluation. Hence the emphasis in postmodern theory that Hassan (1985) detects and categorizes as tendencies toward *indeterminacies*, the recognition of openness, pluralism, randomness, eclecticism, incoherence, paralogism, intertextuality, the primacy of the many over the one; and *immanences*, the acknowledgement of our innerworldliness, our own opaque symbolic self-constitution, our entrapment in a dissemination and diffusion of signs that derealize history and all the other metanarratives. The emergence of antiphilosophical, antifoundational philosophy which is taken under the banner of postmodernism, it has been argued, reflects a loss of confidence on the part of Western intellectuals in the superiority of their project, in their authority and capacity to establish universal standards of truth, morality, and taste, towards which mankind will progress. Bauman (1988) links this acknowledgement of polyculturalism with a change in the societal role of the intellectuals, linking this to the lack of use that today's state has for legitimation to reproduce the structure of domination. The intellectuals' status is further undermined by the massive expansion in the production of cultural goods which they can no longer control nor indeed are consulted about as 'gallery owners, publishers, TV managers', and other 'capitalists' or 'bureaucrats', the 'agents of the market' undermine things (Bauman, 1988: 224). We will say more later about the rise of what I would prefer to describe as 'the new cultural intermediaries' or 'new intellectuals' or 'para-intellectuals' and the general conditions of inflation in the production of symbolic goods.

If we look at the intellectuals' field (bearing in mind the term 'intellectual' is by no means an unproblematic concept that covers a range of specialists in symbolic production, the vast majority of whom today have a base in academic institutions) we are struck by the parallels between their practice and artistic practices. As Bourdieu (1983b: 4) remarks: 'Resembling the artist ... the philosopher sets himself up as an uncreated creator, who owes nothing to the institution.' The intellectuals' 'intellectual centricism' prevents them thinking of their practice as practice, and while the antifoundationalism onto which postmodern theories have latched provides a necessary critique of philosophical universalism, there is often an inability to see this shift in other than dichotomous terms that cloud shades of differences between universalism and relativism and discount the possibility that the emergence of such concepts themselves need to be linked to the development of the fund of human knowledge. Hence the loss of universalism is seen necessarily as leading to pluralism and relativism in which the tendency for the intellectuals is still to see themselves as 'uncreated creators' – if not now as creators of universal axioms, then in terms of selectivity, with the emphasis on the randomness and relativity of their choice between an assumed finite range of positions. The critique of universalism (often inflated into a straw man that it is hard to credit anyone believing) discounts the possibility of various blends and balances between universalism and pluralism, absolutism and relativism, involvement and detachment. There is also sometimes a back door importation of universalism in the assumption that the wheel of history has become fixed at this particular set of aporias, or that we have at last had the exhilarating courage to see through the deceptive representational signifying schemata into the eternal human condition of endless, yet ultimately meaningless and unsubstantiable, word-spinning. In effect all we can do is to join the game of signification. and art becomes the master paradigm for knowledge (Kauffmann, 1986), be it in the sciences, social sciences, or humanities. This may also be used as a justification for postmodern theorists to write 'thin' or philosophical history to establish their points, as Arac (1986) argues is the case with writers like Lyotard and Rorty.

The focus on the apparent naïveté of the intellectuals of yesteryear, with their universalistic schemes, brings in a back-door sense of our own progress in knowledge over theirs with which to castigate their own false belief in progress. It also neglects diversity within the intellectual held and the relation of postmodernism to the substantive antifoundational countercultural subcurrent that has been flourishing within Western intellectual life since at least the Romantics. This tradition sought to develop the relationship between artistic and intellectual modes of theorizing and to establish aesthetic taste as a criterion for knowledge, and the aestheticization of life as a guide for living: tradition in which one would have to place Nietzsche, who is revered by postmodern, poststructuralist and deconstructivist theorists such as Derrida, Foucault, Deleuze, Baudrillard (see Megill, 1985; Rajchman, 1985).

For those intellectuals who, to work off Arac's (1986) metaphor, write 'thicker' histories in that they draw on empirical materials to examine the rise of postmodernism – here Arac cites Anderson, Bell and Jameson – there is at times a tendency to argue for the existence of a widespread postmodern culture by reading off evidence from the intellectuals' experience. Here in particular we can think of the work of Jameson (1984a, 1984b) and Berman (1982). Jameson (1984b), for example, identifies the two basic features of postmodernism as (1) the transformation of reality into images and (2) a schizophrenic fragmentation of time into a series of perpetual presents. The problem is that little evidence is presented as to how men and women engaged in everyday practices actually come to formulate these experiences. We therefore need to build into our analysis the entrepreneurial role and strategies of intellectuals, architects, critics and cultural intermediaries who have an interest in promoting the name and developing a pedagogy for postmodernism with which to educate various publics. In addition, for all the emphasis upon intertextuality and multireadability of texts on the part of some postmodern critics, there are others who, in contrast to the assumed fragmentation and difference, presuppose a unity of experience prior to discourse that corresponds to the global process of capital logic or modernization and that gives rise to a range of expressions that can be read back by the critic as manifestations of the unity of the experience (Tagg, 1985/6). This sense of totality leads to totalizations such as the 'postmodern age', to subtotalizations like 'postmodern culture' and to the cultural sphere', which presuppose an integrated and unified culture, usually deduced from some master system imperative or process such as capital logic', or cultural logic' or 'axial principle' (for example, Jameson, 1984a; Bell, 1976). The actual practices of particular groups engaged in various struggles, power balances, and interdependencies are neatly avoided as a jump is made from experience to 'higher' level integrating concept or vice versa.

Effectively a sociology of postmodernism would have to take into account the processes of competition, monopolization, demonopolization and usurpation, the various strategies of outsiders and the established that take place between different groups of specialists in symbolic production. in which the term 'postmodernism' becomes a stake in the struggle between groups. This would point us toward collecting evidence to enable us to answer the questions: Who is using the term postmodernism? In what specific practices is it used? Which groups resist its use? Where specifically is the term used? Are there particular sites of postmodernism? Part of the answer to those questions we have suggested should come from examining the emergence, development, and use of the term within specific intellectual, academic, and artistic fields and the changing nature of these practices which lead to greater interchanges between the fields. Yet we are also aware that these changes themselves may be dependent on and heightened by changes taking place that have brought into prominence increasing numbers of cultural intermediaries. The destabilization of existing symbolic hierarchies, then, may not occur merely in response to the usurpatory and avant-garde tactics of outsider artists and intellectuals, but in terms of an increase in both the demand for and capacity to supply symbolic and cultural goods of various types (including consumer cultural goods and not just artistic and intellectual goods). The growth of new cultural intermediaries and new audiences for symbolic goods within the middle class itself must also be understood in terms of changes in the wider interdependencies between the state, economic and business specialists and the specialists in symbolic production which are part of a long-term process of the increasing valorization of art. A process that is likely to continue, despite the current round of cutbacks and the more negative evaluation of symbolic specialists as the balance of power shifts more strongly back toward economic specialists. We can now look at some of these changes.

The new cultural intermediaries and the centres of postmodernism

A good deal has been written about the new middle class in sociology. Indeed it has been argued that the rise of sociology itself can be linked to the hegemonic drive of this class in its attempt to increase the societal valorization of intellectual knowledge, symbolic goods, and cultural capital as against economic capital (Gouldner, 1979). While this view at times neglects the interdependencies between economic and symbol specialists and the important sense in which the growing autonomy of economic specialists and their theorists, who developed the autonomy of the science of economics that effectively became the first scientific analysis of society (see Elias, 1984a), it does direct us toward the development of the power potential of the specialists in symbolic production and dissemination within the middle class. There are long debates about the rise and composition of the new middle class and the problems of trying to explain their role within Marxist class theory, too complex to investigate here (see Bruce-Briggs, 1979; Burris, 1986; Carter, 1985; Barbalet, 1986). Some may dispute the terminology and prefer to refer to the 'new petite bourgeoisie' (Bourdieu, 1984) or the 'knowledge class' or the 'new class' after Djilas, Galbraith, and others (Bruce-Briggs, 1979). Others (Lash and Urry, 1987) more recently have referred to the expansion of 'the service class' (employers, managers and professionals) which grew by practically half a million jobs in Britain between 1971 and 1981 and in 1981 made up 13.2 per cent of the labour force as against 11.0 per cent in 1971 (see Cooke, 1988).

There has also been considerable debate (much of it unsympathetic speculations by journalists in the media) about the emergence of the 'Yuppies' (young urban professionals), regarded as an elite segment of the United States baby boom generation, and it has been argued that this rapidly growing segment can be augmented by 'psychographic' Yuppies who, while they cannot be counted as actual Yuppies, exhibit similar attitudes. Burnett and Bush (1986: 27) state that while 14 per cent of the baby boom generation (those born between 1946 and 1964) can be counted as Yuppies, nearly 50 per cent of the baby boom cohort are 'psycho, graphic Yuppies', representing approximately 30 million people in the United States. While a good deal of systematic research is needed on their lifestyles and dispositions to see how far Yuppies are actually the selfish 'perfect consumers' and the narcissistic, calculating hedonists they have been designated (for a useful start see Hammond, 1986), the very formulation of the concept Yuppie does direct attention to the large post-war cohort, many of whom had a childhood of relative prosperity, attained high educational levels, passed through the 1960s in their teens and twenties, and in the 1970s and 1980s have been entering an increasingly competitive occupational market in large numbers. It is possible that a distinct set of tastes and classificatory schemes have been formed in this cohort that may come to have an increasing social effect as some of them move into mid-life and attain positions of power within various organizations.

While definitions of the new middle class often include managers, employers, scientists and technicians, the sector I would like to focus attention on is the expanding group of 'new cultural intermediaries' (see Bourdieu, 1984). These are engaged in providing symbolic goods and services that were referred to earlier – the marketing, advertising, public relations, radio and television producers, presenters, magazine journalists, fashion writers and the helping professions (social workers, marriage counsellors, sex therapists, dieticians, play leaders etc.). If we look at the habitus, the classificatory schemes, and dispositions of the group we should note that Bourdieu (1984: 370) has referred to them as 'new intellectuals' who adopt a learning mode towards life. They are fascinated by identity, presentation, appearance, lifestyle and the endless quest for new experiences (see chapters 4 and 6). Indeed their awareness of the range of experiences open to them, the frequent lack of anchoring in terms of a specific locale or community, coupled with the self-consciousness of the autodidact, who always wishes to become more than he/she is, leads to a refusal to be classified, with the injunction to resist fixed codes as life is conceived as essentially open-ended. Bourdieu (1984: 371) remarks that their quest for distinction via the cultivation of lifestyle, a stylized, expressive life, 'makes available to *almost* everyone the distinctive poses, the distinctive games and other signs of inner riches previously reserved for intellectuals'. They actively promote and transmit the intellectuals' lifestyle to a larger audience and collude with the intellectuals to legitimate new fields such as sport, fashion, popular music and popular culture as valid fields of intellectual analysis. These cultural intermediaries working between the media and academic and intellectual life help to facilitate the transmission of popular intellectual programmes in the media such as the British Channel 4 series *Modernity and its Discontents* and the BBC series on modern art *The Shock of the New* which helps to promote a new breed of celebrity intellectuals who have little distaste for, indeed who embrace, the popular. Effectively they help to collapse some of the old distinctions and symbolic hierarchies that revolve around the popular culture/higher culture axis. This general veneration for intellectual goods and the artistic and intellectual lifestyle thus helps to create an audience within the new middle class and potentially beyond, for new symbolic goods and experiences, for the intellectual and artistic way of life, which could be receptive to some of the sensibilities that are incorporated into and disseminated in postmodernism.

The origins of these sensibilities can, of course, be traced back a long way and should be regarded as a part of a long-term process in which specialists in symbolic production since the Romantics have engaged in a greater emotional exploration and informality (which can be contrasted to the specialists in economic production) that favours a loosening of restraints to facilitate artistic ends and the artistic-bohemian way of life. Clearly the 1960s was a period in which what became known as the 'counterculture' developed an attack on emotional constraints and favoured a relaxation of formal standards of dress, presentation and demeanour.

Contrary to popular perceptions at the time it has been argued by Wouters (1986), following the approach of Elias, that such manifestations of informality do not signal a lack or breakdown of controls, rather they depend upon greater self-control. The ability to confront dangerous and painful. previously repressed emotions effectively requires both a relaxation and a higher level of control: a 'de-controlled control of the emotions'. The less strict canons of behaviour and relaxation of codes that accompanied the informalization process demanded that individuals show greater respect and consideration for each other as well as the ability to identify with and appreciate the other's point of view. It also favoured changes in organizational structures toward management through negotiation as opposed to management by command and a higher degree of fluidity in hierarchical organizational structures and flexibility in performance of roles (de Swaan, 1981; Haferkamp, 1987). It can be argued that while the process of informalization has slackened in the late 1970s and 1980s (Wouters, 1986, 1987), the resultant 'formalization of informalization' has not led to a complete erosion of the 'gains' of the 1960s. It can be argued that sectors of the new middle class, the cultural intermediaries and the helping professions (the latter are referred to as the 'expressive professions' by Martin (1981)) will have the necessary dispositions and sensibilities that would make them more open to emotional exploration, aesthetic experience and the aestheticization of life. Indeed the aestheticization of the body, which has been characterized as one element of postmodern art, necessarily requires an emotional decontrol both to produce and appreciate it. Likewise postmodern theories that detect or promote schizo- or multiphrenic intensities, or a 'return' to a decoded pre-oedipal state of experiencing bodily intensities, are also asking for a greater emotional decontrol. It could also be argued that the style of management by negotiation has penetrated into academic institutions with outsider groups demanding and using more informal procedures and styles of presentation of works of art and selves. (In this context Pollock (1985/6) provides an interesting discussion of challenges to the previous canons of aesthetic taste and modes of exhibiting works sustained by art college lecturers (largely men) by a new generation of young women students.)

The increasing sensitivity to aesthetics, style, lifestyle, the stylization of life, and emotional exploration within the new middle class has developed in parallel to a rise in the numbers of people working as artists and in intermediary art occupations and a more general societal rise in the level of respect that such occupations command. In effect there has been a 'diminution of contrasts' with the artist's bohemian, outsider, difference rendered more intelligible and acceptable. In certain centres the rise in numbers of art occupations has been dramatic. Zukin (1982a, 1982b) in her study of the SoHo area of New York remarks that in the 1960s estimates of numbers of artists working in New York ranged from 1,000 to 35,000, whereas census data at the start of the 1970s showed around 100,000. The increase in numbers of jobs was partly the result of increased state patronage of the arts (see DiMaggio and Useem, 1978) and the change in the attitude of some business leaders toward the arts. From 1965 onwards in the United States the numbers of art jobs in state-supported educational and cultural institutions also increased rapidly. One of the effects was to close the distance between artistic and other occupations, and relatively secure career trajectories could be developed in the arts that brought the 'artistic vision' closer to that of the ordinary middle class. Zukin (1982a: 436) writes that 'far from "shocking the bourgeoisie," art became the aesthetic vision of the bourgeoisie'. This emphasis gave rise to a generation of practitioners, instead of visionaries and innovators. Art became less elitist and more 'professionalized' and 'democratized'. The SoHo area of lower Manhattan in New York became gentrified as part of this process and brought members of the new middle and upper class into a declining inner-city area to redevelop it as a centre of cultural consumption: 'the Disneyland for the aesthete' as one magazine referred to it (quoted in Jackson, 1985). Parallel processes have occurred in other major Western cities through a combination of state promotion of the arts resulting from the strategies of local and national politicians and the adoption of new strategies of capital investment by businessmen and financiers. Within such art centres there is an increasing manifest interdependency between figurations of artists, intellectuals, and various cultural intermediaries and various audiences and publics. While representatives of the business community and especially professional politicians who see themselves as guardians of the old petit-bourgeois values, such as Margaret Thatcher, may express a strong distaste for many of these newer symbolic specialists and seek to cut government spending on the arts, the market inflated by the rise of a new generation of art investors continues unabated. Indeed under the pressure of new money according to a spokesman at Sotheby's in New York, 'the art market has reached the point where it's almost another business' (*Independent*, 28 May 1987).

Hence the wider figuration which has brought together professional politicians, government administrators, local politicians, businessmen, financiers, dealers, investors, artists, intellectuals, educators, cultural intermediaries and publics, has resulted in new interdependencies and strategies that have changed power balances and produced alliances between groups that previously may have perceived their interests as opposed.

In more general terms in the 1980s the power balance may have swung away from centres in which academic, artistic, helping professionals and cultural intermediaries are employed in large numbers toward the commercial and managerial centres who have long developed in a situation of tension and opposition toward their less powerful opponents (Wouters, 1987). Of course this type of tension balance and the peculiar strategies, interdependencies, rivalries and conflicts it engenders occurs today in an extensive and far-reaching figuration of people which may make it harder to delineate. Nevertheless, it deserves more detailed and systematic sociological research, which could usefully draw on studies of similar processes. As Wouters (1987: 424) tells us, in some senses the tension balance between the academic. artistic or social care centres and the commercial or managerial centres resembles the tension balance Elias described between the nobility and the bourgeois intelligentsia in eighteenth-century Germany. At the time there was a similar distinction between the 'depth (of feeling)' 'true virtue' and 'honesty' (of the bourgeois intelligentsia) and the 'superficiality', 'falsity', 'ceremony' and 'outward politeness' (of the nobility).

Of course, as we have argued, we are in a more extensive figuration and set of power balances with more groups involved today than was the case between the bourgeois intelligentsia *(Bildungsbürgertum)* and nobility in eighteenth-century Germany, yet the example may well be instructive in helping us develop a sociology of postmodernism.

Postmodernism and the aestheticization of life

In an influential collection on postmodern culture (Foster, 1984) there is an article by Ulmer entitled 'The Object of Post-Criticism' in which, in an argument that draws heavily on Derrida, he contends that the critic should not attempt to follow the old mode of trying to give a true or correct representation of the text or its meanings; rather the critic should be free to parasitically and playfully engage in non-linear writing to subvert the text's central concepts and strategies. As Kauffmann (1986: 187) argues, such a proposal and the demand for a 'postmodern pedagogy' challenges 'the distinction between art and criticism, arguing that critical writing must also be artistic'. A similar valorization of art in which 'artists are the heroes' who articulate the limits of our world by exploring the very 'source' and limits of our language is detected in the work of Foucault (Rajchman, 1985; see also Wolin, 1986; Megill, 1985). One of the problems with this transgressive strategy is that it is targeted against the intolerant petit-bourgeois consumer who is incapable of conceiving of 'the other', who values speech above writing etc. Yet it may be the case that if we examine the long-term changes that have brought into prominence specialists in symbolic production and dissemination, such a posture now strikes a resonance with a much larger audience – not that we have seen the end of the shockable traditional petit-bourgeois, far from it. Effectively within the new middle class there may be increasing numbers who accept that the aesthetic life is the ethically good life, that there is no human nature or true self, that we are a collection of quasi-selves, and life is open to be shaped aesthetically (Shusterman, 1988). The desire to be continuously learning and enriching oneself, to pursue ever new values and vocabularies, the unending curiosity in which the artist and intellectual are heroes that some postmodernists advocate (Shusterman deals specifically with Rorty) has a long history that can be traced back to the Romantics. It also resonates with the concern for style, the stylization of life, 'the no rules, only choices' slogan of the ever-renewable lifestyle, which is found within the new middle class and that, as cultural intermediaries, they attempt to disseminate to a wider population.

The emphasis on the aesthetic justification of life as a more widespread current within our culture has been met with a nostalgic lament and call for a religious revival by some (such as Bell, 1976) and an equally nostalgic lament to preserve the possibility of a Marxist utopia or truly 'rational society' by others (such as Jameson, 1984a; see O'Neill, 1988 for a discussion of these positions). Jameson himself (1984c) has dealt with the tricky problem of sifting through postmodernism for progressive and retrogressive strains, yet he too cannot escape being instructed ironically by Hutcheon (1987: 23) that his former self-defined progressive modernist stance in (along with Eagleton) denigrating Lukács's realist position as passé is now compromised by the adoption of a reactionary hostility toward postmodernism. Such are the aporias of those who wish to assess and evaluate postmodernism. They arise from the difficulty of trying to understand the beginning of what may be a new movement in whose symptoms we are immersed and involved. They point to the need to understand the rise of postmodernism as part of a long term process that has led to an increase in the power-potential of specialists in symbolic production and dissemination: in effect to the need to work toward a sociology of postmodernism rather than a postmodern sociology.

Notes

1 To follow the method Norbert Elias used in examining the long-term development of concepts like civilization and economics and focus on their derivation from everyday terms and subsequent alteration as a consequence of the changing structure of power balances between interdependent groups to their eventual theorization and canonization as universal or scientific notions, is in the case of the term 'postmodernity' extremely difficult. Not least for the fact that we are looking at signs and traces of the very early stages of a process that may itself go off into a number of directions or even prematurely fizzle out. In effect while we may attempt to uncover traces of postmodernism *avant la lettre* (for example, the 1920s avant-garde) we should be aware that the term itself may not yet be stabilized and may go the way of many recent academic fads and fashions. This would not of course imply that the process would cease, nor that the carriers of 'postmodernism' may arrive at other descriptive terms. A further point is that the concepts of civilization and economics were linked to the rise of particular groups who enjoyed major power gains and a degree of success in monopolizing knowledge and means of orientation. In effect an ability to present their concerns as concerns that were somehow 'in the nature of things'; that is, as foundational. If we try to conceive the trajectory of the concept postmodern there are numerous difficulties – not least that of being at the equivalence of a pre-Quesnay and Physiocrat stage in relation to the development of economics. We do not yet now what the power potential of the specialists in symbolic production and dissemination is. Knowledge specialists (that is, priests) have attained a dominance in shifting power balances in the past; other knowledge specialists may yet do so again in the future. (For Elias's account of the relation between the various specialists of violence, knowledge, economic production, and means of orientation see Elias (1987b).) The current signs suggest, however, that in both the production of theories of postmodernism and postmodern cultural goods the tendency toward demonopolization. In short the hyperreflexivity, antifoundationalism and polycultural 'tolerance' found in postmodern theories and practices, tied as it is to the stylistic and fashion imperatives of the current markets in academic, intellectual, artistic and consumer goods, may in its very dependence on publics educated in the quest for

novelty, resist tendencies toward monopolization and the erection of a new stable symbolic hierarchy. In Elias's terms, then, the capacity to develop relatively autonomous types of knowledge (such as science), on the one *hand*, or a relatively stable body of knowledge linked to the ability of a group to monopolize, on a societal level, a range of power resources, on the other, may not occur in this case. The further element of his approach to refer to (see Elias, 1987b) is his notion of 'functional democratization' which points to a diffusion of the knowledge and the growing power potential of the masses. If continued this will further the tendency toward a certain openness and resistance to monopolization of knowledge. This is not to say that attempts at remonopolization will not occur and stable pedagogies be developed; however. the lack of agreed unifying principles among cultural specialists in conditions of informational overproduction and the development of multiple competing centres of cultural taste may tend to reduce the possibility of a stable recentring and rehierarchization of knowledge and culture. Effectively we should consider those tendencies in terms of monopolization and demonopolization processes, and shifting power balances.

2 This is not to suggest that postmodern theory (and here I am thinking of Lyotard, Deleuze, Foucault, Derrida, Baudrillard, Vattimo and Rorty and aware that some of them would object to be included in the category) is to be regarded as a troublesome, mischievously invented problem that merely represents a regression to earlier forms of irrationalism, and once explained away sociology can proceed much as before. On the contrary postmodern theory is reacting to changed circumstances in the organization of knowledge and culture in contemporary Western societies that have important metatheoretical and methodological implications. The focus on the metaphysics of presence, the hidden metanarrative legitimations of texts and the rhetorical structures, the recurrent figures and devices (metaphor, synecdoche, chiasmus etc.) that can be identified within the schemes of historians at different times in history represents a definite gain in knowledge (see White, 1973; Bann, 1984). We have to be prepared to live with some of the problems that arise in not making a choice between objectivity and relativism – as Giddens does in his wish to retain the insights of postmodern modes of cultural analysis and champion the investigation of long-term, large-scale social processes. In effect we have to be careful not to be misrepresented and emphasize the antifoundational stance that can be built into theories of long-term, large-scale social processes as Elias's and Giddens's work both demonstrate, in their different ways.

4

Cultural Change and Social Practice

The coming into prominence of the term 'postmodernism' has aroused a good deal of interest among academics and intellectuals. While some dismiss it as merely a transient and shallow intellectual fad, others regard it as signifying a deep-seated break not only with artistic modernism but with the larger epoch of modernity. This entails a resultant rejection of all the cultural manifestations of modernity as passé and here the term 'culture' would be extended to include wider cultural production not just in the arts, but also in the spheres of science, law and morality which Weber saw as originating as part of the differentiation process of modernity. The reversal of this differentiation process, or *de-differentiation* as some would refer to it, also suggests a far-reaching transformation of the nature of cultural production and regimes of signification (see Lash, 1988). The implications of the alleged shift towards the postmodern are thus to highlight the significance of culture in a dual emphasis upon (1) the emergence of new techniques of cultural production and reproduction which transform everyday experiences and practices, and (2) the questioning of the deep cultural coding of modernity in which knowledge was given foundational status in the sense that science, humanism, Marxism or feminism claimed or aspired to offer humankind authoritative guidelines for both knowledge of the world and practical action within it. Postmodernism has therefore raised far-reaching questions about the nature of cultural change and the underlying metatheoretical nexus with which we seek to analyse it.

As many critics have pointed out, one of the problems faced by those such as Lyotard who formulate the postmodern as the end of master narratives is that they too require a metanarrative to explain the emergence of the postmodern which necessarily includes some theory of society and social development leading up to the alleged rupture (see for example Kellner, 1988). The fact that to date many of those theorizing the postmodern have done so from a philosophical, literary or humanities background. along with the antisubstantivist and antievidential logic of their theories means that what were formerly regarded as facts and treated with a degree of caution within social science circles, can now be treated in a more cavalier fashion, in its worst excesses postmodernism can legitimate the writing of thin histories and 'anything goes' or the idiosyncratic use of evidence to back up the claim of the eclipse of evidentiality. This is at times coupled with the tendency to generalize and read off the transformation of social processes and social practices from evidence gleaned from the analysis of literary and artistic texts which are regarded as harbingers of the new 'disordered' social order.

It is one of the merits of the work of Fredric Jameson that he seeks to walk this particular tightrope: to treat the postmodern seriously and understand it as a sign of a major cultural transformation and at the same time to attempt to explain it in terms of social processes, as well as to *evaluate* it to assess its practical significance. Jameson's (1984a, 1984b, 1984c, 1987) work on postmodernism has been highly influential, as he has not only sought to detect and understand the particular quality of the cultural experiences designated postmodern, but also sought to locate them within a social framework. Jameson's theory of society and development is derived from Marxism and he locates postmodernism as the cultural dominant which is associated with the move to late capitalism in the post-World War II era. In this chapter I shall examine some aspects of Jameson's characterization of postmodernism, in particular his use of culture. it will be argued that Jameson directs us towards the social processes and structure within which postmodernism should be understood and explained. In this sense his endeavour to totalize – which is the target for much criticism from postmodernists and others – is laudable (see During, 1987; O'Neill, 1988). Yet I shall also argue that there are problems with the way in which Jameson situates culture within late capitalism via his focus upon cultural experiences and not cultural practices.

Late capitalism and social practice

Jameson (1984b: 125) persistently refers to postmodernism as the cultural logic of late capitalism and analyses the ways in which cultural changes such as postmodernism 'express the deeper logic' of the 'late consumer, or multinational' capitalist social system. His periodization of this third stage of capitalism as post-World War II multinational capitalism follows Mandel's scheme in *Late Capitalism* (1975). Apart from the reductionism in regarding historical changes as a consequence of the logic of capital accumulation and technological changes, his analysis is accompanied by a neat cultural periodization. Thus for Jameson (1984a: 78), realism corresponds to market capitalism, modernism to monopoly capitalism, and postmodernism to late/multinational/consumer capitalism. From this perspective, culture seems to be regarded as taking place on 'the superstructural levels' (Jameson, 1984d: xv). While Jameson tries to shy away from the economistic implications of this position, it is clear that his view of culture largely works within the confines of a base-superstructure model which entails a whole series of problems I shall discuss here.

Apart from the fact that Mandel associates High Modernism and the International Style, not Postmodernism, with late capitalism (see Cooke, 1988), we do not find the assumed even spread of modernism in monopoly capitalist societies. indeed, it is noticeable how geographically uneven its distribution is, with England and the Scandinavian countries in the developed West scarcely generating sustained modernist movements whereas Germany, Italy, France, Russia, America and the Netherlands did. It is therefore difficult to link artistic movements with specific stages of the development of capitalism.

In addition, approaches like those of Jameson tend to regard history as the outcome of a particular relentless developmental logic and play down the role played by classes, social movements and groups in creating the preconditions for such a logic in their various power balances, interdependencies and struggles for hegemony. In effect our focus of attention should not just be on the higher-level relatively abstract systems theorization of capital, but on the way capitalism has been practiced by specific groups, classes, and class fractions. Here we can refer to the debate between E.P. Thompson and Perry Anderson on the 'pecularities of the English' which took place in the 1960s, and Anderson's (1987) retrospective on the debate. Anderson defends his earlier position and emphasizes the role of the landed aristocracy in controlling English society in the nineteenth century. Effectively, feudalism did not just slip away and the bourgeoisie reign supreme; rather, contrary to the canons of the established theory, the landowners remained the hegemonic class in Victorian Britain (Wiener, 1981). Hence, it would seem important to acknowledge the different power balances and trajectories of domination in different capitalist societies, and to counter tendencies towards economistic readings with those which are more open to cultural differences, or what has been called by Richard Johnson (1976, 1979) 'culturalism'.

With regard to Jameson's general characterization of culture a number of points can be made. The first one relates to Jameson's designation of the role of culture in late capitalism as one cultural profusion produced by the logic of the commodity form. Jameson (1979: 131), for example, has written that culture is 'the very element of consumer society itself; no society has ever been saturated with signs and images like this one'. This statement has more recently been incorporated into Jameson's writings on postmodern culture when he refers to the destruction of 'the semi-autonomy of the cultural sphere' to be replaced by 'a prodigious expansion of culture throughout the social realm, to the point at which everything in our social life ... can be said to have become "cultural"' (Jameson, 1984a: 87).

The first point I'd like to raise about this statement is the implied contrast between late capitalist culturally saturated societies and other societies. If it is based upon the assumption that nineteenth-century capitalism was more purely economic, that transactions and social interactions were based on pure exchange value, with goods regarded as utilities, not commodity-signs, then some anthropologists and sociologists would take exception. It is possible to conceive of 'the culture of the economy', or the cultural underpinning of economic behaviour as does Elwert (1984) who, following Durkheim refers to 'the culturally embedded economy'. Sahlins (1974, 1976), Douglas and Isherwood (1980) and Leiss (1983) have all pointed to the role goods play as 'communicators', cultural signs, in both 'primitive' and modern societies. We therefore need to take seriously notions of the culture of production and not just focus on the production of culture. Economic transactions themselves take place within a cultural matrix of taken-for-granted assumptions which should not be naturalized. Reddy (1984) has argued in his study of the rise of market culture in France that the notion that capitalist societies became transformed into a competitive market society is largely a mirage. Rather than an effective market in labour working in nineteenth-century England and France, which was not the case, we have to reformulate this economic myth of the industrial revolution to consider the call for unregulated competition and the assumption that people are motivated by gain as elements of a new culture, a market culture, which progressively infiltrated discourse. In addition we need to ask the question how this discourse was transmitted and sustained which points to the need to examine the rise in the power-potential of economic specialists and a change in their relation to other groups. Elias (1984a), for example, has drawn attention to the way in which the growing autonomy of social phenomena such as markets must be related to the growth in the power potential of actual economic specialists in commerce, trade and industry, and the growth of autonomy of thinking about these phenomena (the emergence of a science of economics). Hence we need to inquire into the sociogenesis of economics and the economic sphere and the crucial role of culture in this process.

Furthermore if we look at other writers, such as Baudrillard, who have explored the logic of the commodity form and investigated the profusion of images and the growth of a simulational society which is similar to the postmodern culture Jameson talks of, we note some very different conclusions. In *The Mirror of Production* (1975) and *For A Critique of the Political Economy of the Sign* (1981), Baudrillard has theorized the logic of the commodity to point to the way in which under capitalism the commodity has become a sign in the Saussurean sense with its meaning arbitrarily determined by its position in a self-referential system of signifiers. We can therefore talk about commodity-signs, and the consumption of signs, and in an earlier piece – 'Reification and Utopia in Mass Culture' (1979) – Jameson followed Baudrillard thus far and would agree with his description that consumer culture and television have produced a surfeit of images and signs which have given rise to a simulational world which has effaced the distinction between the real and the imaginary: a depthless aestheticized hallucination of reality. For Baudrillard, however, this discovery of the nihilism at the heart of the logic of the capitalist commodity form – of Nietzsche as the completion of Marx (Kroker, 1985) – is such to break all 'referential illusions'. To use one of Baudrillard's (1983a) favourite metaphors: all the privileged domains of finalities – labour, use-value, sex, science, society, human emancipation and their theorizations (what Lyotard (1984) refers to as metanarratives) – are sucked into a 'black-hole'. For Baudrillard, then, the logic of commodity production has produced a particular reversal in which culture once determined, now becomes free-floating and determining to the extent that today we can talk about the triumph of signifying culture. This means that we can no longer speak of class or normativity which belong to the prior stage of the system as people are reduced to a glutinous mass which refuses to stabilize in its absorption, reflection and cynical parody of media images. It is neither manipulated nor manipulable according to Baudrillard (1983b).

Jameson clearly follows Baudrillard in his depiction of the consumer society as saturated with signs, messages and images and adds that 'the priorities of the real become reversed, and everything is mediated by culture to the point where even the political and ideological "levels" have initially to be disentangled from their primary mode of representation which is cultural' (Jameson, 1979: 139). From the above discussion, it is clear that the distinction between culturally saturated and non-culturally saturated societies needs a higher degree of specificity. As we will see below, it is a distinction which plays off the confusion of two meanings of culture: the anthropological or everyday meaning in the sense that all societies involve signifying practices, and culture in the sense of high culture, the product of specialists of symbolic production whose gain in power-potential since the eighteenth century has given rise to the sense of an autonomous cultural sphere with pretensions to producing universal cultural guidelines for social practices. The assumption that this privileged cultural sphere has been eroded by the profusion of mass consumer cultural images and signs glosses over the long process of competition and interdependencies between the carriers of the market, consumer or mass culture and specialist high culture. We can discuss this by exploring two further aspects.

Many commentators would agree with Jameson's statement that the culture of postmodernism/late capitalism/post-industrial society is less unified than that of earlier capitalism (see Bell, 1976; Touraine, 1985; Habermas, 1975). There is again, however, the danger we have discussed earlier that such a perspective is accompanied by a false dichotomy which implicitly regards the culture of traditional societies as integrated and unified. This viewpoint has been systematically criticized by Norbert Elias (1978b, 1982), the Annales School (see D. Smith, 1988) and Abercrombie, Hill and Turner (1980), much of whose research points to the way in which the popular culture of the fifteenth, sixteenth and seventeenth centuries cannot be simply presented as a relatively unsophisticated forerunner of later developments. Many commentators unfortunately succumb to the writing of 'thin histories' in which they attempt to think backwards from the upheavals of nineteenth-century capitalism to some point of stability and pre-industrial organic unity, usually prior to 1750, and miss the complex, stratified nature of popular culture and its ritual inversions such as carnivals, festivals, and fairs (see Easton et al., 1988: 20). Hence it is dubious to claim that the parameters of order and disorder apply to modernity and postmodernity, respectively. Lyotard also argues that traces of this nostalgia can be found in Baudrillard's thesis that postmodernism has led to the end of the social, the disintegration of the social bond which turns society into an amorphous mass. For Lyotard (1984: 15) this is a point of view 'haunted by the paradisiac representation of a lost "organic society"' – a point which suggests that 'the death of God' and the undermining of master narratives may be a bigger problem for intellectuals and their search for apodictic knowledge, that is to say, the centrality that cognitive beliefs play in their practices in contrast to those of ordinary men and women. Rather than succumb to the nostalgia of the intellectuals as Stauth and Turner point out (1988) we should acknowledge that particular versions of culture are carried and manipulated by various groups in a struggle to appropriate signs and use them in terms of their own particular interests.

It has often been noted that the distinction between high and mass culture has been used in this way by the intellectuals whose distaste for mass culture and preference for elitist high culture also betrays a nostalgia (B.S. Turner, 1987). The conclusion of some commentators has been to regard the shift towards postmodern culture with the erosion of the distinction between mass culture and high culture as particularly threatening to the intellectuals. Jameson (1984b: 112) for example writes:

> This is perhaps the most distressing development of all from an academic standpoint, which has traditionally had a vested interest in preserving a realm of high or elite culture against the surrounding environment of philistinism, of schlock and kitsch, of TV series and *Reader's Digest* culture, and in transmitting difficult and complex skills of reading, listening and seeing to its initiates.

Academics do, of course, have an interest in reclaiming the investments they have made in accumulating their own cultural capital, and the bulwark against popular culture and non-privileged readings of consecrated 'difficult' academic texts is to be seen throughout the academic institution with its pedagogy, examinations, refereeing procedures and 'rigor'. Yet Jameson is perhaps providing too homogeneous a view of the intellectuals here. Not all intellectuals sit back and contemplate the erosion of high culture with horror. Rather, we can think of some groups, such as outsider intellectuals, who may contemplate the threat to the established order with less than concern, and indeed may themselves seek to hasten the process by proclaiming the virtues of popular, mass and postmodern culture. This attack on the existing system of classification in the name of equality and democracy may then itself be followed by an attempted reconstitution of the symbolic hierarchy in favour of the outsider group. We are not of course yet in a situation of remonopolization and it may very well be that this is no longer a realistic possibility today, yet it can be argued that the opening up of the cultural categories creates a space in which new interpretations, readings and translations of the now acceptable mass/popular culture goods are in demand, and in the academy there is every sign that this will lead to the institutionalization of new pedagogies to guide initiates. We will return to the theme of the intellectuals and postmodernism at the end of the chapter; suffice to say at this point that the current phase of cultural declassification both inside and outside the academy which has produced an interest in popular culture and postmodernism may undermine the power of some symbolic specialists while providing great opportunities for other symbolic specialists and cultural intermediaries.

Experience versus practice

The next point about Jameson's approach I would like to raise relates to his focus on the experience of postmodernism to the neglect of the practices of postmodernism. it would seem important to distinguish between the commentator s experience of postmodernism and specific experiences of groups and class fractions who use postmodern cultural goods in particular practices. The latter may entail an analysis of how specialists in symbolic production (artists, intellectuals, academics) use postmodernism in their own practices as well as how members of specific groups (the audiences and publics) use specifically designated postmodern goods and experiences, as well as those experiences deemed to be postmodern by the critics (yet which may remain undesignated by the recipients) in particular everyday practices. To take an example with reference to Marshall Berman's (1982) work on modernity, Janet Wolff in a paper titled 'The Invisible *Flâneuse'* (1985) takes exception to Berman's restriction of the experience of modernity to public life. Berman, following Baudelaire, sees *the flâneur*, the stroller, in the anonymous urban spaces of the modern city, as experiencing the shocks, jolts of the impersonal stimuli of the impressions gained in the crowd. Yet Berman has no place in his account for the *flâneuse*, and the absence of an account of women's experience of modernity is hardly justified by the limited capacity women had to appear in public life. Rather the experience of modernity of women in the private sphere constitutes an important yet missing relational element in any account of the experience of modernity.

The same argument could be presented with reference to two basic features of postmodernism Jameson (1984b: 15) identifies: the transformation of reality into images and the fragmentation of time into a series of perpetual presents. With regard to the first. in a way similar to Baudrillard's discussion of postmodern imagistic culture, Jameson refers to pastiche and simulations, the stylistic diversity and heterogeneity which lead to the loss of the referent, 'the death of the subject', and the end of individualism. Again we must raise the question who is experiencing this loss, and whether we are in danger of succumbing to nostalgia for a referent which may have been of little concern in the day-to-day practices of specific lower-class groups in the *longue durée*. In addition, research into the practice of watching television has shown that a whole host of different activities in different groups takes place – eating, talking, working, sex and so forth. Furthermore the actual reception and reading of programmes is also filtered through a particular class habitus (Mullin and Taylor, 1986; Leal and Oliven, 1988). It is also important to note that television watching can be correlated to class and age. Those with the least capital, the old and the lower class, watch the most with viewing diminishing as one rises up the class scale and descends the age scale. Television for middle-class groups provides a resource which is used in social encounters and is related to the important need to generate and sustain social contacts in the leisure time activities of these groups. Hence television watching is enclaved. TV is not the world and we need to inquire into the differential social uses of television (cf. DiMaggio, 1987).

With regard to the second feature, the fragmentation of time into a series of perpetual presents, Jamesons's paradigm here is schizophrenia. (Incidentally Baudrillard (1983b) has also discussed the channel-hopping TV viewer's fragmented perception of the world as inducing a schizophrenia which is an element of postmodernism.) Schizophrenia is regarded as the breakdown of the relationship between signifiers, the breakdown of temporality, memory, a sense of history. The schizophrenic's experience is of 'isolated, disconnected, discontinuous material signifiers which fail to link up into a coherent sequence' (Jameson, 1984b: 119). Although he/she therefore does not know personal identity, and has no projects, the immediate undifferentiated experience of the presentness of the world, leads to a sense of *intensities*: vivid, powerful experiences which bear 'a mysterious and oppressive charge of affect' (Jameson, 1984b: 120). This loss of a sense of narrative to the individual's life, and the disconnectedness of experience therefore links well with Jameson's first factor: the transformation of reality into images. It is difficult to comment adequately on postmodernism's alleged inducement of schizophrenic intensities, so I shall confine myself to making two brief points.

First, how far have various religious and artistic subcultures down the ages celebrated the notion of such vivid intensities with the aid of group catharsis, drugs and other means? Such liminal experiments are generally well circumscribed, and function as areas of excess demarcated from the seriality of everyday life. Here one thinks also of the discussions of the carnival of the Middle Ages by Bakhtin, Ladurie, and others (Stallybrass and White, 1986; Featherstone, chapter 4 below). Whether or not individuals beyond these subcultures, or other groups outside certain well-defined occasions are experiencing greater intensities and loss of a sense of history, need investigating. Jameson is guilty of overgeneralization, therefore, and a lack of sensitivity to historical concreteness. His interest in totalizing and relating cultural changes to well-defined epochs means that he underestimates the differentiation of culture within pre-capitalist societies and hence the uniqueness of elements of the postmodern. Jameson provides very vivid and suggestive examples to illustrate his theory, yet they are only examples and only illustrative. One gets little sense of an interest in countertendencies and the openness and contingency of the lived structure of history as it is produced and reproduced, albeit blindly, by groups of individuals trapped together in competitive struggles and interdependencies in their everyday lives. This could be the stock objection of a social scientist against the more exploratory and openly imagistic modes of writing common in the humanities. But it is also central to the emergence and the problem of postmodernism which has brought together scholars from the humanities and social sciences on a common terrain. Jameson's totalizing interests and his attempts to outline a social theory of postmodernism do, however, put him firmly into the social science orbit and necessarily open him to their standards of judgement and rigour. This is especially so as Jameson is clearly unwilling to become an advocate of the new methods and practise postmodernism in his writings, which relates to his desire to stand outside postmodernism to explain and judge it.

Second, Norbert Elias's theory of *The Civilizing Process* (1978b, 1982) which describes the internalization of external controls and increasing emotional constraint which accompanies the process of state formation has been recently modified by Cas Wouters (1986) who has worked closely with Elias to take into account tendencies which seem to run counter to this trend – such as the relaxation of emotional controls which took place in the 1960s. The resultant informalization process, a countermovement in the spiral development of the civilizing process, emphasizes that at certain points the balance may shift towards a 'controlled de-control of the emotions' in which (and I would add especially for the new middle class) forms of behaviour and modes of exploration of the emotions which were formerly forbidden and accompanied by strong interpersonal and psychic sanctions, now become permissible and even mandatory. In what follows, it should be possible to discover in more detail the increasing capacity of the new middle class to display a calculating hedonism, to engage in more varied (and often dangerous) aesthetic and emotional explorations which themselves do not amount to a rejection of controls, but a more carefully circumscribed and interpersonally responsible 'controlled de-control' of the emotions which necessary entails some calculation and mutually expected respect for other persons. Hence we should go beyond the rational–emotional dichotomy and investigate those conditions and practices within the new middle class which create the possibility for a loosening of the controls on aesthetic and emotional experiences. which could lead to a greater receptivity to those symbolic goods and experiences which have been designated 'postmodern'.

To take an example suggested by the work of Meyrowitz (1985), on the adult-like child and the child-like adult; he argues that adults today are given greater licence to explore emotions, act 'spontaneously' and depart from former stricter controlled parental roles. Disneyworld and the proliferation of the theme parks clearly offer good examples of sites in which this emotional de-control and appreciation of sensations and adoption of behaviour once restricted to children take place. Jameson (1987: 48) cites Disneyland as paradigmatic of postmodern hyperspace and simulation. It has been argued that increasingly the contemporary tourist (or 'post-tourist') approaches holiday locations such as resorts, theme parks, and increasingly museums in the knowledge that the spectacles offered are simulations and accepts the montaged world and hyper-reality for what it is (Urry, 1988). That is, they do not quest after an authentic pre-simulational reality but have the necessary dispositions to engage in 'the play of the real' and capacity to open up to surface sensations, spectacular imagery, liminoid experiences and intensities without the nostalgia for the real.

If one seeks to approach postmodern culture from this perspective, then it is possible to move away from some of the more abstract and hypostatized discussions of postmodernism and provide sociological evidence in terms of the classic evidential questions 'who, when, why, and how many?' A study of the cultural practices and sites of postmodernism from this point of view could begin by examining what Zukin (1988a) and Cooke (1988) have dubbed 'Postmodernization' to refer to spatial restructuring and the development of urban artistic and cultural centres and the gentrification which accompanies them (see discussion in chapters 1 and 7). In addition the links between this process and the new *petite bourgeoisie* of new cultural intermediaries who provide symbolic goods and services needs investigating. These 'new intellectuals' who adopt a learning-mode towards life (Bourdieu, 1984: 370) are fascinated by identity, presentation, appearance and lifestyle (see chapter 6). Indeed their veneration of the artistic and intellectual lifestyle is such that they consciously invent an art of living in which their body, home and car are regarded as an extension of their *persona* which must be stylized to express the individuality of the bearer. Bourdieu laconically tells us that this quest for distinction via lifestyle cultivation 'makes available to *almost* everyone the distinctive poses, the distinctive games and other external signs of inner riches previously reserved for intellectuals' (Bourdieu, 1984: 371). The new cultural intermediaries therefore help in transmitting both intellectual cultural goods and the intellectual lifestyle to a wider audience.

It is therefore possible to point to the formation of audiences, publics and consumers of postmodern cultural goods, which is part of a long-term process of the growth in the power-potential of symbol producers and the importance of the cultural sphere. These changes have necessarily led to some declassification and demonopolization of the power of the defenders of the long established symbolic hierarchies in artistic, intellectual and academic institutions. The authority of the canon of the established, or of the aspirations of avant-gardes to become established, thus becomes subject to challenge, critique and attack. To take the example of the arts, this is the result of a series of complex changes in the interdependencies between business leaders, state, and local politicians which has increased business and state patronage for the arts and the power for the arts to become a major market in its own right. Zukin (1988b) has pointed to the massive increase in artists working in New York since the 1970s and the growth of ancillary occupations the gentrification of SoHo and other districts which has made art a more acceptable, profitable occupation and art itself appear more democratized. Despite the cry for a return to Victorian values and the obliteration of the 1960s culture by Thatcher and Reagan, it is interesting how difficult it is to remove symbol specialists and cultural centres and return to the old petit-bourgeois mores.

There is not the space here to go into the changes within the various artistic and intellectual fields which have been associated with postmodernism save to make a few brief points (see also discussion in chapters 1 and 3). To understand postmodernism we need to focus upon the power balances and struggles within each particular field in the arts which opened up a space of cultural declassification which made the emergence of the term and its advocacy by new outside groups against the established possible. Here the strategy of naming is important on the part of groups which seek to legitimate the closure and exhaustion of the old tradition and generate a new space ahead of the established. Hence 'postmodern' became the term used in artistic and intellectual circles in the 1960s and 1970s to distance younger artists and critics from what they perceived as the exhausted and institutionalized modernism.

Likewise with the intellectuals, changes in the structures of their particular field may have worked on two levels: (1) to open up pressures from below on the established by outsiders who seek to destabilize existing symbolic hierarchies; and (2) as a result of changes in the demand for intellectual goods in general by state agencies and the democratizing effect of being drawn into a wider cultural consumption market, the intellectuals are led to engage in a searching reconsideration of the value, ends, and purpose of their endeavours. This latter position has been argued by Bauman (1988) in that he sees postmodernism as a direct articulation of the experience of the intellectuals who face a status and identity crisis as a result of the decline in demand for their goods which transforms them from the position of legislators with a universal project to the lesser role of interpreters, who must play with and translate for enlarged popular 'transient' audiences the multiplicity of life-words and language games from the human cultural archive. Lyotard (1988) as well as others have pointed to the eclipse of the universal authority of the intellectuals. Some are happy to accept the move in which intellectuals have to more openly acknowledge their interests as a positive one and welcome the emergence of particular as opposed to universal intellectuals (see Bourdieu, 1986). For others such as Jacoby (1987), the destruction of the universal intellectual project of the 'last intellectuals' who have no successors in the generation that follows them is a cause for concern.

Authority and cultural practice

From Jameson's perspective, there is a definite need on the part of intellectuals to resist the democratizing, populist spirit of postmodernism and retain the authority to speak for humankind. For example he argues from his Marxist perspective that the decay of the concept of socialism must be resisted and 'it is a matter of re-inventing that concept as a powerful cultural and social vision' (Jameson, 1987: 5). It is a retention of the utopian aspect of Marxism which has laid Jameson open to accusations of a nostalgic neo-Durkheimian reaction to postmodernism such as that by O'Neill

(1988). It could be that Jameson here has adopted an overintellectualist approach to culture in which he overestimates the power-potential of cultural images in producing social changes, and the necessity of integrative beliefs to sustain or produce social changes to the neglect of the ways in which culture is used and enacted on a 'lower' taken-for-granted level in everyday practices. While many have welcomed the secularization of religion, perhaps the same should be said for the secularization of science (Douglas, 1982). Indeed one way of understanding both forms of secularization, and that of intellectual knowledge in general, is to see it not in terms of the replacement of one set of beliefs or world-views by another, but a decline in the relative power-potential of the symbol specialists in question – the clergy, scientists and intellectuals – which is manifest in their inability to sustain the authority of their knowledge in the day-to-day power balances involving figurations of people. Of course there are clear differences in the nature and social effectivity of the types of knowledge involved. Bendix (1970) follows Weber in pointing out that religious specialists supplied beliefs which had a mundane meaning and practical usefulness for ordinary people. Yet the knowledge of artists and intellectuals does not offer similar practical benefits, despite the convictions of their advocates. Although artists and intellectuals possess formidable skills. these skills do not provide power in the religious sense, and arcane knowledge without apparent purpose makes cultural elites suspect to the populace.

It is therefore fitting that Jameson (1987: 53) has referred to the democratization of culture as one aspect of postmodernism, yet he does so with a certain ambivalence, for he evaluates postmodernism negatively and wants to develop modes of analysis and artistic production which dissolve the postmodern pastiche and provide some renewed sense of social or global totality and history. In this sense, for Jameson (1984a: 89–90), knowledge and art must retain some pedagogical function. While this may be an understandable reaction to the acceptance of the disorder and playfulness of postmodernism as the paradigm for future social life and cultural production, it does leave him open to the postmodernist's riposte that he is nostalgically bemoaning the loss of authority of the intellectual aristocracy over the population (see Hutcheon, 1986–7; During, 1987).

To understand postmodernism then, we need to approach it on a number of levels. First, it involves changes in the artistic intellectual and academic fields manifest in the competitive struggles in particular fields over the canon. Second, it involves changes in the broader cultural sphere in terms of the modes of production, circulation, and dissemination of symbolic goods which can be understood in terms of changes in the power-balances and interdependencies between groups and class fractions on inter- and intrasocietal levels. Third, it involves changes in the everyday practices and experiences of different groups who as a result of the first and second set of changes start to use regimes of signification in different ways and develop new means of orientation and identity structures. In many ways postmodernism stands as a sign for contemporary cultural change and should direct our attention to the interrelationship between the above areas or 'levels' of culture and the necessary reflexivity which entails the inclusion of the academic intellectuals as socially interested parties in the process.

Like many other commentators, Jameson focuses on the experiential dimension of these changes, which is usually deciphered from texts and other modes of signification. Yet he has the merit of going beyond mere cultural analysis by attempting to locate postmodern cultural production in terms of the move to the third 'purer' stage of late capitalism which has globalized the social. Here he rightly focuses on the eclipse of the state–society couplet with nation-states undermined by the expanded international market with its rapid capital and information flows. Yet while in this sense we could speak of the end of the social, for long the referent of sociology in the form of the identity of the state–society couplet, this does not mean the eclipse of social relations. Widening interdependencies and more complex balances of power between larger figurations of people can still be understood sociologically. The problem with Jameson's approach is that he moves from the economic to the cultural and misses out the mediating effect of the social, understood here as social relationships. That is, to understand postmodern culture, we need not just to read the signs but look at how the signs are used by figurations of people in their day-to-day practices. Of course a proliferation of signs, a flood of new cultural goods and commodities such as took place in eighteenth-century England or mid-nineteenth-century Paris has a culturally democratizing effect and makes it more difficult to 'read the signs' to attribute a particular status and social position to the bearers of particular cultural goods and practices. Yet it can be argued that attempts will be continuously made to reassign and read the attributes of cultural goods.

In short, the tendency is for social groups to seek to classify and order their social circumstances and use cultural goods as means of demarcation, as communicators which establish boundaries between some people and build bridges with others. Such a focus on the social usages of cultural goods firmly directs our attention to the practices of embodied persons who read off and necessarily have to make judgements about others by decoding the cultural signs which others practice, display and consume. Postmodernism offers the prospect of the end of this social game, of a move beyond the social. Yet although we live in a phase of cultural declassification, we must not discount the possibility of the reestablishment of a cultural order, nor fall for the temptation of treating liminoid enclaves of cultural disorder as coextensive with culture as such.

In conclusion, then, postmodernism should be understood not only on the level of the unfolding of the logic of capitalism; it needs to be studied concretely in terms of the dynamic of the changing power balances, competitive struggles and interdependencies between various groups of specialists in symbolic production and economic specialists. That means we need to inquire into the role of the producers, transmitters and disseminators of the alleged new forms of cultural production and consumption both inside and outside the academy. If postmodernism is a symptom of a societal or global shift towards cultural declassification (DiMaggio, 1987) which is manifest in a number of other areas such as the destabilization of long-established symbolic hierarchies which has opened up a space for the pop-ularization and legitimation of the study of popular culture, then we need to locate it within the dynamic of changing intragroup struggles and inter-dependencies both on an inter and intrasocietal level. To understand the postmodern, therefore, demands a good deal of reflexivity. We need to focus upon the carriers and transmitters of postmodernism who have an interest in the success of the term and all it implies within their struggles in the academy with the guardians of established symbolic hierarchies, and an interest in the creation and education of audiences and publics who can recognize and use postmodern cultural goods in practices.

Finally, we cannot ignore the role of academics, artists and intellectuals in detecting traces of cultural change which they articulate and fashion as postmodernism. This is not to dismiss their interest in postmodernism as a cynical manipulation or moves within intellectual distinction games. Clearly, we are currently witnessing cultural changes which have raised the profile of culture within the culture–economy–society configuration and which demand careful research and theorization. Yet today the numerical force and power-potential of the specialists in symbolic production has grown, particularly so if we compare the current debate over postmod-ernism with the earlier debate between the ancients and the moderns. If postmodernism points to a rise in the significance of culture – here one thinks of Baudrillard's (1983b) assertion that today everything is cultural – then we should not just understand this as an extension of the logic and technology of commodity production but also inquire into modes of trans-mission and consumption the practices of symbolic specialists, cultural intermediaries and audiences which have dispositions which make them receptive to those sensibilities designated postmodern.

5

The Aestheticization of Everyday Life

If we examine definitions of postmodernism we find an emphasis upon the effacement of the boundary between art and everyday life, the collapse of the distinction between high art and mass/popular culture, a general stylistic promiscuity and playful mixing of codes. These general features of postmodern theories which stress the equalization and levelling out of symbolic hierarchies, antifoundationalism and a general impulse towards cultural declassification, can also be related to what are held to be the characteristic postmodern experiences. Here one can build upon the use of the term *modernité* by Baudelaire to point to the new experience of modernity, the shocks, jolts, and vivid presentness captured by the break with traditional forms of sociation which the modern cities such as Paris seemed to bring forth from the mid-nineteenth century onwards. In a similar way one might also be able to speak of the experience of *postmodernité* and draw upon perceived shifts in cultural experiences and modes of signification. Here we find an emphasis upon the aestheticization of everyday life and the transformation of reality into images in the work of Baudrillard (1983a). Jameson (1984a) too emphasizes the loss of a sense of history and the fragmentation of time into a series of perpetual presents in which there is the experience of multiphrenic intensities. A similar aestheticization of experience and breaking down of the ordered chain of signifiers can be detected in the writings of their followers where one finds an emphasis upon 'the liquefaction of signs and commodities', 'the effacement of the boundary between the real and the image', 'floating signifiers', 'hyperreality', 'depthless culture', 'bewildering immersion', 'sensory overload' and 'affect-charge intensities' (Kroker and Cook, 1987; Crary, 1984). While many of these examples draw this inspiration from the intensification of image production in the media and consumer culture in general, one also finds it in descriptions of the contemporary city. Here the emphasis is not only on the type of new architecture specifically designated postmodern, but also on the more general eclectic stylistic hotchpotch which one finds in the urban fabric of the built environment. In addition a similar decontextualization of tradition and a raiding of all cultural forms to draw out quotations from the imaginary side of life are found among the young 'de-centred subjects' who enjoy the experimentation and play with fashion and the stylization of life as they stroll through the 'no place' postmodern urban spaces (Chambers, 1987; Calefato, 1988). There are clearly strong linkages and crossovers between the project of the aestheticization and stylization of everyday life on the part of such groups and the romantic, bohemian art-school tradition which has fed into rock music, particularly since the 1960s, and which has sought in various ways to transgress the boundary between art and everyday life (see Frith and Horne, 1987). This suggests then that the experience of *postmodernité*, in particular the emphasis upon the aestheticization of everyday life and its formulation, articulation and promotion by cultural specialists may have a long history. In short it would be useful to explore the *genealogy* of *postmodernité* and in particular examines the linkages between *modernité* and *postmodernité* which may yet direct us back to still earlier forerunners. This is not to argue that the postmodern does not exist or that it is a misleading concept. Rather it is only by exploring its antecedents and the long-term cultural process in which there may have been earlier similar developments, that we can attempt to understand, and differentiate between, what is specific to the postmodern and what may represent an accumulation and intensification of tendencies long present within the modern, and even pre-modern.

The aestheticization of everyday life

There are three senses in which we can speak of the aestheticization of everyday life. First we can refer to those artistic subcultures which produced the Dada, historical avant-garde and Surrealist movements in World War I and the 1920s, which sought in their work, writings, and in some cases lives, to efface the boundary between art and everyday life. Postmodern art in the 1960s with its reaction to what was regarded as the institutionalization of modernism in the museum and the academy built on this strategy. It is interesting to note that Marcel Duchamp, who was centrally involved in the earlier Dada movement with his infamous 'readymades', became venerated by the New York postmodern trans-avant-garde artists in the 1960s. Here we detect a double movement. In the first place there is the direct challenge against the work of art, the desire to beauraticize art, to dissemble its sacred halo and challenge its respectable location in the museum and the academy. There is also the assumption that art can be anywhere or anything. The detritus of mass culture, the debased consumer commodities, could be art (here one thinks of Warhol and pop art). Art was also to be found in the antiwork: in the 'happening', the transitory 'lost' performance which cannot be museumified, as well as in the body and other sensory objects in the world. It is also worth noting that many of the strategies and artistic techniques of Dada, Surrealism and the avant-garde have been taken up by advertising and the popular media within consumer culture (see Martin, 1981).

Second the aestheticization of everyday life can refer to the project of turning life into a work of art. The fascination of this project on the part of artists and intellectuals and would-be artists and intellectuals has a long history. It can, for example, be found in the Bloomsbury Group around the turn of the century in which G.E. Moore argued that the greatest goods in life consisted of personal affectations and aesthetic enjoyment. A similar ethic of life as a work of art can be detected in the late-nineteenth-century writing of Pater and Wilde. Wilde's assumption was that the ideal aesthete should 'realize himself in many forms, and by a thousand different ways, and will be curious of new sensations'. It can be argued that postmodernism – especially postmodern theory – has brought aesthetic questions to the fore and there are clear continuities between Wilde, Moore and the Bloomsbury Group, and the writings of Rorty whose criteria for the good life revolve around the desire to enlarge one's self, the quest for new tastes and sensations, to explore more and more possibilities (Shusterman, 1988). We can also detect the centrality of the aesthetic approach to life in the work of Foucault, as Wolin (1986) has argued. Foucault (1986: 41–2) approvingly refers to Baudelaire's conception of modernity in which a central figure is 'the dandy who makes of his body, his behaviour, his feelings and passions, his very existence, a work of art'. In effect the modern man is 'the man who tries to invert himself'. Dandyism, which first developed with Beau Brummel in England in the early nineteenth century, stressed the quest for special superiority through the construction of an uncompromising exemplary lifestyle in which an aristocracy of spirit manifested itself in a contempt for the masses and the heroic concern with the achievement of originality and superiority in dress, demeanour, personal habits and even furnishings – what we now call lifestyle (see R.H. Williams, 1982: 107 ff.). It became an important theme in the development of artistic countercultures, the bohème and avant-gardes in mid- to late-nineteenth-century Paris, and one finds a fascination with it in the writings and lives of Balzac, Baudelaire, Comte d'Orsay down to Edmond de Goncourt, de Montesquieu and Huysmans' Des Esseintes. This dual focus on a life of aesthetic consumption and the need to form life into an aesthetically pleasing whole on the part of artistic and intellectual countercultures should be related to the development of mass consumption in general and the pursuit of new tastes and sensations and the construction of distinctive lifestyles which has become central to consumer culture (Featherstone, 1987a).

The third sense of the aestheticization of everyday life refers to the rapid flow of signs and images which saturate the fabric of everyday life in contemporary society. The theorization of this process has drawn much from Marx's theory of the fetishism of commodities which has been developed in various ways by Lukács, the Frankfurt School, Benjamin, Haug, Lefebvre, Baudrillard and Jameson. For Adorno the increasing dominance of exchange value not only obliterated the original use-value of things and replaced it by abstract exchange value, but it left the commodity free to take on an ersatz or secondary use-value, what Baudrillard was later to refer to as 'sign-value'. The centrality of the commercial manipulation of images through advertising the media and the displays, performances and spectacles of the urbanized fabric of daily life therefore entails a constant reworking of desires through images. Hence the consumer society must not be regarded as only releasing a dominant materialism for it also confronts people with dream-images which speak to desires, and aestheticize and de-realize reality (Haug, 1987: 123). It is this aspect which has been taken up by Baudrillard and Jameson who emphasize the new and central role which images play in the consumer society which gives culture an unprecedented importance. For Baudrillard it is the build-up, density and seamless, all-encompassing extent of the production of images in contemporary society which has pushed us towards a qualitatively new society in which the distinction between reality and image become effaced and everyday life becomes aestheticized: the simulational world or postmodern culture. It is worth adding that this process has generally been evaluated negatively by the above writers who stress the manipulative aspects (Benjamin to some extent and Baudrillard in his later writings being exceptions). This has prompted some to argue for a more progressive integration of art and everyday life – as, for example we find in Marcuse's (1969) *Essay on Liberation*. We also find this in the notions of cultural revolution developed in various ways by Henry Lefebvre (1971), with his plea to 'let everyday life become a work of art', and the International Situationists (see Poster, 1975).

This third aspect of the aestheticization of everyday life is of course central to the development of consumer culture and we need to be aware of its interplay with the second strand we have identified: in effect we need to examine the long-term process of their relational development which has entailed the development of mass consumer culture dream-worlds and a separate (counter)cultural sphere in which artists and intellectuals have adopted various strategies of distantiation, as well as attempting to thematize and comprehend this process. First we will examine in more detail the writings of Baudrillard to gain a stronger sense of the meaning of the aestheticization of everyday life in relation to postmodernism.

In his earlier writings on the consumer society Baudrillard developed a theory of the commodity-sign, in which he pointed to the way in which the commodity has become a sign in the Saussurean sense with its meaning arbitrarily determined by its position in a self-referential set of signifiers. In his more recent writings Baudrillard (1983a, 1983b) has pushed this logic even further to draw attention to the overload of information provided by the media which now confront us with an endless flow of fascinating images and simulations. so that 'TV is the world'. In *Simulations* Baudrillard (1983a: 148) states that in this hyperreality the real and the imaginary are confused and aesthetic fascination is everywhere so that 'a kind of non-intentional parody hovers over everything, of technical simulating, of indefinable fame to which is attached an aesthetic pleasure'. For Baudrillard (1983a: 151) art ceases to be a separate enclaved reality; it enters into production and reproduction so that everything 'even if it be the everyday and banal reality, falls by this token under the sign of art, and becomes aesthetic'. The end of the real and the end of art moves us into a hyperreality in which the secret discovered by Surrealism becomes more widespread and generalized. As Baudrillard (1983a: 148) remarks:

It is reality itself today that is hyperrealist. Surrealism's secret already was that the most banal reality could become surreal, but only in certain privileged moments that are still nevertheless connected with art and the imaginary. Today it is quotidian reality in its entirety – political, social, historical and economic – that from now on incorporates the simulating dimension of hyper-realism. We live everywhere already in an 'aesthetic' hallucination of reality.

The contemporary simulational world has seen the end of the illusion of relief, perspective and depth as the real is emptied out and the contradiction between the real and the imaginary is effaced. Baudrillard (1983a: 151) adds

And so art is everywhere, since artifice is at the very heart of reality. And so art is dead, not only because its critical transcendence is gone, but because reality itself, entirely impregnated by an aesthetic which is inseparably from its own structure, has been confused with its own image.

In this third stage of simulational culture, which Baudrillard now calls postmodern (Kellner, 1987), one of the forms often used as an illustration is MTV (see Chen, 1987; Kaplan, 1986, 1987). According to Kaplan (1986) MTV seems to exist in a timeless present with video artists ransacking film genres and art movements from different historical periods to blur boundaries and the sense of history. History becomes spacialized out, aesthetic hierarchies and developments are collapsed with the mixing of genres and high art, popular and commercial forms. It is argued that the continuous flow of diverse images makes it difficult to chain them together into a meaningful message; the intensity and degree of saturation of signifiers defy systematization and narrativity. Yet we should raise the question of how those images work: has MTV moved beyond a sign system which forms a structured language in the Saussurean sense?

The distinction between *discourse* and *figure* which Scott Lash (1988) takes from the work of Lyotard (1971) may go some way toward helping to answer this question. Lash points to a number of features which make postmodern culture figural: its emphasis upon primary processes (desire) rather than secondary (the ego); upon images rather than words; upon the immersion of the spectator and investment of desire in the object as opposed to the main-tenance of distance. Lash also associates these qualities with the process of de-differentiation. This notion is based on a reversal of the process of cultural *differentiation* Weber and Habermas refer to (which entails the differentiation of aesthetic forms from the real world) to *de-differentiation*, which implies a reversal to favour the de-auraticization of art, and an aesthetics of desire, sensation and immediacy. For Lash, then, de-differentiation and figural regimes of signification point to the way in which images unlike language are based upon perceptual memories which draw on the unconscious, which is not structured like language with systematic rules. Images signify iconically, that is through resemblances. While the figural is found in visual regimes of signification such as the cinema, television and advertisements, it can also be said to be a general feature of consumer culture, Here we can refer to Benjamin's (1982b) emphasis upon the sense of intoxication and the poetization of the banal in the dream-worlds of mass consumption, which is central to his discussion of the mid-nineteenth-century Paris arcades in his *Passagen-Werk*. A study which, with its focus on nineteenth-century Paris, brings together in time and space the origins of the second and third sense of the aestheticization of everyday life we have discussed.

The aestheticization of everyday life through the figural regimes of signification, which Lash (1988) holds as central to postmodernism, then, may have its origins in the growth of consumer culture in the big cities of nineteenth-century capitalist societies, which became the sites for the intoxicating dream-worlds, the constantly changing flow of commodities, images and bodies (the *flâneur*). In addition those big cities were the sites of the artistic and intellectual countercultures, the bohemias and artistic avant-gardes, members of whom became fascinated by and sought to capture in various media the range of new sensations, and who also acted as a intermediaries in stimulating. formulating and disseminating these sensibilities to wider audiences and publics (see Seigel 1986) While the literature on modernity pays attention to the centrality of this experience of *modernité*, the shocks, jolts, and phantasmagoria of the new urban centres captured in Baudelaire's discussion of the *flâneur* and Benjamin's discussion of the arcades, we need to consider how relevant it is to understanding the experience of *'postmodernité'*.

Hence we need to investigate the continuities and discontinuities with late-twentieth-century practices and sites. This would point us towards a consideration of urban renewal through the process of postmodernization (Cooke, 1988; Zukin, 1988a) with the gentrification of inner city areas and the emergence of simulational environments which use spectacular imagery in malls, shopping centres, theme parks and hotels. In addition, it has been argued that significant changes are taking place in institutions (which were formerly) designated as restricted spaces for the educated connoisseur and serious viewer: museums. Today museums seek to cater for larger audiences and discard their exclusively high-culture label to become sites for spectacles, sensation, illusion and montage; places where one has an experience, rather than where knowledge of the canon and established symbolic hierarchies are inculcated (Roberts, 1988). We also need to inquire into the process of the articulation, transmission and dissemination of the experience of these new spaces by intellectuals and cultural intermediaries to various audiences and publics and examine the way in which pedagogies of these 'new' sensibilities are incorporated into everyday practices.

This points to the need to investigate the aestheticization of everyday life in specific locations in time and space. While the total aestheticization of everyday life would entail the breaking down of the barriers between art, the aesthetic sensibility and everyday life so that artifice becomes the only reality available, we should not assume this is a given, or something in the nature of human perception which once discovered can be read back into all previous human existence. Rather we should investigate the process of its formation. It is therefore necessary to raise the stark sociological questions of the specific locations and degree of generality. Here we investigate the sociogenetic historical origins of particular cognitive styles and modes of perception which arise in the changing interdependencies and struggles between figurations of people. To take two brief examples: as Robbins (1987) has shown in his study of nineteenth-century British mountaineers the process whereby mountains, long regarded with indifference by travellers and locals alike, became objects of beauty which would yield up aesthetic pleasures was a definite social process involving the development, education and institution-alization of new tastes in the middle classes; likewise in the early eighteenth century the emergence of the Grand Tour began to attract nobles and upper-class people who desire to experience the ruins and art treasures of Europe, whereas previously the general attitude had been a reluctance to leave one's own locality which was usually conceived of as providing all the sensations and pleasures that one could possibly ever need (Hazard, 1964: 23).

It is clear that we need to work towards a more precise sense of what is meant by the aestheticization of everyday life. More generally aesthetics has sought to investigate the nature of art, beauty, aesthetic experience and the criteria for aesthetic judgement (Wolff, 1983: 13, 68 ff.). Since the devel-opment of modern aesthetics in the eighteenth century one influential tra-dition has developed from Kant's *Critique of Aesthetic Judgement*, in which the distinguishing characteristic of aesthetic judgement of taste is disinter-estedness and from this perspective anything can be looked at in the aes-thetic attitude, including the full gamut of objects in everyday life. Hence Simmel shows the influence of this tradition when he refers to the plea-sures involved in looking at objects from a detached, contemplative point of view, without direct immersion (Frisby, 1981: 151). This distanced, voyeuris-tic attitude is to be found in the stroller in the large cities whose senses are overstimulated by the flood of new perspectives, impressions and sensations that flow past him. Yet we also face the question of the necessity of distantiation and whether the reversal of it in the figural can also be described as entailing an aesthetic orientation. In the same way that Lash (1988) speaks about de-differentiation, it may also be useful to refer to de-distantiation or instantiation – that is, the pleasure from immersion into the objects of contemplation. (Here we are using distantiation in a different way from that used by Mannheim (1956) in his discussion of the democ-ratization of culture.) De-distantiation has the benefit of capturing the capacity to view objects and experiences usually placed outside the range of institutionally designated aesthetic objects in the way it points to the immediacy of the object, the immersion into the experience through the investment of desire. Effectively it involves the capacity to develop a de-control of the emotions, to open oneself up to the full range of sensations available which the object can summon up. A further question which needs to be considered is to what extent can the figural and de-differentiation dis-cussed by Lash as well as the above use of de-distantiation, be used to sug-gest further related categories, pre-differentiation and pre-distantiation, which point to a similar immersion and abandonment of coded controls and enframing of experiences which occurs prior to differentiation and distantiation processes, or can be said to emerge and be cultivated along them in circumscribed liminal moments. On a theoretical level it may be useful to approach this at a later point in terms of the changing balances that occur between involvement and detachment. Elias (1987c) points to the way in which the artist swings between extreme emotional involvement and detachment. Indeed it is a central capacity generated within artistic subcultures to cultivate and manage the capacity to shift between the full exploration and control of the emotions both in the process of producing the work of art and in developing an associated style of life. (This will be discussed in more detail below.) Finally it should be added that if aesthetics is held to revolve around questions of taste, Bourdieu (1984) has developed an opposition between the high Kantian aesthetics involving cognitive appreciation, distantiation, and the controlled cultivation of pure taste and what it denies, the enjoyment of the immediate, sensory, 'grotesque' bodily pleasures of the popular classes. In terms of the aestheticization of everyday life we have to ask how far the direct impressions, sensations and images of the consumer culture 'dream-worlds' in the big cities, which find resonances in postmodernism's figural regimes of signification, have a much longer history within the process of development of the popular classes and their culture. But first we must turn to a brief consideration of the experience of modernity in the large cities of mid- and late-nineteenth-century Europe as discussed by Baudelaire, Benjamin and Simmel.

Modernité

Baudelaire, Benjamin and Simmel all sought to account for the new experiences of *modernité* in the big cities of the mid- to late-nineteenth century. Baudelaire focused on the Paris of the 1840s and 1850s, which was subsequently to fascinate Benjamin. Baudelaire's world with its growth of mass culture became the subject of Benjamin's (1982b) unfinished *Passagen-Werk*. Simmel's *Philosophy of Money*, written in the 1890s and published in 1900, also focuses on the experience of strollers and consumers in the new crowded urban spaces of Berlin. Simmel's Berlin was also the subject for Benjamin's reflections on his childhood: *Berliner Kindheit um 1900*, and 'Berlin Chronicle' (Benjamin, 1979).

Baudelaire was fascinated by the fleeting transitory beauty and ugliness of life in mid-nineteenth-century Paris: the changing pageants of fashionable life, the *flâneurs* strolling through the fleeting impressions of the crowds, the dandies, the heroes of modern life – referred to by Lefebvre (1978) as 'spontaneous (as opposed to professional) artists' – who sought to turn their lives into works of art (quoted in Frisby, 1985b: 19). For Baudelaire art should endeavour to capture these modern scenarios. He despised contemporary artists who painted pictures with the costumes and furnishings of ancient Rome, Greece, the Middle Ages or the Orient. Rather the artist should be aware that 'every age has its own gait, glance and gesture ... not only in manners and gestures, but even in the form of the face' (Baudelaire, 1964: 12). Likewise every trade or profession stamps its marks in terms of beauty or ugliness on the face and body. Hence the painter of modern life, such as Constantine Guys, whom Baudelaire admired, should endeavour to seek out the transitory, fleeting beauty which is being ever more rapidly reconstituted.

Baudelaire was fascinated by the crowd. Benjamin (1973: 169) contrasts the distaste Engels felt for the crowd and Poe's depiction of the fear and menace of the crowd with Baudelaire's *flâneur* who inhabited a different crowd in the arcades where he had elbow-room to stroll in comfort and leisure (Benjamin, 1973: 194). The new Parisian arcades were the subject of Benjamin's (1982b) *Passagen-Werk*. Literally they are passages, worlds without windows which are 'soul spaces of the psyche' (van Reijen, 1988). These consumer culture 'dream-worlds', the arcades and department stores, were for Benjamin materializations of the phantasmagoria which Marx talked about in his section on 'the fetishism of commodities' in volume 1 of *Capital*. The new department stores and arcades were temples in which goods were worshipped as fetishes. Benjamin sought to give expression to the 'sex appeal of the anorganic in the fetish character of commodities' (van Reijen, 1988). (For a discussion of the department store and arcades see R.H. Williams, 1982; Geist, 1983.)

Within the age of industrialism art's power as illusion, its authority as an original work, the source of its 'aura', became shifted over into industry with painting moving into advertising, architecture into technical engineering, handicrafts and sculpture into the industrial arts, to produce a mass culture. Paris exemplified this new urban panorama of visual representations. As Buck-Morss (1983: 213) remarks:

> One could say that the dynamics of capitalist industrialism had caused a curious reversal in which 'reality' and 'art' switch places. Reality becomes artificial, a phantasmagoria of commodities and architectural construction made possible by the new industrial processes. The modern city was nothing but the proliferation of such objects, the density of which created an artificial landscape of buildings and consumer items as totally encompassing as the earlier, natural one. In fact for children (like Benjamin) born into an urban environment, they appeared to be nature itself. Benjamin's understanding of commodities was not merely critical. He affirmed them as utopian with images which 'liberated creativity from art, just as in the XVIth century the sciences freed themselves from philosophy' [*Passagen-Werk*: 1236, 1249]. This phantasmagoria of industrially-produced material objects, buildings, boulevards, all sorts of commodities from tour-books to toilet articles – for Benjamin *was* mass culture, and it is the central concern of the *Passagen-Werk*.

The mass media of the twentieth century, with Hollywood films, the growing advertising industry and television could replicate this commodity world endlessly, although Benjamin still held that the mass media, especially film, could be used in a more critical way not to duplicate the illusions, but to demonstrate that reality was illusion.

The constant recycling of artistic and historical themes in the aestheticized commodity world meant that the city landscape conferred on childhood memories the quality of alluring half-forgotten dreams. In the mythical and magical world of the modern city the child discovered the new anew, and the adult rediscovers the old in the new (Buck-Morss, 1983: 219). The capacity of the ever-changing urban landscape to summon up associations, resemblances and memories feeds the curiosity of the stroller in the crowds. To the idler who strolls the streets, objects appear divorced from their context and subject to mysterious connections in which meanings are read on the surface of things (Buck-Morss, 1986: 106). Baudelaire (1964: 4) sought to capture this in his use of the metaphor of the post-illness ability to see everything anew in its immediacy. Convalescence, he tells us, is like a return to childhood: the 'convalescent, like the child is possessed in the highest degree of the faculty of keenly interesting himself in things, be they apparently of the most trivial ... The child sees everything in a state of new-ness, he is always *drunk*' (quoted in Frisby, 1985b: 17). This passage is inter-esting because it resembles one in which Fredric Jameson (1984b: 118) talks about 'intensities' as in schizophrenia being one of the key features of postmodern culture and refers to vivid powerful experiences charged with affect. This leads to a breakdown of the relationship between signifiers and the fragmentation of time into a series of perpetual presents which is found in schizophrenia or post-illness perceptions. This, then, would seem to be a good example of the figural aesthetic.

In his discussion of Georg Simmel as the first sociologist of modernity, David Frisby (1985a) points to the way in which the themes of neurasthenia, the big-city dweller and the customer which Benjamin (1973: 106) detected in Baudelaire's work are also paramount in Simmel's discussion of modernity. Simmel develops interesting insights into the aesthetic dimensions of the architecture of world exhibitions whose transitory and illusory nature echoes the aesthetic dimension of commodities we have already spoken of A similar process of the introduction of aesthetics into non-aesthetic areas can also be found in fashion. The intensified pace of fashion increases our time-consciousness, and our simultaneous pleasure in newness and oldness gives us a strong sense of presentness. Changing fashions and world exhibitions point to the bewildering plurality of styles in modern life. For the middle classes the retreat to the interior of the household offered little refuge from style, for at the turn of the century when Simmel was writing, the contemporary *Jugendstil* movement (in Britain there was the parallel movement known as Aestheticism) sought to stylize 'every pot and pan'. The stylization of the interior was a paradoxical attempt to provide a toning down and relatively stable background to the subjectivism of modern life (Frisby, 1985a: 65).

For Frisby (1985a: 52) Simmel's theory of cultural modernity is preferable to that of Habermas. Although Habermas (1981a) discusses the aesthetics of modernity in terms of Baudelaire his definition of cultural modernity draws on Max Weber's theory of modernity involving the differentiation of the spheres of life (Habermas, 1984). For Frisby Simmel's position is preferable, as it attempts to ground the aesthetic sphere in the modern life world rather than see it as separate from the other spheres of life.

We can use these contrasting positions to make a number of points with which to conclude the section. First it may not be a question of Habermas or Simmel, but rather that both are looking at different aspects of the same process. Habermas's position builds on Weber's discussion of the emergence of separate artistic countercultures such as the bohemias of the mid-nineteenth century. While the term 'cultural sphere', which includes science, law, religion as well as art, may direct us away from the interdependencies it has with the rest of society, it has the merit of focusing attention on the *carriers* – to the growth in numbers and power-potential of specialists in symbolic production, and in particular for our purposes, artists and intellectuals. The artistic countercultures were also spatially located in the big cities of the nineteenth century, and in particular in Paris (Seigel, 1986), which Benjamin called 'the capital of the nineteenth century'. We therefore have to consider the position of the artist and intellectual as stroller, moving through the new urban spaces and taking in the shocks, jolts, flows of the crowd and dream-worlds we have talked about.

What is important about this group, whose members are by trade predisposed to observe and record experiences, is that the experiences they captured while floating through the urban spaces were taken to be *the* definitive experiences of these places. In Baudelaire, Simmel and Benjamin we have numerous references to the observer's sense of detachment, then swings of immersion (involvement), but they all presume the city crowd to be a mass of anonymous individuals which they can slip into and which carries them along. Baudelaire (1964: 9) for example talks of the pleasure of seeing 'the world, to be at the centre of the world, and yet to remain hidden from the world'. Yet the spectator is not invisible, and we could follow Bourdieu (1984) and cite good reason why the petit bourgeois intellectual or artist may seek such invisibility and feel he is floating in the social space. He is, however, not a perfect recorder, or camera taking snapshots, he (and we need to use the term advisedly, as Janet Wolff (1985) points out in her essay 'The Invisible *Flâneuse*') is an embodied human being whose appearance and demeanour give off readable impressions and signs to those around him. These signs are to be found not only inscribed in the professions and the prostitute, but in the artist and intellectual too. Although the crowd, with its rapid flow of bodies, may be a place of unspoken encounters, the process of decoding and delight in reading other people's appearances goes on apace as Baudelaire points out. Baudelaire was not only aware of the ways in which intellectual and artistic activities, including his own work, had become commodified, he disdained the attempts of the ethereal, spiritually minded artist to escape the process of appropriation in public life. Hence in his prose piece 'Loss of a Halo' he mocks the poet who thinks he can float invisibly through the crowds and shows that his art is profane and his persona socially recognizable (see Spencer, 1985: 71; Berman, 1982: 155).

Once we move from this liminal sphere into direct social encounters in shops, offices, institutions, the flow is slowed down and the reading process goes on more precisely as participants are able to detect, monitor and react to the symbolic power manifest in the unconscious bodily signs and gestures: the dress, style, tone of voice, facial expression, demeanour, stance, gait; and incorporated in body volume, height, weight etc., which betray the social origins of the bearer. In effect, the artist and intellectual must be understood in terms of their lifestyle, which is socially recognizable and locatable in the social space. They also have a social interest in (1) the wider acceptance of their perceptions on life, namely, the value of the aesthetic gaze even while challenging and negating it: the value of cultural and intellectual goods in general and the need for instruction into how to use and experience them; and (2) the proclamation of the superiority of their lifestyle manifest in their subcultures so that others will adopt the 'off-duty' fashions, styles and perceptions they embody – if not those of the very moment, put forth by the avant-garde, then those of yesterday which would maintain the useful distance between the cognoscenti and their eager, but lagging behind, audiences and followers.

While we can use Weber and Habermas to direct us towards the artists' and intellectuals' tastes and lifestyles, and their interest in the generalization of aesthetic perceptions and sensibilities, Simmel and Benjamin can be used to direct us towards the way in which the urban landscape has become aestheticized and enchanted through the architecture, billboards, shop displays, advertisements, packages, street signs etc., and through the embodied persons who move through these spaces: the individuals who wear, to varying degrees, fashionable clothing, hair-styles, make-up, or who move, or hold their bodies, in particular stylized ways. The aestheticization of everyday life in this second sense points to the expansion and extension of commodity production in the big cities which has thrown up new buildings, department stores, arcades, malls and so on, and which has produced an endless array of goods to fill the shops and clothe and cater for those who pass through them. It is this double capacity of the commodity to be exchange value and ersatz use-value, to be the same and different, which allows it to take up an aestheticized image, whatever may be the one currently dreamt up. Sennett (1976), for example, tells of how in the first Parisian department store, Bon Marché, shortly after it was opened in the 1850s one of the first window displays featured pots and pans. The pots and pans were stylistically arranged into a South Sea Island display with shells, coral beads, palms and the like to produce an aesthetic effect. We have also to ask the question 'Who arranged the display?' The answer would be window dressers, but we can also point to other related workers in fields such as advertising, marketing, design, fashion, commercial art, architecture and journalism who help to design and create the dream-worlds. In many ways their tastes, dispositions and classificatory schemes are similar to those of the artists and intellectuals, and they usually keep in touch with the latest developments in this sphere. Hence in many overt and subtle ways they also transmit aesthetic dispositions and sensibilities, and the notions of 'the artist as hero' and the importance of the 'stylization life' to wider publics (see Allen, 1983; Frith and Horne, 1987; Zukin, 1988b). In effect, as cultural intermediaries they have an important role in educating the public into new styles and tastes.

The second point we can note is that many of the features associated with the postmodern aestheticization of everyday life have a basis in modernity. The predominance of images, liminality, the vivid intensities characteristic of the perceptions of children, those recovering from illness, schizophrenics and others, and figural regimes of signification can all be said to have parallels in the experiences of *modernité* as described by Baudelaire, Benjamin and Simmel. In this sense we can point to the links between modernism and post-modernism as Lyotard (1984: 72) does when he says that postmodernism 'is not modernism at its end but in the nascent state, and that state is constant'. While Lyotard is referring to artistic modernism and takes a Kantian per-spective on postmodernity as the avant-gardist attempt to constantly express the inexpressible and represent the unpresentable, we can also extend this to late-twentieth-century spectacles and simulated environments in malls, shop-ping centres, department stores, theme parks, 'Disneyworlds' etc. (see Urry, 1988), which have many features in common with the department stores, arcades, world fairs etc. described by Benjamin and Simmel and others. To mention a brief example: the Paris Exposition of 1900 involved a number of simulations including an exotic Indian landscape with stuffed animals, trea-sures and merchandise; an exhibit representing Andalucian Spain at the times of the Moors with simulated interiors and courtyards; a Trans-Siberian panorama which placed spectators in a real railway car which moved along a track, while a canvas was unrolled outside the window to give an impression of Siberia. There was also a demonstration of a multi-projector spectacle, an early forerunner of Cinerama (see R.H. Williams, 1982).

Third the figural emphasis upon primary processes, the flows of images, dreamlike quality of modernity with its vivid intensities and sense of won-der at the commodity aesthetics on display may itself be traceable back fur-ther than modernity. We will shortly look at the forerunners in carnivals, fairs, theatres and other public spaces. Such locations offered excitement, a new range of sensations and the general de-control of the emotions, a con-trast and temporary relief from the general control of affects which results from civilizing processes.

Fourth we will have little to say about the progressive or retrogressive aspects of this process, save to note that a good deal has been made of the antinomial, transgressive qualities of the artistic and intellectual subcultures of modernism, and their invasion of everyday life through the development of consumer culture. In effect for Bell (1976) art has undermined morality, and the puritan work ethic gives way to the hedonistic search for new sen-sations and gratifications on the part of the untrammelled self'. It is possi-ble that Bell has overemphasized the social threat and demoralizing effect on society through an overemphasis on the transgressive socially destabiliz-ing qualities of art and an overestimation of the role of beliefs as opposed to practices in producing a viable social order. In addition despite many attempts by artists to outbid each other in their quest to scandalize the petite bourgeoisie, it can be argued that rather than being a naïve uncontrolled emotional regression many of the practices and lifestyles of artists necessarily involve 'a controlled de-control of the emotions', which may entail, and indeed require, the mutual respect and self-restraint of the participants as opposed to a narcissistic regression which threatens to destroy the social bond (see Wouters, 1986).

The middle classes and the control of the carnivalesque

For Daniel Bell (1976) modernism with its antinomial and transgressive qualities has dominated in the arts since the mid-nineteenth century. Certainly since the mid-nineteenth century, especially in Paris after the 1848 revolution, we see the emergence of bohemias which adopt the strategies of transgression in their art and lifestyle (Seigel, 1986). The representatives of the bohème existed outside the limits of bourgeois society and were identified with the proletariat and the Left. Hauser (1982) refers to the bohemians as the first true artistic proletariat consisting of people whose existence was completely insecure. Indeed they lived cheek by jowl with the lower orders in the low-rent areas of the large cities. They cultivated similar manners, valuing spontaneity, an antisystematic work ethos, and a lack of attention to the sense of ordered living space and controls and conventions of the respectable middle class. Yet while the symbols and lifestyle may have seemed to be new within the middle classes, there is a long history of the transgressive strategies they adopted. Within the middle classes there are attempts to use transgressive symbols to shock which runs parallel to civilizing processes which sought to bring about the control of emotions through manners. It is therefore possible, following Stallybrass and White (1986) to see bohemias as producing 'liminoid symbolic repertoires' similar to those afforded by earlier carnival forms. Middle-class bohemias, especially surrealism and expressionism, took over in a displaced form much of the symbolic inversion and transgressions which were found in the carnival. It may be possible therefore to trace back to the carnival of the Middle Ages many of the figural aspects, the disconnected succession of fleeting images, sensations, de-control of the emotions and de-differentiation which have become associated with postmodernism and the aestheticization of everyday life.

In their *Politics and Poetics of Transgression* (1986) Stallybrass and White discuss the relational nature of carnivals, festivals and fairs which are seen as symbolic inversions and transgressions in which the distinction between high/low, official/popular, grotesque/classical are mutually constructed and deformed. They draw on Bakhtin's (1968) work to point to the ways in which the carnival involves the celebration of the grotesque body – fattening food, intoxicating drink, sexual promiscuity – in a world in which official culture is turned upside down. The grotesque body of the carnival is the lower body of impurity, disproportion, immediacy, orifices – the material body, which is the opposite of the classical body, which is beautiful, symmetrical, elevated, perceived from a distance and which is the ideal body. The grotesque body and the carnival represent the otherness which is excluded from the process of formation of middle-class identity and culture. With the extension of the civilizing process into the middle classes the need for greater controls over the emotions and bodily functions produced changes in manners and conduct which heightened the sense of disgust at direct emotional and bodily expressivity (Elias, 1978b, 1982). In effect the other which is excluded as part of the identity formation process becomes the object of desire.

Stallybrass and White provide an interesting discussion of the dual role of fairs as, first, the open space of the marketplace in which commercial exchanges take place in a local market which is connected to, and displays wares from other national and international markets. Second, fairs are sites of pleasure: they are local, festive and communal and unconnected to the real world. Fairs were therefore not just guardians of local traditions, they were sites of transformation of popular tradition through the intersection of different cultures; they were sites of what Bakhtin refers to as *hybridization*, which brought together the exotic and familiar, the village and townsmen, the professional performer and bourgeois observer. As agents of cultural pluralism they were not, then, just 'otherness' to official discourse, but involved the disruption of provincial habits and local traditions via the introduction of different, more cosmopolitan people and cultural objects. They displayed the exotic and strange commodities from different parts of the world and along with a flood of strange signs, bizarre juxtapositions, people with different dress, demeanour and languages, freaks, spectacles and performances stimulated desire and excitement. They were in effect outdoor forerunners of the department stores and world exhibitions of the late nineteenth century, and we can surmise produced some of the same effects in a less tamed and controlled manner. Aspects of the untamed emotions, inversions and transgressions which still produced a kind of 'social vertigo' and festive disorder survived in the music halls (see Bailey, 1986a, 1986b; Clark, 1985), The excitement and fears the fair can arouse is still captured today in films which highlight the way in which these liminal spaces are sites in which excitement, danger, and the shock of the grotesque merge with dreams and fantasies which threaten to overwhelm and engulf the spectators. Today funfairs and theme parks such as Disneyland still retain this aspect, albeit in a more controlled safer way, to provide enclaved environments for the controlled de-control of the emotions, where adults are given permission to behave like children again.

Elements of the carnivalesque were diplaced from the fair into literature. Writing about the fair could be an act bent on producing carnivalesque outrage or dissociation from these lower pleasures. In the seventeenth century we also find attempts by Dryden and others to transform theatre audiences from the inattentive, noisy, carnivalesque rabble into the disciplined, controlled, polite and appreciative bourgeois theatre public. These contrary pulls towards popular culture and a more genteel educative culture in the middle classes opened up spaces for cultural entrepreneurs. Sir Robert

Southwell in 1685 wrote to advise his son that he should consider Bartholemew Fair as a suitable subject for a profitable book. To write the book his son would have to learn the rules of resemblances and differentiation of the fair by watching it from some high window to survey the crowd. He was also advised to read Ben Jonson's play on the fair (Stallybrass and White, 1986: 118–19). Here we have an early example of the education project of the middle class in developing structured accounts and pedagogies for new publics about how to read popular cultural experiences in an aestheticized way. Southwell is clear about the dangers of the enterprise, that his son will be lost in endless distinctions which end in 'blank confusion'. This is the threat of disorder which demands elevation and not immersion in order to produce the detached aesthetic appreciation.

We find a similar example in Wordsworth's account of Bartholemew Fair in *The Prelude* (1805). While the fair is 'monstrous' he revels in the 'colour, motion, shape, sight and sounds' of the wonders from all parts of the world which are jumbled up together to produce a transgression and confusion of boundaries in which animals become human, humans become animals etc. (Stallybrass and White, 1986: 120). For Wordsworth the proliferation of difference and the erosion of boundaries in the fair and the city threaten to 'cast loose the chain of signifiers' and dissolve his identity into 'blank confusion' (Stallybrass and White, 1986: 123). The fear of total immersion, the loss of boundaries and the loss of self is resolved by Wordsworth by invoking the classical 'Muse'. In effect the symbolic hierarchies of a classical aesthetic are invoked to retain some neoclassical notion of an education project in which the lower orders and forms will be raised up and ennobled by the poet. For the varieties of modernism that developed in the late nineteenth century and postmodernism in the late twentieth century the neoclassical option was ruled out and the figural disorders explored and cultivated. This is not to imply that the educative mission was abandoned; far from it. Rather the educative project becomes one in which the techniques necessary for a controlled de-control of the emotions are developed. Techniques of the self which will permit the development of sensibilities which can allow us to enjoy the swing between the extremes of aesthetic involvement and detachment so that the pleasures of immersion and detached distantiation can both be enjoyed.

The civilizing process therefore involved an increasing control of the emotions, sense of disgust at bodily betrayal, the smells, sweating and noises of the lower body, and sensitivity to one's own bodily space. It involved the middle class in a process of complex distancing from the popular, the grotesque other. Yet Stallybrass and White (1986: 191) argue that this rise in the threshold of the disgust function which Elias (1978b) talks about also bears the offprint of desire for the expelled other which became the source of fascination, longing and nostalgia. Hence we have the attractions of the forest, fair, theatre, circus, slum, savage, seaside resort for the bourgeois. If the experience of these sites were not acknowledged, if the structures of the civilizing process were too strong, then there was the possibility that this danger zone *outside* of consciousness would become one *inside*, in the subconscious fed by the struggle to exclude it. Hysteria in late-nineteenth-century middle-class women is an example of the price of excluding the lower body and associated symbolic disorders. We should also add that rather than see a strong polarization derived from the 'binaryism of symbolic functioning' which is held by Stallybrass and White (1986: 189) to be at the centre of cultural production, it is also possible to detect shifts in the balances between civilizing and informalizing (emotional de-controlling) processes which themselves represent a higher level of control of the emotions and not a regression: that is, a 'controlled de-control of the emotions' (Wouters, 1987). In this sense, as I have argued elsewhere (chapter 3), postmodernism has drawn much from the social and cultural wave of informalization in the 1960s. The elements of the carnivalesque which became displaced into art, and retained in consumer cultural sites and spectacles, and in the media of film and television, now have larger middle-class audiences who have moved away from the more rigid personality structure associated with the puritan ethic which Bell (1976) speaks of, and are better able to cope with threatening emotions. In effect fractions of the new middle class have become more educated into a controlled de-control of the emotions and the sensibilities and tastes that support a greater appreciation of the aestheticization of everyday life.

Concluding remarks

In this chapter I have attempted to sketch out some of the features of the aestheticization of everyday life and have argued that it is not unique to post-modernism but that it can be traced back to the experience of the big cities of the mid-nineteenth century as described by Baudelaire, Benjamin and Simmel. We have also argued that similar aesthetic experiences seem also to have been generated in the carnival and fairs in which the emergent middle classes struggled to grapple with the symbolic inversions and the grotesque body of the lower orders which remained an ever-present otherness running parallel to the civilizing process. In effect to construct an identity, to know who you are, you need to know who you are not, and the material excluded or confined to the boundaries may continue to exhibit a fascination and allure, and to stimulate desires. Hence the attraction of the sites of 'ordered disorder': the carnival, fairs, music halls, spectacles, resorts, and today theme parks, malls, tourism. As Stallybrass and White (1986) wryly comment, the bourgeoisie never really returned from Bougainville's voyage and still succumbs to the fascination of the constructed exotic otherness.

Note

I would like to thank David Chaney, Peter Bailey, Steve Best, Bryan Turner and Andy Wernick for commenting on an earlier version of this chapter.

6

Lifestyle and Consumer Culture

The term 'lifestyle' is currently in vogue. While the term has a more restricted sociological meaning in reference to the distinctive style of life of specific status groups (Weber, 1968; Sobel, 1982; Rojek, 1985), within contemporary consumer culture it connotes individuality, self-expression, and a stylistic self-consciousness. One's body, clothes, speech, leisure pastimes, eating and drinking preferences, home, car, choice of holidays, etc. are to be regarded as indicators of the individuality of taste and sense of style of the owner/consumer. In contrast to the designation of the 1950s as an era of grey conformism, a time of *mass* consumption, changes in production techniques, market segmentation and consumer demand for a wider range of products, are often regarded as making possible greater choice (the management of which itself becomes an art form) not only for youth of the post-1960s generation, but increasingly for the middle-aged and the elderly. Three phrases from Stuart and Elizabeth Ewen's *Channels of Desire* (1982: 249–51), which they see as symptomatic of the recent tendencies within consumer culture, come to mind here: 'Today there is no fashion: there are only *fashions*.' 'No rules, only choices.' 'Everyone can be anyone.' What does it mean to suggest that long-held fashion codes have been violated, that there is a war against uniformity, a surfeit of difference which results in a loss of meaning? The implication is that we are moving towards a society without fixed status groups in which the adoption of styles of life (manifest in choice of clothes, leisure activities, consumer goods, bodily dispositions) which are fixed to specific groups have been surpassed. This apparent movement towards a postmodern consumer culture based upon a profusion of information and proliferation of images which cannot be ultimately stabilized, or hierarchized into a system which correlates to fixed social divisions, would further suggest the irrelevance of social divisions and ultimately the end of the social as a significant reference point. In effect the end of the deterministic relationship between society and culture heralds the triumph of signifying culture. Are consumer goods used as cultural signs in a free-association manner by individuals to produce an expressive effect within a social field in which the old coordinates are rapidly disappearing, or can taste still be adequately 'read', socially recognized and mapped onto the class structure? Does taste still 'classify the classifier'? Does the claim for a movement beyond fashion merely represent a move within, not beyond the game, being instead a new move, a position within the social field of lifestyles and consumption practices which can be correlated to the class structure?

This chapter is an attempt to develop a perspective which goes beyond the view that lifestyle and consumption are totally manipulated products of a mass society. and the opposite position which seeks to preserve the field of lifestyles and consumption, or at least a particular aspect of it (such as sport), as an autonomous playful space beyond determination. An attempt will also be made to argue that the 'no rules, only choices' view (celebrated by some as a significant movement towards the break-up of the old hierarchies of fashion, style and taste in favour of an egalitarian and tolerant acceptance of differences, and the acknowledgement of the right of individuals to enjoy whatever popular pleasures they desire without encountering prudery or moral censure) does not signify anything as dramatic as the implosion of the social space but should be regarded merely as a new move within it. A perspective informed by the work of Pierre Bourdieu will be developed to argue that the new conception of lifestyle can best be understood in relation to the habitus of the new petite bourgeoisie, who, as an expanding class fraction centrally concerned with the production and dissemination of consumer culture imagery and information, is concerned to expand and legitimate its own particular dispositions and lifestyle. It does so within a social field in which its views are resisted and contested and within, in Britain, especially, an economic climate and political culture in which the virtues of the traditional petite bourgeoisie have undergone a revival. Nevertheless it would seem to be useful to ask questions about consumer culture not only in terms of the engineering of demand resulting from the efficiencies of mass production or the logic of capitalism, but to discover which particular groups, strata, or class fractions are most closely involved in symbol production and, in particular, in producing the images and information celebrating style and lifestyles. What follows is very much a schematic account, written at a high level of generality, and acknowledges that these questions can ultimately only be answered by empirical analyses which take into account the specificity of particular societies.

Consumer culture

To use the term 'consumer culture' is to emphasize that the world of goods and their principles of structuration are central to the understanding of contemporary society. This involves a dual focus: first, on the cultural dimension of the economy, the symbolization and use of material goods as 'communicators' not just utilities; and second, on the economy of cultural goods, the market principles of supply, demand, capital accumulation, competition and monopolization which operate *within* the sphere of lifestyles, cultural goods and commodities.

Turning first to consumer culture it is apparent that the emphasis in some popular and academic circles on the materialism of contemporary consumer societies is far from unproblematic. From an anthropological perspective (Sahlins, 1974, 1976; Douglas and Isherwood, 1980; Leiss,

1983) material goods and their production, exchange and consumption are to be understood within a cultural matrix. Elwert (1984) too has referred to the 'embedded economy' to draw attention to the cultural preconditions of economic life. The movement away from regarding goods merely as utilities having a use-value and an exchange-value which can be related to some fixed system of human needs has also occurred within neo-Marxism. Baudrillard (1975, 1981) has been particularly important in this context, especially his theorization of the commodity-sign. For Baudrillard the essential feature of the movement towards the mass production of commodities is that the obliteration of the original 'natural' use-value of goods by the dominance of exchange-value under capitalism has resulted in the commodity becoming a sign in the Saussurean sense, with its meaning arbitrarily determined by its position in a self-referential system of signifiers. Consumption, then, must not be understood as the consumption of use-values, a material utility, but primarily as the consumption of signs. It is this refusal of the referent, which is replaced by an unstable field of floating signifiers, which has led Kroker (1985) to describe Baudrillard as 'the last and best of the Marxists'. For Kroker, Baudrillard has pushed the logic of the commodity form as far as it will go until it releases 'the referential illusion' at its heart: the nihilism Nietzsche diagnosed is presented as the completion of the logic of capitalism.

It is this dominance of the commodity as sign which has led some neo-Marxists to emphasize the crucial role of culture in the reproduction of contemporary capitalism. Jameson (1981: 131), for example, writes that culture is 'the very element of consumer society itself; no society has ever been saturated with signs and images like this one'. Advertising and the display of goods in the 'dream-worlds' (Benjamin, 1982b; R.H. Williams, 1982) of department stores and city centres plays upon the logic of the commodity-sign to transgress formerly sealed-apart meanings and create unusual and novel juxtapositions which effectively rename goods. Mundane and everyday consumer goods become associated with luxury. exotica, beauty and romance with their original or functional 'use' increasingly difficult to decipher. Baudrillard (1983a) has drawn attention to the key role of the electronic mass media in late-capitalist society. Television produces a surfeit of images and information which threatens our sense of reality. The triumph of signifying culture leads to a simulational world in which the proliferation of signs and images has effaced the distinction between the real and the imaginary. For Baudrillard (1983a: 148) this means that 'we live everywhere already in an "aesthetic" hallucination of reality'. The 'death of the social, the loss of the real, leads to a *nostalgia* for the real: a fascination with and desperate search for real people, real values, real sex' (Kroker, 1985: 80). Consumer culture for Baudrillard is effectively a postmodern culture, a depthless culture in which all values have become transvalued and art has triumphed over reality.

The aestheticization of reality foregrounds the importance of style, which is also encouraged by the modernist market dynamic with its constant search for new fashions, new styles, new sensations and experiences. The formerly artistic countercultural notion embodied in modernism that life is/should be a work of art is thus accorded wider currency. William Leiss (1983) has noted in his investigation of advertisements in Canada a shift over the last fifty years (especially marked in television) from advertisements which contain product information to those which incorporated looser, lifestyle imagery.[1]

The concern with lifestyle, with the stylization of life, suggests that the practices of consumption, the planning, purchase and display of consumer goods and experiences in everyday life cannot be understood merely via conceptions of exchange value and instrumental rational calculation. The instrumental and expressive dimensions should not be regarded as exclusive either/or polarities, rather they can be conceived as a balance which consumer culture brings together. It is therefore possible to speak of a calculating hedonism, a calculus of the stylistic effect and an emotional economy on the one hand, and an aestheticization of the instrumental or functional rational dimension via the promotion of an aestheticizing distancing on the other. Rather than unreflexively adopting a lifestyle, through tradition or habit, the new heroes of consumer culture make lifestyle a life project and display their individuality and sense of style in the particularity of the assemblage of goods, clothes, practices, experiences, appearance and bodily dispositions they design together into a lifestyle. The modern individual within consumer culture is made conscious that he speaks not only with his clothes, but with his home, furnishings, interior decoration, car and other activities which are to be read and classified in terms of the presence and absence of taste. The preoccupation with customizing a lifestyle and a stylistic self-consciousness are not just to be found among the young and the affluent; consumer culture publicity suggests that we all have room for self-improvement and self-expression whatever our age or class origins. This is the world of men and women who quest for the new and the latest in relationships and experiences, who have a sense of adventure and take risks to explore life's options to the full, who are conscious they have only one life to live and must work hard to enjoy, experience and express it (Winship, 1983; Featherstone and Hepworth, 1983).

Against the view of a grey conformist mass culture in which individuals' use of goods conforms to the purposes which have been dreamed up by the advertisers, it has often been pointed out that the meaning and use of consumer goods, the de-coding process, is complex and problematic. Raymond Williams (1961: 312), for example argues that cross-class uniformities in housing, dress and leisure are not significant in understanding the class structure. Rather, different classes have different ways of life and views of the nature of social relationships which form a matrix within which consumption takes place. It should also be noted that the uniformities progressively decline with (1) changes in technical capacity which allow greater product variety and differentiation to be built into production runs, and (2) increasing market fragmentation. Effectively individuals increasingly consume different products. This, coupled with the tendency for more diffuse, ambiguous lifestyle imagery in advertising noted by Leiss, encourages a variety of readings of messages (which increasingly use modernist and even postmodernist formats: a sales pitch which educates and flatters at the same time). Consequently the consumer culture is apparently able to come nearer to delivering the individuality and differences it has always promised.

The tendency for consumer culture to differentiate, to encourage the play of difference, must be tempered by the observation that differences must be socially recognized and legitimated: total otherness like total individuality is in danger of being unrecognizable. Simmel's (Frisby, 1985a) observation that fashion embodies the contradictory tendencies of imitation and differentiation and his assumption that the dynamic of fashion is such that its popularity and expansion lead to its own destruction, suggest that we need to examine more closely the social processes which structure taste in consumer goods and lifestyles, and raise the question of whether the concern for style and individuality itself reflect more the predispositions of a particular class fraction concerned with legitimating its own particular constellation of tastes as the *tastes* of the social, rather than the actual social itself. To do so we must still place the emphasis upon the production of distinctive tastes in lifestyles and consumer goods, but move down from the high level of generality which emphasizes the social and cultural process, the logic of capitalism, which can be regarded as having pushed lifestyle to the fore, to a consideration of the production of lifestyle tastes within a structured social space in which various groups, classes and class fractions struggle and compete to impose their own particular tastes as *the* legitimate tastes, and to thereby, where necessary, name and rename, classify and reclassify, order and reorder the field. This points towards an examination of the economy of cultural goods and lifestyles by adopting an approach which draws on the work of Pierre Bourdieu.

The economy of cultural goods and the social space of lifestyles

In the first place it should be emphasized that when speaking about an economy of cultural goods we do not imply a reductionism which reduces the production of goods and lifestyles to *the* economy: rather, to follow Bourdieu's approach is to acknowledge the autonomy of particular practices which need to be understood in terms of the internal dynamic, structuring principles and processes which operate within a particular field, and act in a way which is analogous to an economy. Hence there are processes of market competition, pulls from production and consumption, the tendencies of market segments and groups to monopolize, which operate within all social practices in specific ways – within fields as diffuse as science, sport, art, ageing, linguistic exchanges, photography, education, marriage, religion. In addition each social field is to be regarded as a system in which each particular element (the agents, groups or practices) receives its distinctive values (in the Saussurean sense) from its relationship to other elements. Bourdieu, however, is no structuralist and is conscious of the need to analyse the history of a field, to examine *process* – the changing trajectories of particular elements within the field over time which alter the relative positions which produces both the structure of the fixed and the meaning of the individual elements within it.

To make the approach more concrete and to introduce the analysis of lifestyles it is useful to examine Bourdieu's *Distinction* (1984). For Bourdieu taste in cultural goods functions as a marker of class and in *Distinction* Bourdieu seeks to map out the social field of the different tastes in legitimated 'high' cultural practices (museum visits, concert-going, reading) as well as taste in lifestyles and consumption preferences (including food, drink, clothes, cars, novels, newspapers, magazines, holidays, hobbies, sport, leisure pursuits). Both culture in the 'high' sense and culture in the anthropological sense are therefore inscribed on the same social space. The oppositions and relational determination of taste, however, becomes clearer when the space of lifestyle is superimposed onto a map of the class/occupational structure whose basic structuring principle is the volume and composition (economic or cultural) of capital that groups possess. To give some examples of the resultant correlations (see Bourdieu, 1984: 128–9): those who have a high volume of economic capital (industrialists, commercial employers) have a taste for business meals, foreign cars, auctions, a second home, tennis, water-skiing, right-bank galleries. Those who possess a high volume of cultural capital (higher-education teachers, artistic producers, secondary teachers) have a taste for left-bank galleries, avant-garde festivals, *Les Temps Modernes*, foreign languages, chess, flea markets, Bach, mountains. Those low in both economic and cultural capital (semi-skilled, skilled, unskilled workers) have a taste for football, potatoes, ordinary red wine, watching sports, public dances.

To pick out examples such as these does an injustice to the complexities of the social space in which the intermediary positions have a definitive role in producing the relational set of taste choices of particular groups (see Featherstone, 1987a). It also provides a static account which masks the relational dynamics of the field in which the introduction of new tastes, or inflation, results when lower groups emulate or usurp the tastes of higher groups. causing the latter to respond by adopting new tastes which will re-establish and maintain the original distance (for example, popularity or mass marketing, be it the William Tell Overture or the introduction of a relatively inexpensive champagne in supermarkets and stores such as Marks and Spencer, which will necessarily mean the upper groups move on to more avant-garde pieces of music or purchase a new rarer drink or drink vintage champagne). Dominant groups, therefore, seek to possess or establish what William Leiss (1983) calls 'positional goods', goods which are prestigious because an artificial scarcity of supply is imposed. One of the problems generated by the dynamic of consumer culture is that inflation is constantly introduced as scarce and restricted goods become marketed to the wider population or passed down the market causing a leapfrogging social race to maintain recognizable distinctions. Satisfaction depends upon possession or consumption of the socially sanctioned and legitimate (and therefore scarce or restricted) cultural goods.

It therefore makes sense to talk about the genesis of taste for lifestyles and cultural goods in terms of the possession of volume of cultural as well as economic capital. To attempt to map taste purely in terms of income is to miss the dual principles in operation, for cultural capital has its own structure of value, which amounts to convertibility into social power, independent of income or money. The cultural realm thus has its own logic and currency as well as rate of conversion into economic capital. For the possessors of a high volume of cultural capital, the intellectuals and academics, the prestige, legitimacy, relative scarcity and therefore social value of this cultural capital, is dependent on a denial of the market in cultural goods and a denial of the relevance and necessity to convert cultural capital into economic capital. This misrecognition of the fact that there is an exchange rate, that prestigious cultural goods are redeemable as money, points to the maintenance of a 'higher', 'sacred' cultural sphere in which artists and intellectuals struggle to bring forth the products of their 'natural' talents (the ideology of charisma). It points also to the prestige accorded to symbolic production *vis-à-vis* economic production, and to the way in which intellectuals have been able to establish a monopoly in defining legitimate taste within the cultural realm, to distinguish, judge and hierarchize between what is tasteful and tasteless, between the pure gaze and the vulgar, between aesthetic distancing and direct sensory enjoyment.

The intellectuals (the dominated fraction of the dominant class), therefore, use the logic of symbolic systems to produce distinctions which contribute to the reproduction of the existing relations between classes and class fractions. In this they share with the bourgeoisie (the dominant fraction of the dominant class) an interest in maintaining the existing state of material class relations in which economic capital enjoys high prestige and a high exchange rate when converted into cultural capital. They will therefore always seek to increase the autonomy of the cultural field and enhance the scarcity of cultural capital by resisting moves towards a democratization of culture.

While the intellectuals as the specialists in symbolic production seek to monopolize access to this field they work within a situation in which inflation and instability increasingly become the norm: the *internal* avant-garde dynamic of artistic modernism creates a new supply of accredited cultural goods, while the *external* dynamic of the consumer marketplace itself generates a popular demand for rare artistic goods. It would be useful to examine the latter dynamic in relation to the disseminators of symbolic production, the new petite bourgeoisie, and raise the question of the relationship between this class fraction and the intellectuals which will point us towards some tentative answers to our original speculation about the role of the new petite bourgeoisie in stimulating the demand for the stylization-of-life form of lifestyle.

In one of the most penetrating chapters of *Distinction* (1984: 359) Bourdieu analyses the new petite bourgeoisie, the cultural intermediaries, who provide symbolic goods and services. The important thing to note about the class fraction is its rising trajectory within the social space. In contrast to groups like peasants and farmers who decline numerically through changes taking place in the division of labour and therefore tend towards a pessimistic, nostalgic view of the world, the new petite bourgeoisie is numerically on the increase, and therefore has a progressive view of the world. Bourdieu defines the petit bourgeois as 'a proletarian who makes himself small to become a bourgeois'. Typically they invest in cultural and educational capital. The new petite bourgeoisie stands apart from the old petite bourgeoisie and the working classes in its attraction for the most naive aristocratic qualities (style, distinction, refinement) in the pursuit of expressive and liberated lifestyles.

Here Bourdieu's concept of habitus is useful to outline the set of dispositions which determine tastes and which characterize this stratum. By habitus Bourdieu is referring to the unconscious dispositions, the classificatory schemes, taken-for-granted preferences which are evident in the individual's sense of the appropriateness and validity of his taste for cultural goods and practices – art, food, holidays, hobbies etc. It is important to stress that habitus not only operates on the level of everyday knowledge-ability, but is inscribed onto the body, being revealed in body size, volume, shape, posture, way of walking, sitting, ways of eating, drinking, amount of social space and time an individual feels entitled to claim. degree of esteem for the body. pitch, tone of voice, accent, complexity of speech patterns, body gestures, facial expression, sense of ease with one's body – these all betray the habitus of one's origins. In short the body is the materialization of class taste: class taste is *embodied*. Each group, class and class fraction has a different habit us, hence the set of differences, the source of the distinctions and vulgarity of taste, can be mapped onto a social field which should in effect form a third grid to be superimposed onto the space of lifestyles and class/occupational capital discussed earlier.

If we turn to the new petit bourgeois habitus it is clear that whereas the bourgeois has a sense of ease and confidence in his body, the petit bourgeois is uneasy with his body, constantly self-consciously checking, watching and correcting himself. Hence the attraction of body maintenance techniques, the new Californian sports and forms of exercise, cosmetics, health food, where the body is treated as a sign for others and not as an instrument. The new petit bourgeois is a pretender, aspiring to more than he is, who adopts an investment orientation to life; he possesses little economic or cultural capital and therefore must acquire it. The new petit bourgeois therefore adopts a learning mode to life; he is consciously educating himself in the field of taste, style, lifestyle.

An approach to life which is characterized by a 'why can't I have my cake and eat it' attitude quests for both security *and* adventure. The new narcissism where individuals seek to maximize and experience the range of sensations available, the search for expression and self-expression, the fascination with identity, presentation and appearance makes the new petit bourgeois a 'natural' consumer. At one point Bourdieu (1984: 370) refers to the new petite bourgeoisie as the 'new' intellectuals

> who are inventing an art of living which provides them with the gratifications and prestige of the intellectual at the least cost: in the name of the fight against 'taboos' and the liquidation of 'complexes' they adopt the most external and easily borrowed aspects of the intellectual life-style, liberated manners, cosmetic or sartorial outrages, emancipated poses and postures and systematically apply the cultivated disposition to not-yet-legitimate culture (cinema, strip cartoons, the underground), to everyday life (street art), the personal sphere (sexuality, cosmetics, child-rearing, leisure) and the existential (the relation to nature, love, death).

They are the perfect audience and transmitters, intermediaries for the new intellectual popularization which is not just a popularization of bodies of knowledge, but a popularization of the intellectual *lifestyle* too. An approach which fulfils the functions of distinction since 'it makes available to *almost* everyone the distinctive poses, the distinctive games and other external signs of inner riches previously reserved for intellectuals' (Bourdieu, 1984: 371). In effect the new ethic espoused by the vanguard of the new bourgeoisie and the new petite bourgeoisie may well be in the process of creating *the perfect consumer*.

The new petite bourgeoisie, therefore, identifies with the intellectuals' lifestyle and acts as intermediaries in transmitting the intellectuals' ideas to a wider audience. They also act as cultural entrepreneurs in their own right in seeking to legitimate the intellectualization of new areas of expertise such as popular music, fashion, design, holidays, sport, popular culture etc. which increasingly are subjected to serious analysis. Here it is not a question of the new petite bourgeoisie promoting a particular style, but rather catering for and promoting a general interest in style itself, the nostalgia for past styles, the interest in the latest style, which in an age which itself lacks a distinctive style – what Simmel referred to as the peculiar styleless quality of modern life – have a fascination, and are subjected to constant interpretation and reinterpretation.

While the new petite bourgeoisie has affinities to and similarities with the intellectuals, it also finds a natural ally in the new bourgeoisie. The 'new' in both implies that they are travelling in the social space, they have abandoned the narrow asceticism of the petite bourgeoisie in favour of promoting more hedonistic and expressive consumption norms. Both groups generate parvenus and an autodidacticism which can be seen in the learning mode they adopt towards culture – to sacred 'high' culture, but also popular culture and also more general consumption style and practices. The generation of a fulfilling, expressive lifestyle mediated through affluent consumption and a stylized presentation of the performing self (Featherstone, 1982) partners and commodities can be seen as central to the worldwide popular TV series about the American sun-belt new rich: *Dallas* and *Dynasty*. Part of their fascination is within 'the context of a consumer society which asks individuals of all classes, within different targeted markets, to harness their rising expectations to venture along the road to self-improvement and stylization.[2]

Finally, in having pointed to affinities between the intellectuals and new petite bourgeoisie in their role as symbol producers a number of points can be made about the dynamics of the field of lifestyles and cultural goods which tend to throw the two groups closer together:

1 Time must be introduced into the social space and is one (perhaps the best) dimension for measuring the distance between styles and lifestyles. The introduction of new styles pushes the existing rank order of distinctions out of balance. Outmoded styles and lifestyles may generate loyalty from those whose formative years occurred when 'their' style enjoyed endorsement and legitimated popularity. For the avant-garde, of course, the opposite situation pertains. The field, therefore, generates a devaluation of established styles over time. Tastes and styles are subjected to a further market slippage due to the dynamic of popularization within consumer culture. To the avant-garde and *cognoscenti* popularization is essentially a devaluation. This occurs with a whole range of popular cultural activities and practices not just in artistic modernism which is the exemplar. Within popular music (itself an unacceptable term to the avant-garde who seek to legitimate their practice by quasi-monopolization and closure practices which impose new hierarchies of expertise and a renaming of the field: 'rock music'), as Bernice Martin (1981) has noted, popularity is double-edged: teenagers abandoned Rod Stewart or the Beatles once they had been passed down the market to teeny-weeny-boppers and kiddypop and up the market to the adults and middle aged.

2 Within strata such as the intellectuals (and here one especially thinks of art and the dynamics of modernism) there is a struggle between the established and the outsiders/newcomers (Bourdieu, 1979: Elias and Scotson, 1965). Newcomers adopt subversive strategies, they seek difference, discontinuity and revolution or a return to origins to detect the true meaning of a tradition – strategies to create a space for themselves and displace the established. In the post-war era the numbers of individuals entering higher education and intellectual pursuits in the 1960s created a confrontation with the established 'high culture' which can be read in this manner.[3]

3 One of the subversive strategies of outsider intellectuals and the new culture entrepreneurs is to seek to legitimate new fields to stand alongside and undermine the traditional restricted definitions of taste provided by the established intellectuals and embodied into a high culture. Rock music, fashion, the cinema become canonized as legitimate intellectual areas for critics, interpreters and popularizers.

The strategy need not be seen as one way; the imposition of new rules for the game on the part of outsider intellectuals allied with the new petite bourgeoisie cultural intermediaries may also create conditions in which the established intellectuals are forced to enter the new game, to adopt strategies which popularize and interpret texts, styles, practices in the popular media in order to seek to maintain or reestablish some semblance of their former monopoly of cultural authority. Two related points should be noted here: first the demand on the part of the cultural intermediaries, with their financial resources and expertise to present and *realize* their cultural interests (albeit for a mass audience) is flattering to the established intellectuals. It also combats both the accusation of elitism and outmoded taste. Hence 'classical' composers conduct pop operas, conductors of orchestras play jazz intellectuals seek to and are drawn into quiz shows, chat shows etc. via the 'voracious appetite for expertise' and new interpretation of old styles, the discovery of new styles. Second, we should note the emergence of the celebrity-intellectuals (Vaughan, 1986) who carry out this very process but in doing so undermine their closed, sacred authority by venturing into popularization. Even without venturing into mass popular programmes (for example, on science and natural history – Magnus Pike and David Bellamy in the UK – where they overplay the stereotype of the mad, arms-flailing scientist) the late-night or minority channel debates among the cultural experts devalues their expertise by putting it on the same level as other programmes. In short their skills as communicators and performers thus have priority over the *sacred* content of their messages.

4   New institutions for recording, preserving, analysing cultural products (for example, an archive or museum of popular culture will appear near to or as an annexe of 'sacred' art galleries) new journals to popularize television and radio programmes and interpret taste, consumer associations to test products are established. The number of personnel employed in the role of cultural intermediary has also increased. In short. the market in culture is an expanding one which undermines the traditional currency and its authenticators. (See Bourdieu, 1971, on this dynamic in art.)

5   The capacity to circulate information has increased. Styles and works of art are rapidly passed from producers to consumers. Old sacred works of art (such as the Mona Lisa) are put on the road to be surveyed by mass audiences in different cultures. Here the globalization process contributes to strengthen the role of the cultural intermediaries who administrate the new global media distribution chains (via satellite etc.). It also draws in the intellectuals to interpret traditions and styles in a new global circumstance which is one of polyculturalism. This further weakens the (Enlightenment) authority of established Western hierarchies of (high) cultural taste. The intellectuals therefore have to adopt a new role as *interpreters* of the great variety and *wealth* of the different cultural

traditions which can be presented to new audiences as meaningful and exotic without venturing into areas of judgement or value-hierarchization (Bauman, 1985).

6 This can be linked to one strategy for outsider intellectuals, which is to appear to attempt to subvert the whole game – postmodernism. With postmodernism, traditional distinctions and hierarchies are collapsed, polyculturalism is acknowledged which fits in with the global circumstance; kitsch, the popular, and difference are celebrated. Their cultural innovation proclaiming a *beyond* is really a *within*, a new move within the intellectual game which takes into account the new circumstances of production of cultural goods, which will itself in turn be greeted as eminently marketable by the cultural intermediaries.

Notes

1 It therefore becomes less important to endorse product quality (although functional information is still required about certain consumer goods) since an experience is associated with and consumed alongside the commodity. While this experience has a psychological dimension in relation to fantasy fulfilment it also has a social dimension which relates to the role goods play as communicators. The more general tendency for not only goods but experiences to become commodified and sold should also be noted – sport spectacles, tourism theme parks, Disney World etc. increasingly involve an aesthetically mediated – that is, distanced – perception of 'reality'.

2 There is not the space here to provide an analysis of the working class in this respect. Suffice to say that Bourdieu's analysis of the French working class who have to make do with 'the choices of necessity' while ringing true for the lumpen, traditional or unemployed working class does not take into account the privatized, consumer-orientated fractions, which of course, have different consumption patterns to the new petite bourgeoisie and the bourgeoisie and a very different habitus, but can identify with the latter groups via the problematics of autodidacticism: embarrassment and the learning mode.

3 For a discussion of the process of informalization which took place in the 1960s from a perspective which builds upon Elias's theory of the civilizing process, see Cas Wouters (1986).

7

City Cultures and Postmodern Lifestyles

How are we to understand the recent growth of interest in city cultures and urban lifestyles? On one level we can rightfully argue that cities have always had cultures in the sense that they have produced distinctive cultural products, artefacts, buildings and distinctive ways of life. It is possible to be even more 'culturalist' and assert that the very organization of space, the layout of buildings, is itself a manifestation of particular cultural codes. In this case particular 'deep' culture codes may dispose us to see cities as for example primarily economic, functional or aesthetic entities. If there is a switch from say a more economic and functional emphasis to a more cultural and aesthetic emphasis does it help to try to relate this to the asserted shifts from modernity and modernism towards postmodernity and postmodernism? If we set aside this question for the moment and focus in the first level, the notion that cities have always had cultures, we can take this to imply two senses of the term culture: culture as a way of life (the anthropological sense); and culture as the arts, spiritually elevating cultural products and experiences (high culture). One of the central themes which I will address in this chapter is that there has been a blurring of the boundaries between these two senses of culture which has broadened the range of phenomena designated as culture from the arts (high culture) to take in a wide spectrum of popular and everyday cultures in which practically any object or experience can be deemed to be of cultural interest. This has been accompanied by a shift in attention from lifestyles conceived as a relatively fixed set of dispositions, cultural tastes and leisure practices which demarcate groups from each other to the assumption that in the contemporary city lifestyles are more actively formed. Hence the focus turns away from lifestyle as class- or neighbourhood-based to lifestyle as the active stylization of life in which coherence and unity give way to the playful exploration of transitory experiences and surface aesthetic effects. It is the compound effects of these shifts which prove to be a source of fascination for a number of cultural commentators who are disposed to regard them as indicators of a more fundamental social and cultural displacement which is increasingly referred to as postmodernism.

This chapter will seek to understand these changes via a dual focus, first, on the transformations in lifestyles and city cultures which are taking place and alleged to amount to a postmodern shift; and, second, to raise the question of the changes in social structures and relationships which dispose particular sets of cultural specialists and intermediaries to exploit and develop new markets for cultural goods and experiences. In short, attention needs to be given to the role of the interpreters, carriers and promoters of both a range of new cultural goods and experiences and the perception of those goods and experiences as significant, meaningful and worthy of investment.

Before going into these questions in more detail we can briefly refer to a number of factors which point to the ways in which the culture of cities and urban lifestyles have become thematized. First, there is the assumption that particular cities (for example, Florence, Venice) are cultural centres containing the art treasures and cultural heritage of the past which are housed both in museums and galleries and in the fabric of the buildings and layout which represents the prime source of their cultural capital. Alongside the notion that the city can be regarded as 'work of art' (Olsen, 1986) as in the above cases, or in the case of the outstanding natural beauty of the site (for example, Rio de Janeiro, San Francisco) which can be regarded as an alternative source of prestige, or cultural capital, we have the view that cities can also be cultural centres to the extent to which they house leisure and entertainment industries. Particular metropolises (such as New York, Paris, Los Angeles, London) may be strong in cultural capital in terms of the extent to which they are centres of cultural production, housing not only the arts (still an expanding sector), but also the mass culture industries of fashion, television, cinema, publishing, popular music, tourism and leisure. The employment of the notion of cultural capital (Bourdieu, 1984) in this context is to point to alternative sources of wealth than economic (financial and industrial) capital whose value may nevertheless be redeemable and reconvertible back into economic value, through a whole series of direct and indirect routes. Hence the willingness of national policy-makers, city administrations and private capitalists to encourage and seek investment in culture (Fisher et al., 1987) and their sensitivity to the importance of the city's image under conditions of intensified competition.

Second, the general expansion of the cultural sphere within contemporary Western societies not only points to the enlarged market for cultural goods and information, but also to the ways in which the purchase and consumption of commodities, an allegedly material act, is increasingly mediated by diffuse cultural images (via advertising, display and promotion) in which the consumption of signs or the symbolic aspect of goods become the major source of the satisfaction derived (Baudrillard, 1981). Here one can point to the increasing salience of forms of leisure consumption in which the emphasis is placed upon the consumption of experiences and pleasure (such as theme parks, tourist and recreational centres) and the ways in which more traditional forms of high cultural consumption (such as museums, galleries) become revamped to cater for wider audiences through trading-in the canonical, auratic art and educative–formative pretensions for an emphasis upon the spectacular, the popular, the pleasurable and the immediately accessible. In addition it can be argued that there are further convergences between these two cultural forms and a third, the development of malls and shopping centres.

Third the extension of the range of cultural and leisure pursuits available has not only extended the range of leisure lifestyles available but has resulted in some qualitative shifts too. As I mentioned earlier, there is a tendency on the part of some groups (especially the young, highly educated, sectors of the middle classes) to take on more active stance towards lifestyle and pursue the stylization of life. Here we can point not only to the imitation and popularity of the lifestyles of artistic subcultures (bohemias, avant-gardes) in contemporary metropolises, but also to what has been referred to as 'artist of life', the painters who do not paint but adopt the artistic sensibilities in order to turn their lives into a work of art. The concern with fashion, presentation of self, 'the look' on the part of the new wave of urban *flâneurs*, points to a process of cultural differentiation which in many ways is the obverse of the stereotypical images of mass societies in which serried ranks of similarly dressed people are massed together. If the contemporary age can be characterized as an era of 'no style', to borrow a phrase of Simmel's, then it points to the rapid circulation of new styles (fashion, appearance, design, consumer goods) and the nostalgic invocation of past ones.

Here we can point to a further convergence in the process of the stylization and aestheticization of everyday life between the popularity of artistic lifestyles and stylistic presentation and display and the development of a differentiated and sophisticated range of consumer goods, leisure-time pursuits and experiences which incorporate a high input of design, style, and artistic and fashionable cultural imagery. It can also be argued that certain modernist artistic currents (such as Dada and surrealism) which became central to postmodernism in the 1960s themselves sought to collapse the boundary between art and everyday life to show that the most banal consumer cultural objects and the kitsch and detritus of mass culture could themselves be aestheticized and introduced as the subject of, or incorporated into, the formal structure of artworks. Postmodern art also focused upon the body, living art and the happening (see chapter 3). Hence we have an interchange between a number of currents: a higher input of style, design and cultural imagery into consumer goods, sites of leisure and consumption and the fabric of the city; an expansion of artistic professions, intermediaries and ancillary workers with the growth of specific artistic enclaves and neighbourhoods (e.g. SoHo in New York); the move towards postmodern art with its aestheticization of everyday life and mass consumer cultures; the growing prominence of social agglomerates which show a concern with stylistic display, fashionable clothing and presentation of self (which often entails a playful or parodic emphasis which allegedly seeks to transcend traditional status games), as people move through city spaces and consumption, leisure and entertainment sites. We will now turn to a more detailed examination of these strands.

Postmodern city cultures

Some commentators have referred to some of the tendencies we have just mentioned as postmodern (Cooke, 1988; Zukin, 1988a; Chambers, 1987). While the term 'postmodern' and its most common derivatives 'postmodernism' and 'postmodernity' are generally used in a confusing range of ways (see chapters 1 and 3), they do sensitize us to a series of cultural changes which may presage a more fundamental set of transformations of social structures and relationships. Among the most frequently cited characteristics associated with postmodernism are (1) an antifoundational stance in philosophy and social and cultural theory which suggests that the foundational meta-narratives which ground Western modernity's claims for privileged universality in its notions of science, humanism, socialism etc. are flawed and that we should seek to produce less pretentious modes of knowledge which are more sensitive to local differences as intellectuals swap their role as confidant legislators to that of interpreters (see Lyotard, 1984; Kellner, 1988; Bauman, 1988); (2) this privileging of the local and the vernacular is translated into a democratic and populist collapsing of symbolic hierarchies within the academy and intellectual and artistic circles in which for example the distinctions between high culture and popular or mass cultures, art and everyday, are contested – put simply we should 'learn from Las Vegas' (Venturi, Scott Brown and Izenour, 1977); (3) there is a shift from discursive to figural forms of culture manifest in an emphasis upon visual images over words, primary processes of the ego over secondary and immersion rather than the distanced appreciation of the detached spectator (Lash, 1988); and (4) these aspects are captured in the phrase 'postmodern depthless culture' (Jameson, 1984a) and the notion that ordered historical development should give way to the perception of the past as a conglomerate of images, fragments and spectacles which are endlessly reduplicated and simulated without the possibility of discovering an essential order or point of value judgement. These features have been noted by commentators within a wide range of academic fields, and however suitable the emphasis on the move beyond the modern implied by the term 'postmodernism', the use of the term has the merit of directing us towards what are perceived to be significant changes in artistic and popular cultural practices, regimes of signification and modes of orientation within everyday life. The populist and de-hierarchizing spirit of postmodernism directs our attention to the way in which culture has surfaced as an issue, as something to be theorized and explored alongside the de-monopolization of long-established symbolic hierarchies whose former dominance meant that particular notions of culture were taken for granted and unthematized. Hence it is possible to follow DiMaggio (1987) and regard the Western world as entering a phase of 'cultural de-classification' in which there will be heightened competition between a wide variety of notions of culture and a reduced ability to impose a value-hierarchy.

For our particular purposes it is interesting to note that commentators have adopted the rhetoric of postmodernism to understand the changes to the culture of cities and urban lifestyles we have alluded to. Particularly influential has been the work of Baudrillard (1983a, 1983b) with his notion of a simulational culture. Arguing that consumer commodities in late capitalism have developed the capacity to take up a wide range of imagistic and symbolic associations which overlay their initial use-value and hence become commodity-signs, he detects a qualitative shift in the intensification of this process which leads to the loss of a sense of concrete reality as the consumer–television culture with its floating mass of signs and images produces an endless series of simulations which play off each other. Baudrillard refers to this as a 'hyperreality', a world in which the piling up of signs, images and simulations through consumerism and television results in a destabilized, aestheticized hallucination of reality. For Baudrillard, culture has effectively become free-floating to the extent that culture is everywhere, actively mediating and aestheticizing the social fabric and social relationships. A move beyond the discursive reflexive primacy of language towards figural cultural forms which emphasize the immediacy and intensity of aural and visual sensations which provide inchoate and dispersed pleasures for decentred subjects.

If these perceptions are translated into an urban context it is apparent that the old notion of pre-modern city cultures which implies certain cities are sedimented in tradition, history and the arts, housing famous buildings and landmarks which provide a strong sense of place and collective identity – or the 'de-cultured' city, the modernist functional economic city whose spatial form is dominated by the grid iron layout and high rise modernist architecture – both give way to the postmodern city which marks a return to culture, style and decoration, but within the confines of a 'no-place space' in which traditional senses of culture are decontextualized, simulated, reduplicated and continually renewed and restyled. The postmodern city is therefore much more image and culturally self-conscious; it is both a centre of cultural consumption and general consumption, and the latter, as has been emphasized, cannot be detached from cultural signs and imagery, so that urban lifestyles, everyday life and leisure activities themselves in varying degrees are influenced by the postmodern simulational tendencies.

To take some examples: postmodern tendencies in architecture can be seen as a revolt against architectural modernism with its austere Miesian functionalism and abstract formalism (Jencks, 1984; Davis, 1985) by the reintroduction of decoration, the mixing of styles and a playful pop art simulation of commodities (such as Philip Johnson's Chippendale ATT Building in New York). It also introduces what Venturi and associates (1977) in *Learning from Las Vegas* refer to as 'Roadside Eclecticism': the eclectic stylistic hotchpotch of big signs and little buildings which run along the highway. Words, pictures, sculpture and neon are mixed together and in contrast to modernism's austerity, symbolism is reintroduced to produce a hedonistic consumer culture landscape. Here pop art's parodic duplication of mass consumer cultural objects are fed back into the urban landscape and culture industries. Not only the billboard, but especially electronic media images, provide sources of inspiration. There is a plethora of ornamental, overcoded multicoloured façades whose impact is immediate with no opportunity for distanciation (Cooke and Onufrijchuk, 1987).

If architecture and art take quotations from everyday consumer culture and play them back to produce postmodern cities 'where everything is "larger than life", where the referents are swept away by the signs, where the artificial is more "real" than the real' (Chambers, 1987: 1), then what of the people who move through these urban spaces? In many ways the people are regarded as engaging in a complex sign play which mimics or resonates with the surfeit of signs in the built environment. Contemporary popular culture (fashion, music, television, videos, drinking. dancing, clubbing) is regarded as dominated by the 'as if ...' world of advertising. Clothes, bodies, faces become 'quotations drawn from the other, imaginary side of life: from fashion, the cinema, advertising and the infinite suggestibility of urban iconography' (Chambers, 1987: 7). These signs, which are decontextualized from tradition or subcultural ordering, are played with in a superficial way, with people revelling in the fact that they are artificial, opaque and 'depthless' in the sense that they cannot be decoded to offer access to some revelatory meaning or fundamental sense of truth. Everyday life becomes a 'fantastic *mélange* of fiction and strange values' which captures the sense of the surreal as an everyday presence both as excess, style and experimentation and as randomness, banality and the repetition of street images (Calefato, 1988: 225). The contemporary is a dandy of a new and more democratic bohemia', a new metropolitan figure who 'explores routes already travelled by avant-garde art, crossing the boundary between the museum and mass culture, but transfers the game from the art gallery to the fashion catwalk of the street' (Del Sapio, 1988: 206–7).

It should be apparent that this group of people who seek to cross, re-cross and transgress the boundaries between art and everyday life are predominantly the young and are the inheritors of the tradition of youth subcultures. The latter operated as fixed symbolic structures which are now rejected or ironically parodied and collaged. Yet there is the assumption on the part of commentators that these new tendencies are indications of the processes which are breaking up traditional patterns of social regulation which link lifestyles closely to class, age and normativity (Baudrillard, 1983a; Chambers, 1987: 7). Hence Chambers (1987: 2) quotes Robert Elms, a writer for the fashionable youth magazine *The Face*, as remarking 'nobody is a teenager any more because everybody is'. Certainly there is some evidence that youth styles and lifestyles are migrating up the age scale and that as the 1960s generation ages they are taking some of their youth-orientated dispositions with them, and that adults are being granted greater licence for childlike behaviour and vice versa. This relationship between lifestyle, habitus and class will be discussed towards the end of this chapter.

One interesting aspect of the new urban lifestyles and depth less stylistic eclecticism commentators label as postmodern is that it is linked to the notion of a movement beyond individualism, to a de-centring of the subject. The de-centred subject has a greater capacity to engage in a controlled de-control of the emotions and explore figural tendencies, immediate sensations and affective experiences formerly regarded as threatening, as something which needs to be kept at bay or strictly controlled. It has been argued by Maffesoli (1988b) that in the postmodern city we have a move beyond individualism with a sense of communal feeling being generated, a new 'aesthetic paradigm' in which masses of people come together in temporary emotional communities. These are to be regarded as fluid 'postmodern tribes' in which intense moments of ecstasy, empathy and affectual immediacy are experienced. Of course it should be emphasized that these tendencies are not in themselves historically new. One can find examples of the disorientating *mêlée* of signs and the aestheticization of everyday life in the carnivals and fairs of the Middle Ages and mid-nineteenth-century Paris with its *flâneurs*, or the great world exhibitions in metropolises like Berlin and Paris (see chapter 5 above). What is new is not only the capacity to reduplicate and simulate these previously enclaved examples of the aestheticization of everyday life – and indeed any other cultural experience – on a hitherto unexperienced level of intensity and vividness of reproduction. Also new is the attitude of intellectuals and theorists towards the process. Whereas Simmel was troubled by the threat to art posed by the de-auratization of art and the ways in which the stylization of everyday objects lead to an interference with the distanced appreciation demanded by the artwork Benjamin especially in his *Passagen-Werk*, celebrated the fragmented images of mass culture and the shocks and jolts of the perceptions in everyday city life from a theoretical perspective clearly influenced by surrealism, Dadaism and montage (see Wolin, 1982) which resonates well with postmodernism.

If postmodern cities have become centres of consumption, play and entertainment, saturated with signs and images to the extent that anything can become represented, thematized and made an object of interest, an object of the 'tourist gaze', then it is to be expected that leisure activities such as visiting theme parks, shopping centres, malls, museums and galleries should show some convergence here. To take some examples, Disney World is often taken as the prototype for postmodern simulational experiences (Baudrillard, 1983a) and it is interesting to see that the format of moving between spectacular experiences (white-knuckle rides, hologram illusions etc.) and the simulation of historical national-founder or childhood worlds (the Magic Kingdom) or wandering through simulations of building, which are chosen to symbolize selected national cultures (such as the Merry England pub) or futuristic scenarios (EPCOT) in sanitized, highly controlled surroundings, has not only been imitated by theme parks around the world, but has also been merged with other formats such as museums. The growth of open-air museums directed at a wider spectrum of people has broadened the range of objects worthy of preservation (such as working coal mines, miner's terraced houses, trams, metal advertising signs dubbed 'street jewellery', as at the Beamish Open Air Museum in Tyne and Wear in north-east England). It has also encouraged a new attitude on the part of spectators with actors (often the unemployed on government schemes) trained to play historical roles to enliven the recreated physical settings, so that the mood of walking through a film set is extended as spectators are encouraged to participate and bring the simulation to life (Urry, 1988). The range of sites worthy of the tourist gaze and exploration is extended. One increasingly lives in a 'heritage country' in which the sense of historical past gives way to myths. Hence if one crosses the north of England one moves rapidly from Wordsworth country, to Brontë country, to Herriot country, to Captain Cook country – and to show working-class popular culture is respectable too – to Catherine Cookson country, each with tour guides, itineraries, museums and souvenirs. Even former non-attractive locations are clamouring to join the queue with towns like Bradford capitalizing on its 'Northern Grit' industrial past and current large Asian community to become the site for 'getaway break weekends'. Here we have typical sites for what have been referred to as 'post-tourists' (Feifer, 1985; Urry, 1988), people who adopt a postmodern de-centred orientation towards tourist experiences. Post-tourists have no time for authenticity and revel in the constructed simulational nature of contemporary tourism which they know is only a game. They welcome the opportunity to explore backstage regions and tackle the experience from many points of view.

Similar orientations are also to be found in contemporary museums, many of which are abandoning their commitment to the cultural canon and education project, in which the old and the new were organized in terms of a hierarchy of progress developed in the nineteenth century to reflect the values of ascendant Western modernity (Bann, 1984; Bennett, 1988), in favour of a more populist ethos. From this perspective, museums should cease to be dull places of education; rather, they should incorporate the features of postmodernism and become 'amazing spaces' which present spectacular imagery and simulations. This encourages a different, more playful, orientation from much broader-based crowds whose mass-media-influenced perceptions are at home with the abandonment of symbolic hierarchies and a more playful approach to montaged exhibits that offer experiences organized in terms of the equality of a plurality of styles, which shows the abandonment of a civilizing mission and hierarchized vision of a unitary culture (Roberts, 1988; Horne, 1984). This is captured in Baudrillard's (1982) description of the Beaubourg Museum in Paris which draws in the masses to what he calls this 'hypermarket of culture'. He states:

> The people want to accept everything, eat everything, touch everything. Looking, deciphering, studying doesn't move them. The one mass effect is that of touching or manipulating. The organizers (and the artists, and the intellectuals) are alarmed by this uncontrollable impulse, for they reckoned only with the apprenticeship of the masses to the *spectacle* of culture. They never anticipated this active, destructive fascination – this original and brutal response to the gift of an incomprehensible culture, this attraction which has all the semblance of housebreaking or the sacking of a shrine. (Baudrillard, 1982: 10)

It can be argued that the conflict between populism and elitism is a perennial feature of museums (Zolberg, 1984), yet the populist tendencies certainly have come to the fore in the 1980s.

This populism is hardly an unexpected feature of shopping centres, malls and department stores. Within these sites it is apparent that shopping is rarely a purely calculative rational economic transaction to maximize utility, but is primarily a leisure-time cultural activity in which people become audiences who move through the spectacular imagery designed to connote sumptuousness and luxury, or to summon up connotations of desirable exotic faraway places, and nostalgia for past emotional harmonies. In short shopping has to become an experience. As cities de-industrialize and become centres of consumption one of the tendencies in the 1970s and 1980s has been the redesigning and expansion of shopping centres which incorporate many of the features of postmodernism in their architectural design of interior space and simulated environments: use of dreamlike illusions and spectacles, eclecticism and mixed codes, which induce the public to flow past a multiplicity of cultural vocabularies which provide no opportunity for distanciation (de-distanciation) and encourage a sense of immediacy, instantiation, emotional de-control and childlike wonder. One of the major North American examples is the West Edmonton Mall – or more appropriately 'mega-mall' – which has a supplementary sixty-four-acre entertainment centre with a 'Fantasyland' funfair and water park which includes an indoor saltwater lake containing dolphins, mini-submarines and Spanish galleons (Shields, 1987: 9). Europe's largest shopping centre is the Metrocentre in Gateshead, in north-east England. The Metrocentre is a good example of the de-industrialization process and switch of cities to become centres of consumption being built upon derelict industrial land in an economically depressed metropolitan region. The Metrocentre has promoted itself as a tourist attraction with its 'Antiques Village', fantasy fairytale 'Kingdom of King Wiz', Ancient Roman Forum gallery and general eclectic smattering of symbolism to evoke the myths of a communal past via Christmas card and chocolate-box iconography (Chaney, 1990).

There are therefore common features emerging between shopping centres, malls, museums, theme parks and tourist experiences in the contemporary city in which cultural disorder and stylistic eclecticism become common features of spaces in which consumption and leisure are meant to be constructed as 'experiences'. As Lefebvre (1971: 114) remarks, in the contemporary city we have 'consuming displays, displays of consuming, consuming of signs, signs of consuming'. This convergence takes place not only on the level of the common form to the sets of experiences which are sought to be generated by advertisers, designers, architects and other cultural intermediaries, but also in terms of the alliances forged between the proprietors, patrons, trustees and financiers of these institutions. For example, a New York department store promoted a China Week in which art works and museum treasures were exhibited in the store. The Metropolitan Opera in New York hosts fashion shows (Silverman, 1986). Japanese department stores regularly display art treasures and hold exhibitions of paintings. Such promotion phases and exhibitions blur the distinctions between high culture and low culture and the distinctions between commerce and culture.

These convergences are not without forerunners, although they are new to the extent that the mixing of codes and the deconstruction of the symbolic hierarchies involving discriminations between high and mass culture, now takes place across a wider range of cultural forms and within what were almost exclusively regarded as places of inculcation of high cultural values and a coherent education formative process (such as museums). With regard to forerunners, the department stores which developed first in Paris and then in other cities in the second half of the nineteenth century were essentially conceived as 'palaces of consumption', 'dream-worlds' and 'temples' in which goods were worshipped by new consumers (largely female) who were able to wander through display areas which introduced simulations and an evocative, exotic imagery (R.H. Williams, 1982; Chaney, 1983). Similar experiences were also generated by the world exhibitions and expositions which became regular events until the early years of the twentieth century, in the wake of the Crystal Palace Great Exhibition of 1851. These presented simulation involving stuffed animals and ethnographic scenarios, stands for various nations involving replicas of cultural treasures and everyday life (for example, a Moorish palace, a Chinese house) and even simulations of experiences (for example, a Trans-Siberian Railway journey) (see R.H. Williams, 1982). In addition the phantasmagorical distractive overload of signs and impressions which Simmel (1978) refers to in *The Philosophy of Money* produced many similar experiences to those which have been labelled postmodern (Frisby, 1985b). We have a similar emphasis upon play and display. As the 'Short Sermon to Sightseers' at the 1901 Pan-American Exposition instructed 'Please remember when you get inside the gates you are part of the show' (cited in Bennett, 1988: 81). In effect the crowd itself became part of the spectacle and the reason for going just as much in the Great Exhibition of 1851 and the Berlin Trade Exhibition of 1896 as in the Parisian Beaubourg Museum described by Baudrillard in the 1980s. Yet to be a *flâneur*, a stroller, who watches others and displays him or herself, necessitates an ordered space as much in the Parisian Arcades so dear to Baudelaire in the 1840s and 1850s which became central to Benjamin's *Passagen-Werk* (Berman, 1982), as in the exhibitions and department stores of the late nineteenth century and as much in the theme parks, shopping centres and museums of today. In short, to wander through goods or art treasures on display demanded discipline. The imagery may summon up pleasure, the carnivalesque and disorder, yet the emotional decontrol these encouraged must itself take place within a framework of self control. And for those who lacked it or were in danger of losing it there existed a battery of external controls designed along the principles of panopticism (Foucault, 1977). These entail surveillance and exclusion. It is a central principle of theme parks and shopping centres that these are privately owned public spaces in which the public are under the watchful eye of video-cameras, and rowdy, troublesome elements are excluded before the disorder might disturb others.

This suggests that before going along with the thesis that de-industrialization and the shift to cities as centres of consumption have entailed the accumulation of spectacles, mixing of codes and merging of high and low cultures, a shift towards postmodern lifestyles, we need to ask specific questions about (1) the extent of forerunners and (2) the extent to which such lifestyles represent minor enclaved experiences in the lives of specific groups of people in specific urban locations. In short, we need to ask the stark sociological questions about not only where the postmodern lifestyles take place; but how many people from which range of groups participate and for how long. We need also to attempt to understand the forces which are propelling culture to greater importance within the contemporary city and investigate the interdependencies and conflicts between specific groups (such as cultural specialists, economic specialists, policy makers) which are bringing this about.

Cultural capital, gentrification and the stylization of life

In recent years there has been increasing recognition of the value of culture industries to the economy of cities and the many direct and indirect ways in which the presence of cultural institutions, activities and a general sensitivity to ways in which the enhancement, renovation and redevelopment of the cultural façades, fabric and lived space of cities carries benefits. The awareness that culture industries such as publishing, recorded music, broadcasting, and tourism generated by arts and cultural institutions, can play a growing role in national and local economies has grown alongside the general expansion in the production and consumption of symbolic goods in contemporary Western societies. Here we might usefully refer to the concept of *cultural capital* which has been developed by Pierre Bourdieu (1984, 1987) and others (see Lamont and Lareau, 1988). The concept points to the way in which in parallel to economic capital which is immediately calculable, exchangeable and realizable, there also exist modes of power and processes of accumulation based upon culture in which the value of the latter, the fact that culture can be capital, is often hidden and misrecognized. Bourdieu (1987: 243) points to three forms of cultural capital: it can exist in the *embodied* state (style of presentation, mode of speech, beauty etc.), *objectified* state (cultural goods like pictures, books, machines, buildings etc.), and in the *institutionalized* state (such as educational qualifications). It is the objectified state which is of particular interest with respect to cities and I have already mentioned the ways in which specific cities may have accumulated cultural capital because of their exemplary preservation of buildings, artefacts and goods which have become defined as 'art treasures (Olsen, 1986). From this perspective one could construct a symbolic hierarchy of cities according to their accumulated prestige in terms of culture capital with Florence, Paris, Rome near the top. Conventionally the culture industries are defined as producing mass cultural goods (Horkheimer and Adorno, 1972; Garnham, 1987) which traditionally have featured low on the scale of cultural capital. Yet one can argue that the legitimacy of particular forms of cultural capital and the legitimacy of the existing symbolic hierarchy and structural features of the field of cultural capital should not be eternalized. Rather, they should themselves be conceived as a process which is the result of the intentional and unintentional outcome of particular groups who are bound together in interdependencies and struggles (often misrecognized or masked by claims to disinterestedness) to maximize their own particular form of cultural capital. Hence it is possible that particular forms of cultural capital, such as popular and mass culture (jazz, rock music, cinema, theme parks) may themselves become regarded as more legitimate and the source of prestige and further up the symbolic hierarchy. Hence New Orleans and districts of large cities may gain attraction and cultural capital as sites of formerly defined 'low life', now elevated to respectability and worthy objects of the tourist gaze.

There are therefore an expanding range of criteria on which cities may be ranked in terms of cultural capital. What the shift towards postmodern culture is held to introduce is a movement away from agreed universal criteria of judgement of cultural taste towards a more relativistic and pluralistic situation in which the excluded, the strange, the other, the vulgar, which were previously excluded can now be allowed in. In this sense the tendency is for the long-held Western universally based symbolic hierarchy to become spatialized out with a greater tolerance of difference and diversity. From the perspective of the economic utility of cultural capital this means that while traditional smokestack industrial towns of the 'rust belt' are to be regarded as low in cultural capital (with the exception of those who are able to repackage and museumify these elements as assets), the range is extended from traditional historic value and treasures to include newly created and simulated environments that take in some of the postmodern and more popular cultural forms we have mentioned, which are perceived as attractive and saleable. In short, those who seek to invest in new service, information and high-tech industries may be swayed by the ambience and cultural capital of cities and may have helped to speed up the reconversion strategies such as the redevelopment and gentrification of docklands and inner-city areas. Under global conditions of intensified competition and the freeing of market forces for investment and capital flows, cities have become more entrepreneurial and aware of their image and the ways in which image translates into jobs for the local economy. As Harvey (1988) puts it, cities have to mobilize culture to become 'lures for capital'. Hence in the early 1970s Seattle attempted to remove mass unemployment by bringing together business leaders and planners who lobbied for investment to expand the arts infrastructure, and gained much favourable publicity as a self-proclaimed 'quality of life capital'. Baltimore develops its Harbor Place, Hamburg becomes a 'media city', Gateshead has its Metrocentre and so on.

This is the process which has been referred to as *postmodernization* (Cooke, 1988: Zukin, 1988b) to point to the global restructuring of sociospatial relations by new patterns of investment which lead to some counter-tendencies to urban decentralization through the redevelopment of inner city areas. This process entails the de-industrialization of inner city areas and docklands, which become gentrified by members of the new middle class and developed as sites of tourism and cultural consumption. At the same time the working class and poor who previously resided in these areas are moved out or driven into other enclaves. A good example of this is Battersea in London, where large blocks of working-class council housing were sold and redeveloped for the yuppie market. In this case the new inhabitants were made to feel secure from the neighbouring lower orders by security fences and guards. This process of increased segregation as the middle classes move back into the central areas is also symbolized in the postmodern architecture with towers, moats and drawbridges which create defensible privatized spaces free from the unemployed, the poor, rebellious youth, and other residues of the 'dangerous classes'. It creates what David Harvey (1988) has called 'voodoo cities' in which the postmodern façade of cultural redevelopment can be seen as a carnival mask which covers the decline of everything else. In Los Angeles, for example, side-by-side but segregated from the financial node of the Pacific Rim economy and gentrified area, we have an Hispanic-Asian enclave of one million people fuelled by Third-World migration and the demand for labour which results in undocumented homeworkers and child labour (Davis, 1985). It is those processes which have helped to destroy the former fragile consensus within the middle classes that supported high culture and the culture industries and which raise the questions of the political uses of the arts and other forms of cultural capital within the city and whether there can be a more democratic cultural policy (Garnham, 1987). It also entails, in a wider sense, the question of resistance to redevelopment, to what some refer to as 'urbicide' (Berman, 1982).

The process of gentrification is of interest because it not only points to the redevelopment of the cultural fabric of inner-city areas, it also provides a higher profile for groups within the new middle class who are in many guises the producers, carriers, consumers of lifestyles which entail the culturally sensitive 'stylization of life' and have developed dispositions which make them receptive to postmodern cultural goods and experiences. They therefore have direct and indirect interests in the accumulation of cultural capital both on a personal basis, and in terms of that of their neighbourhood and the wider city.

The location which has been widely studied and can best illustrate this process is SoHo in New York City (Zukin, 1987, 1988a; Simpson, 1981; Jackson, 1985). As Zukin (1988a) points out, the regeneration of SoHo into an artist's colony and then a gentrified new middle-class neighbourhood with incomers attracted by the ambience of the artist's lifestyle is a complex story. It is based upon the rise in the investment value of art in the post-war era which has seen art become a strong international market in its own right. It also entails an elevation in the status of artists and ancillary occupations to the extent that other groups become more favourably disposed to associate themselves with artistic lifestyles. It is further based on the fact that city governments begin to realize the potential for redevelopment and reversal of the negative side of de-industrialization and general enhancement of the city's image by granting such enclaves a protected status. New York replaced Paris as the centre for Modern Art in the post-war era and a dramatic increase in the numbers of artists, galleries, museums and exhibiting outlets occurred (see Crane, 1987; Zukin, 1988b; DiMaggio, 1986). There was also a more general change on the part of national and local governments, foundations and corporations who began to perceive the arts as socially useful. In short, the economic value of cultural capital increased and from the 1960s the artistic avant-garde ceased to be seen as a troublesome and transgressive bohemian counterculture and were regarded by city politicians, speculators and developers as a different avant-garde, as those who beat the trail to large-scale low-rent rundown areas ripe for redevelopment through gentrification.

This was coupled with a more general reevaluation of the status of the artist in American society which made art less high-culture and elitist and more democratic. Artists now made money; some of them made a good living from art. With the transition from artistic modernism to postmodernism their oppositional pretensions and austere indecipherability of artworks were displaced and celebrity artists such as Andy Warhol gained much media attention and coverage. The artist became perceived as an attractive persona and his studio – the loft – an interesting place to be, and live. The new middle classes (Burris, 1986), and in particular those sectors which Bourdieu (1984) has referred to as 'new cultural intermediaries', have a fascination for artists' and intellectuals' lifestyles and a general interest in the stylization of their lives. Theirs is a lifestyle which focuses very much on identity, appearance, presentation of self, fashion design, decor; and considerable time and effort have to be expended in cultivating a sense of taste which is flexible, distinctive and capable of keeping abreast of the plethora of new styles, experiences and symbolic goods which consumer culture and the culture industries continue to generate.

The habitus of the cultural specialists within the new middle class points to a flexible, learning mode towards life. Here it may be that the new cultural intermediaries have an important role in the transmission of new style. Their interest may be less in the attempt to impose a particular style on consumer audiences and more in terms of a general interest in the full range of styles from different cultures, civilizations and traditions which they can play and replay. Hence there is an interest in the stylization and aestheticization of life on the part of particular factions within the new middle classes who have been referred to as 'para-intellectuals' in their role of admiring intellectual and artistic pursuits and lifestyles. They, therefore, are able to transmit the latest styles such as postmodernism to wider audiences and themselves form part of the reception class for postmodern goods and experiences.

Conclusion

The proponents of postmodernism detect a major shift in culture taking place in which existing symbolic hierarchies are deconstructed and a more playful, popular democratic impulse becomes manifest. Here we have spa-tialization out of the previous more firmly structured symbolic hierarchies which became dominant motifs within Western modernity and established particular notions of universal history, progress, the cultivated person, state political structures and aesthetic ideals. With respect to the contemporary Western city it has been argued that postmodern and postmodernizing ten-dencies can be observed in the new urban spaces which point to a greater aestheticization of the urban fabric and the daily lives of people, the devel-opment of new consumption and leisure enclaves (such as shopping cen-tres, theme parks, museums) and the drawing back of new middle-class gentrifying populations into the inner city. These postmodern impulses sug-gest less strong neighbourhood identifications and a less fixed habitus or rigid set of dispositions and classifications into which encounters are framed. Some of the new urban lifestyles point to a de-centring of identity and a greater capacity to engage in a de-control of the emotions and aestheticized play. It can also be argued that on the global level we are wit-nessing the end of the dominance of a few metropolitan centres over artis-tic and intellectual life (R. Williams, 1983). Paris and New York as centres of culture, the arts, fashion, culture and entertainment industries, television, publishing and music, now face greater competition from a variety of direc-tions. New forms of cultural capital and a wider range of symbolic experi-ences are on offer within an increasingly globalized – that is, more easily accessible via financial (money), communications (travel), and information (broadcasting, publishing, media) – field of world cities.

Hence it could be argued by those who emphasize the novelty and his-torical events which postmodernism is purported to bring, that we are entering a phase in which the old cultural hierarchies are becoming obso-lete. The de-hierarchizing impulse suggests that high/low, elite/popular, minority/mass, taste/tasteless, art/life, vertical classificational hierarchies (Goudsblom, 1987; Schwartz, 1983) which are held to be endemic features of social life, no longer apply.

Against this seductively oversimplified postmodern story of the end of history we have to point to the persistence of classification, hierarchy and segregation within the city. As we mentioned, the new middle class and new rich live in enclaved areas of gentrification and redevelopment which are designed to exclude outsiders. These enclaves are areas of high investment in designed environments, stylized form and the aestheticization of everyday life. Such groups expect to be entertained while they shop and shop at places of entertainment. They seek to cultivate a style of life and have an interest in the arts and a pleasurable aestheticized living environment (Boyer, 1988). For certain fractions of the new middle class this style of life certainly has affinities with the range of characteristics and experience designated postmodern. There are tendencies which point to an overload of information and signs, which make the ordered reading of bodily presentation, fashion, lifestyle and leisure pursuits much more difficult. People are able to draw from a much wider repertoire of instantly accessible symbolic goods and styles from the 'global showcase' and it is more difficult to make a judgement of class from taste and lifestyle. Since the 1960s there has been a more general informalization and elaboration of previously restricted codes of behaviour. Notions of beauty prominent in consumer culture, for example, widened beyond the classic Western one in the 1960s to take into account standards of other cultures (Marwick, 1988). Yet for all the democratizing tendencies there are status differences. As Douglas and Isherwood (1980) points out, the informational component of consumer goods rises as one moves up the class scale. Those in the middle and upper reaches continue to use information about consumption goods to build bridges with like-minded people and close doors to exclude outsiders. This is very much the case with knowledge of the arts.

If, then, we are arguing that it is still possible to read bodily presentation and lifestyles as indicators of social status it is clear that the game is much more complex now. If postmodern points to something it is the eclipse of a particular coherent sense of culture and associated way of life which was dominant in the Western upper and middle classes which set the tone for the culture as a whole. This happens as the historical generations which carried them slowly recede in numbers and influence. Here one thinks of the notion of a common culture as a goal; as based on an educational formative project, as something unified, a totality of knowledge (the classics in literature, music and the arts), which had to be struggled through to improve the person. Along with it went the notion of a cultured or cultivated person, the ideal of a gentleman, the product of a civilizing process (Elias, 1978b, 1982). The middle and upper classes in the second half of the nineteenth century were prime carriers of this cultural ideal and sought to extend it through museums and educational institutions.

Since the 1960s the process of cultural declassification has seen the decline and relativization of this ideal. The question is whether these tendencies, which have been labelled postmodern, merely point to a collapse of an established hierarchy, a temporary phase, a cultural intermezzo of intensified competition, varied standards and value complexes, before a re-monopolization by a new establishment. Or should we see the extension of the current tendencies *ad infinitum* – the end of history? In this context it is salutary to refer to similar historical ages of cultural turmoil and incoherence. If it is proclaimed today that there is no fashion, only fashions, then we should bear in mind that Simmel discovered similar tendencies in Florence around 1390 when the styles of the social elite were not met with imitation and each individual sought to create his own style. Fashion and other lifestyle pursuits, to use Simmel's metaphor, are used as 'bridges and doors' to unite and exclude. If these functions appear to decline does it mean that we are merely in a temporary intermezzo? Or does the extension of the game to draw more groups, cultures and nations into a widened global system mean that the conditions for particular dominant elites to exercise global hegemony over taste and culture are destroyed with the unlikelihood of foreseeable re-monopolization, thus pointing us towards a historical development in which some of the impulses detected and labelled postmodern may become more widespread?

8

Consumer Culture and Global Disorder

One of the noticeable features of sociology in the 1980s has been the growth of interest in the cultural dimension of social life which has propelled the sociology of culture from a marginal position towards the centre of the sociological field (Robertson, 1988; and chapter 3 above). At the same time a reverse process seems to have taken place which has seen the sociology of religion move towards a more marginal and isolated place within the field (Fenn, 1982; Beckford, 1985). Save for a few notable exceptions there has generally been little interest in religious phenomena on the part of those engaged in theorizing the contemporary cultural complex. Yet we hardly need to recall that the classic sociological theorists Weber and Durkheim, whose writings have long been held up as exemplary texts for the sociology of culture, both treated religion as central to the understanding of the structure and development of social life. Indeed the progressive demise of the influences of religion in social life, which can be related to the processes of industrialization, rationalization, urbanization and social differentiation, has been held by some to have provoked a peculiarly modern crisis of meaning or crisis in the effectiveness of the social bond, which could only be adequately allayed through the creation or emergence of some new meaning complex or *morale*. The decline of religion and the erosion of its institutional bases within society, then, is often held to have left behind a vacuum with deleterious effects for both the individual and society. Yet for some the dissipation of religion into numerous quasi-religious and non-religious meaning complexes which supply individuals with the knowledge to help them cope with the intractable existential questions of ultimate meaning, the sacred, birth, death, sexuality and so on has merely rendered religion invisible. Max Weber's (1930) famous metaphor in *The Protestant Ethic* of religion striding into the marketplace of worldly affairs and slamming the monastery door behind it, becomes further transformed in modern society with religion placed very much in the consumer marketplace alongside other meaning complexes. Here we think of the writing of Peter Berger (1969) and Thomas Luckmann (1967) with individuals able to select from a plurality of suitably packaged bodies of knowledge in the supermarket of lifestyles. Individuals' sense of fulfilment, happiness and ultimate life-meaning become located in the private sphere where 'man is free to choose and decide on his own what to do with his time, his home, his body, and his gods' (B. Luckmann, 1971); see also Hammond (1986) and B.S. Turner (1983) on the market model of religion.

If the tendency in modern Western societies is for religion to become a private leisure-time pursuit purchased in the market like any other consumer culture lifestyle, then we need to ask a number of questions about the effect of this shift on religion. Has this brought religion close to other consumer commodities and experiences, does it have to present itself as a way of life and meaning complex which offer similar kinds of emotional refreshment to other leisure pursuits? Have other leisure-time experiences such as consumer culture spectacles taken on the aura of the sacred? How significant are questions of ultimate meaning, of belief, in the habitual day-to-day practices and power balances individuals are enmeshed in? What effective practical knowledge is provided by religious, quasi-religious and non-religious meaning complexes? Are questions of meaning and belief more relevant to particular social groups and classes – for example, the intellectuals? How does the 'choice' of particular types of religious and quasi-religious meaning complexes relate to other cultural taste and lifestyle pursuits which can be mapped onto the universe of tastes and lifestyles which operate with a specific society? In addition to a discussion of religion in relation to consumer culture we need also to speculate about the possible role of religion in relation to a postmodern culture. Consumer culture can clearly be located as arising within modernity yet it displays tendencies which point towards the *post*modern.

Consumer culture and the sacred

Consumer culture is generally presented as being extremely destructive for religion in terms of its emphasis on hedonism, the pursuit of pleasure here and now, the cultivation of expressive lifestyles, the development of narcissistic and egoistic personality types. Before we examine some of the ways in which religion has accommodated to consumer culture and consumerism continues to support a religious dimension, it would be useful to outline briefly some of the salient features of consumer culture. The term, as it suggests, refers to the culture of the consumer society. It is based on the assumption that the movement towards mass consumption was accompanied by a general reorganization of symbolic production, everyday experiences and practices. A number of studies have traced its origins back to the eighteenth century for the middle classes in Britain (McKendrick, Brewer and Plumb, 1982) and to the nineteenth century for the working classes in Britain, France and the United States, with the development of advertising, department stores, holiday resorts, mass entertainment and leisure etc. (Bailey, 1978; Ewen and Ewen, 1982; R.H. Williams, 1982). Other studies emphasize that the inter-war years in the United States saw the first sustained development of a consumer culture with new tastes, dispositions, experiences and ideals publicized through advertising, the motion picture industry, the fashion and cosmetic industries, mass circulation tabloid newspapers and magazines and mass spectator sport (Susman,

1982; Ewen, 1976; Bell, 1976). It is often alleged that consumerism led to spiritual impoverishment and hedonistic selfishness with its 'live now, pay later' philosophy which ran directly counter to the ascetic regimes, industry, foresight and thrift which religion in general, and the puritan heritage in particular, taught. Malcolm Cowley (1951) writing in the 1930s drew attention to what he called the new 'consumption ethic' which was initially developed by bohemian artists and intellectuals in Greenwich Village as an overt attack on the business-Christian ethic. The new consumption ethic which was taken over by the advertising industry by the late 1920s celebrated living for the moment, hedonism, self-expression, the body beautiful, paganism, freedom from social obligations, the exotica of faraway places, the cultivation of style and the stylization of life.

It is evident that one of the central features of consumer culture is the availability of an extensive range of commodities, goods and experiences which are to be consumed, maintained, planned and dreamt about by the general population. Yet this consumption is far from being just the consumption of utilities which are addressed to fixed needs (Adorno, 1967; Jameson, 1979; Leiss, 1983). Rather, consumer culture through advertising, the media, and techniques of display of goods, is able to destabilize the original notion of use or meaning of goods and attach to them new images and signs which can summon up a whole range of associated feelings and desires. The overproduction of signs and loss of referents, which we have already spoken of in the context of postmodern culture, is therefore an immanent tendency within consumer culture. Hence within consumer culture the tendency is to push culture towards the centre of social life, yet it is a fragmented and continually reprocessed culture which does not cohere into anything like a dominant ideology. Of course, we need to beware of treating culture on the level of sign and image systems without asking how they are used in everyday practices, and who is engaged in their production and dissemination. To answer the second question will entail a discussion of the role of specialists in symbolic production and various cultural intermediaries who handle, circulate and purvey cultural goods and this will be discussed shortly. To answer the first question points to the significance of the active cultivation of lifestyle within the imagery of consumer culture. That is, individuals are encouraged to adopt a non-utilitarian attitude towards commodities and carefully choose, arrange, adapt and display goods – whether furnishings, house, car, clothing, the body or leisure pursuits – to make a particular stylistic statement which expresses the individuality of the owner.

The concern with constructing an expressive lifestyle, to achieve some sense of satisfying order from the commodities and practices that surround the individual, generates a constant demand for information about lifestyles. For the individual who has 'only one life to live' there is a vast array of interpretations of cultural goods experiences and lifestyles all of which point to the capacity for self and lifestyle transformation. Warren Susman (1979: 220) has suggested that one of the key changes in identity formation which took place with the move towards consumer culture occurred with a shift from the proclamation of the virtues of character to those of personality. He quotes advice manuals from the early decades of the twentieth century to point to this transition. O.S. Marsden, for example, wrote a book *Character: The Grandest Thing in the World* in 1899 which stressed the ideals of the Christian gentleman: integrity, courage, duty and the virtues of hard work and thrift. In 1921 he published a new advice manual *Masterful Personality*, which emphasized 'the need to attract and hold friends', 'to compel people to like you', to develop 'personal charm' and 'fascination'.

This type of advice manual was, of course, hardly restricted to the development of consumer culture. The manners books examined by Norbert Elias (1978b, 1982), and his discussions of the taming of the medieval knights and the emergence of a court society in which the nobility became specialists in the art of consumption, point to the care individuals had to take with fashion, demeanour, style of presentation, as well as in developing the skills to read the appearance of others in order to survive in the fluctuating power balances of the court figuration. While these types of status games (which contrary to Sennett (1976) were anything but playful games) led to an emphasis upon distinctions and differences which has been adopted within consumer culture and is the central focus of one of the major recent analyses of consumption practices, tastes and lifestyles, Bourdieu's (1984) *Distinction*, this should not blind us to the existence of the countertendency which mass consumption and democratization favoured, the tendency towards equalization and the diminishing of contrasts (Gellner, 1979; B.S. Turner, 1986). Consumer culture here seen as part of a process of functional democratization offered the transcendence of sumptuary laws and was accompanied by a greater levelling out of balances of power (between the classes, men and women, parents and children), as the less powerful were for the first time able to emulate, within the limitations of mass fashion, the consumption practices and styles of the more powerful.

The tendencies towards emulation, equalization and imitation on the one hand and differentiation, individuality and distinction on the other have been noted by Georg Simmel (1978) as central to the dynamic of fashion, which is seen as a compromise between adherence and absorption into the social group and individual differentiation and distinction from other group members. Simmel relates fashion to the fragmentation of modern life. the neurasthenia, the overstimulation and nervous excitement which accelerated with the growth of the metropolis. The modern individual is confronted by a feverish change of fashion and bewildering plurality of styles. Yet the peculiar stylessness of the times manifest in the objective culture, the visible public culture, was for Simmel compensated for by the stylization of the interior by which individuals sought to express their subjectivity (Frisby, 1985a: 65).

Two other points of interest can be drawn from Simmel's turn of the century discussion of fashion which are relevant to our understanding of consumer culture. First he regards fashion as most closely associated with a particular social stratum, the middle classes, and a specific location, the metropolis. Second, the stylization of everyday household objects, part of the project of the *Jugendstil* and Aestheticism movements, can be related to a larger project of the 'stylization of everyday life' and the 'beautification of life'. Both point to a close relationship between art, fashion and consumer culture and the various producers, consumers, audiences, transmitters and intermediaries within sectors of the middle class which developed similar dispositions, tastes, classificatory schemes and lifestyle practices despite the apparent quest for individuality and distinction which seemingly distanced artists and their lifestyles from the more worldly commercial, design and retail occupations. They further point to the need to investigate the long-term process involving the growth of specialists in symbolic production, and the growth of separate intellectual artistic disciplines, institutions and movements which has taken place since the late eighteenth century. This process, which involved the development of movements such as Romanticism, Aestheticism, Modernism and Dadaism, and the constant avant-gardist negation and re-creation of the artists' oppositional bohemian lifestyle, entailed the transmission of aesthetic dispositions and sensibilities, with notions such as 'the artist as a hero' and 'the stylization of life' to a larger audience. It also fed into consumer culture in a host of different ways which changed the design of everyday objects, commodities and the fabric of the urban industrial landscape that it is possible to speak of, to use the title of James Allen's (1983) book, as the romance of commerce and culture.

Hence there is a good deal of interest in highlighting the antinomial, out-to-shock and transgressive qualities of artistic countercultures (for example, Bell, 1976). Yet we should be careful not to just look at texts and art objects and assume that their meanings are self-evident and can be read off, but must inquire into how they are used *practically* in everyday activities. There is a danger of overestimating the significance of beliefs which are produced, classified and discussed primarily by symbol specialists, and underestimating the significance of practical knowledge, taken-for-granted, commonsense classificatory schemes and dispositions which do not operate as norms, but are called upon as social life unfolds practically by individuals held together in various shifting power balances with other people (see Bourdieu, 1977; Elias, 1978a). Here we would want to emphasize power-balances and the practical uses of knowledge, because power exists as an aspect of every human relationship from the fact that people, groups or individuals, have the capacity to withhold or monopolize what other people need – food, love, meaning, protection from attack, knowledge etc. (Elias, 1984b: 251).

Daniel Bell (1976: 28), for example, tells us that 'The real problem of *modernity* is the problem of belief.' Secular systems of meaning have proved illusory solutions to the spiritual crisis once the anchorage of society in religion has been severed, and only a religious revival is capable of restoring the continuity of generations and producing images of cosmic order, humility and caring which can satisfactorily address our sense of the existential predicaments. Rather than deal with the question in terms of a void in belief which needs to be filled to produce some meaningful moral order and adequate social bonding – a void which, for Bell (1976: 156), the aesthetic justification of life with its emphasis upon hedonism and self-expression is incapable of filling – we need to inquire into the specific ways in which beliefs, especially those produced by specialists in symbolic production such as priests, intellectuals and artists, played a central role in holding together everyday life. There is a tendency arising out of the practical day-to-day use and valuation of beliefs and ideas for symbol specialists (artists, intellectuals, priests) to overvalue the importance of coherent belief systems as relevant guidelines structuring activities in everyday life. Indeed, there is also a tendency noted by (Bourdieu, 1983b) for intellectuals and artists to set themselves up as 'uncreated creators' in the sense that they draw upon what Bourdieu calls the 'ideology of charisma', 'talent' and 'giftedness' which should rather be seen as arising from the gradual sedimentation of dispositions and practical aptitudes which is reinforced within institutional contexts. Hence there is the tendency for artistic and intellectual pursuits such as writing or producing works of art to be regarded as creative and not to be understood as practices involving sedimented dispositions, institutional frameworks and power-balances. In short, artists and intellectuals have an interest in parading their own disinterestedness, in that their contempt for material things in the world (economic capital, money, property), their apparent disinterestedness, may conceal their interest in accumulating cultural capital in which status and prestige accumulation act effectively as an alternative form of currency and power. To understand the changes in belief in modernity we therefore need to examine the long-term processes which led to a shift in the balance of power away from religious knowledge specialists to favour the growth of scientific, artistic and intellectual knowledge in various institutions and practices (cf. Elias, 1983: 262). This would entail an investigation of the development of the emergence of a relatively separate cultural sphere since the eighteenth century which paralleled the struggle to overturn the church authorities' monopoly hold on the societal fund of knowledge (see Featherstone, 1988). Therefore, while it is possible to conceptualize one strand of this process as taking place on the level of belief, we also have to consider the practical use of beliefs in relation to group alliances, interests and struggles.

Although it is possible for specific sets of beliefs or ethical complexes to generate intense emotional fulfilment and commitment on she part of specific groups, it is generally noted that (1) such phases are difficult to sustain in the long run, and (2) the commitment may be stronger on the part of certain groups or class fractions who may be more predisposed to taking ideas seriously and rarely applies universally across a society, although it may be possible that particular groups of carriers may sustain it as a long-term project. Hence Cowley's (1951) and Bell's (1976: 63) references to the active propulsive force of a 'consumption ethic' must be treated with caution. The term 'consumption ethic' also features in Colin Campbell's (1987) book *The Romantic Ethic and the Spirit of Modern Consumerism.* Campbell (1987: 8) takes as his model the cultural approach Weber (1930) adopted in *The Protestant Ethic and Spirit of Capitalism*, in which an assumed affinity between a particular ethic and spirit gave rise to psychological impulses which gave direction to an individual's everyday life. Yet in his later writing Weber (1968) developed a much stricter sociological account of the relationship between religious beliefs and the status and power structure of groups in society. He emphasized that status groups will endeavour to preserve and enhance their present style of life by maintaining a social distance and by closing off economic opportunities to outsiders (see Bendix, 1959: 258 ff.). In addition to the monopolization strategies of established groups to maintain visible differences in style of life, we can add that outsider groups will endeavour to de-monopolize, to adopt usurpatory tactics to break down exclusivity and privilege (cf. Elias and Scotson, 1965; Bourdieu, 1983a; Parkin, 1979). In doing so, of course, they may claim to have wider ambitions to join the established and emphasize the sincerity of their beliefs, their disinterested return to fundamentals in a quest to address their particular field or even the fate of a people or humanity in general.

An objection, then, to approaches which see modernity as entailing the replacement of religion by art to fill a vacuum in belief, or which would like to explain consumer culture in terms of an ethic, is that they tend to rely on a view that society needs, or that individuals operate through, basic beliefs. Of course, under certain circumstances specialists in symbolic production may have an interest in increasing the circulation and demand for new symbolic and intellectual goods. Some groups then have an interest in dealing with men and women as 'cultural beings', and form alliances with other groups who have an interest in becoming cultivated, in treating life as a learning project; yet we cannot assume this applies equally across the social structure. Still other groups may effectively dilute, transpose and integrate articulated meaning complexes such as religion into their existing everyday mundane practices more on their own terms. 'Big culture', then, may have a different impact and practical relevance for different groups (cf. Robertson, 1978: 80). For the intellectuals a central concern may be to search for coherence and to universalize their particular interpretation of the world to the extent that the disorder within culture is eliminated.

Bell's (1976; 1980: 333) definition of culture as the modalities of responses to the core existential questions – love, death, tragedy, obligation – gives his view of culture and religion an intellectualist bias (see Douglas, 1982: 7). When religion is defined as providing the most coherent set of answers to these core existential questions, a decline in religion must necessarily be seen as providing a threat to social integration and the social bond, and this is Bell's verdict on the culture of modernism. Yet such perspectives should also consider the extent to which culture diversity and disorder occurred both in pre-modern and modern societies. There is the danger that we will accept what Margaret Archer (1988: 1 ff.) has referred to as 'the myth of cultural integration', which became prevalent both in anthropology and German historicism. In doing so our sense of cultural coherence may be derived from assumed exemplary literary texts to the extent that we read off popular practices from intellectualist accounts and neglect the integrity and diversity of popular traditions. If we look at popular mainstream culture we may find little of the penetration of adversarial cultural modernism which so worries Bell. Rather, it tends to be retained within its cultural enclave to be consumed by specialist, if expanding, audiences and publics. Popular mainstream culture, such as soap operas, films, television advertisements, newspapers and magazines, are generally much freer from cultural exploration, criticism and protest. Here we frequently find a concern for respectability, cleanliness, good food, clothes, service, concern for law and order and property and individual success (see Douglas, 1982: 16). In addition, mass consumption is rarely the endless modernist round of cultivation of new pleasures and sensations which Bell stresses. Mary Douglas (1982: 16) argues that 'To the consumers themselves, consumption is less like a pleasure for its own sake and more like a pleasurable fulfilment of social duties.' Before pronouncing about the danger which art and intellectual pursuits represent to culture and social integration we need to investigate the actual everyday practical uses of culture by different social groups which directs us to the way in which culture interrelates with social structures and cannot be regarded as an autonomous sphere. If we do not, there is a danger that we will follow mass society theorists and read off mass consumption from mass production and miss the diverse ways in which cultural meaning and commodities can be reworked and de-commodified.

The ways in which new sets of ideas, be they religious or modernist, which are articulated by a cultural elite, influence large numbers of people must be demonstrated and not assumed. This applies as much for Protestantism in seventeenth-century England as for modernism in the United States in the twentieth century. A great deal of high culture may develop with little or no influence on the people. Weber's (1930) *Protestant Ethic* essay also demonstrates a caution about the extent to which the reformed doctrines successfully bridged the gulf between high culture and everyday behaviour (Bendix, 1970: 147). Seventeenth-century puritan divines in England were concerned about the spiritual slumber of their flocks, and evidence suggests that there was a continuing tradition of scepticism and irreligion (Reay, 1985b: 101). The 'theatre and counter-theatre of popular culture' with its charivaris, mock church ceremonies, ritual of popular protest, and festivals was still strong (Reay, 1985a: 8). Indeed, as Reay (1985a: 16) reminds us, 'the carnivalesque was surprisingly strong in early modern England'. The carnivals, festivals and fairs in early modern Europe celebrated transgressions of the classical and official culture with symbolic inversions and promotion of grotesque bodily pleasures. They provided sites of 'ordered disorder' in which otherness and desire could be explored (Stallybrass and White, 1986; see discussion in chapter 5 above). While it is possible to follow Bell (1976) and consider the diffusion of cultural modernism into the consumer culture of the lower classes, it is also important to examine the ways in which the liminal symbolic repertoires, the transgressions, inversions and celebration of otherness, made their way from the carnivalesque and popular traditions to be taken up both in the artworks and lifestyles of the burgeoning bohemias which became sites of cultural modernism in the large cities of the nineteenth century.

It is therefore important to avoid the temptation of the strand in current sociology which seeks to 'retreat into the present' (Elias, 1987b) and to avoid projecting backwards from our self-designated troubled times to some point of order and stability, a pre-industrial organic unity which existed prior to 1750 (Easton et al., 1988: 20). Daniel Bell's (1976, 1980) concern about the deleterious effects of cultural modernism can also be related to the German tradition of societal rationalization and *Kulturpessimismus* (Kalberg, 1987), in which contemporary mass consumer society is perceived as atomized, impersonal and bereft of meaningful social bonds and means of integration. It is therefore not surprising that Bell has been accused of nostalgia in seeking to advocate a religious revival to restore the social bond apparently endangered by cultural modernism (O'Neill, 1988).

In summary, then, to understand contemporary culture and the place of religion within it we need to adopt a broader definition of culture than does Bell, one which allows us greater sensitivity to cultural diversity and disorder. Those groups which are disposed to take ideas seriously may be restricted to specific locations within the class structure (for example, symbol specialists and cultural intermediaries within the middle class). On the other hand, other groups may exhibit a disregard for formal beliefs. It is possible that particular national state formation processes may give rise to a range of outcomes in which different societies develop a range of orientations towards beliefs and religions and intellectual goods. In some state formation processes in which the aristocracy play a minor role the particular conjunction of symbol specialist (for example, Puritans) and economic specialists within the middle classes may help to produce a national culture and character structure which favour the importance of beliefs. It is possible to regard middle-class culture in the United States from this perspective (see Bellah et al., 1985). Finally, the attraction of belief systems may differ historically, with a temporary diffusion of particular sentiments to a wider population taking place at certain points in time. It is to such a Durkheimian perspective that we now turn.

Durkheim (1974: 92) emphasized that societies experience moments of collective ferment and enthusiasm. Such moments are, however, difficult to sustain both over time and across the span of social groups within a differentiated society. Durkheim emphasized the deep and enduring layer of affectivity at the heart of society which is manifest in symbols which embody social sentiments, collective representations and rituals (Tiryakian, 1978).

From this perspective, modernity with its processes of rationalization, commodification, secularization and disenchantment does not lead to the eclipse of religious sentiments, for while formal religions may decline, symbolic classifications and ritual practices which embody sacred/profane distinctions live on at the heart of secular social processes. As Durkheim pointed out, any thing can become sacred, so why not the 'profane' goods of capitalism? If we focus on the actual use of commodities it is clear that in certain settings they can become de-commodified and receive a symbolic charge (over and above that intended by the advertisers) which makes them sacred to their users. It is therefore possible for mundane consumer goods to become transformed into cherished possessions (see Rochberg-Halton, 1986: 170).

Modern society, then, is far from being a symbolically impoverished mundane material world in which commodities, goods and things are regarded as mere 'utilities'. As I have argued, consumer culture produces a vast shifting web of signs, images and symbols and these symbols cannot be conceptualized as merely profane. Alexander (1988: 189), building on Durkheim's later work, argues that in modern society

> social symbols are *like* sacred ones, in that they are powerful and compelling; the conflict between social values is *like* the conflict between the sacred and profane, or pure and impure sacredness; political interaction is like ritual participation in that it produces cohesion and value commitment.

This is not to imply that social symbols are harmonious and integrating: they may be contested and subjected to competitive processes. Here one thinks, for example, of the way in which the cultural dimension of the state formation process with its legitimate moral regulation and unifying collective representations must be seen as a product of an ongoing struggle to discredit and exclude alternative cultures and traditions (Corrigan and Sayer, 1985). Alexander's (1988) own study of the Watergate crisis in the United States in the early 1970s is a good illustration of the outcome of the struggle between differentiated elites which led to the creation of a ritual communitas via the televised hearings affirming the sacred democratic myths of American civic religion.

From one perspective, television within consumer culture can be regarded as trivializing the sacred in its capacity to put out a flood of information and arrive at bizarre juxtapositions as once-sealed-off signs and symbols are now placed in contiguity. Yet it can also be argued that televised ceremonies, events and spectacles are also capable of generating a sense of festive occasion (Dayan and Katz, 1988). Such events (for example, coronations, royal weddings, state funerals and even rock concerts and sports championship finals), may heighten the sense of the sacred to generate and reaffirm the moral consensus which underpins social conflicts and competition. Because in modern societies we are made more aware of attempts to invent tradition, to manufacture charisma and the sacred, to manipulate consensus through television, it should not blind us to those events in which a new sense of the sacred is generated for successive generations. As Durkheim pointed out, such occasions generate intense feelings of excitement, 'liquid emotion', and are reinforced in the accompanying communal activity by chants, dancing, ritual gestures. The 1960s can be regarded in this way with its happenings, music festivals like Woodstock, and general sense of excitement and effervescence. Such festive moments in which the everyday routine world becomes transformed into an extraordinary sacred world enabled people to temporarily live in unison, near to the ideal (Tiryakian, 1978; Durkheim, 1974). Subsequent gatherings often incorporate rituals which reinvoke the aura of the sacred of the original events and in effect act as 'batteries' which charge up the liquid emotion which can be carried over to sustain people in the more mundane everyday world (Collins, 1988b: 111). Televised rock music spectacles such as Band Aid, Food Aid, the Nelson Mandela concert and other transnational link-ups may also invoke a more direct sense of emotional solidarity which may reawaken and reinforce moral concerns such as the sense of common humanity, the sacredness of the person, human rights, and more recently the sacredness of nature and nonhuman species.

We have been arguing, then, that consumer culture has not resulted in the eclipse of the sacred by a debased materialism. This is in contrast to theorists who want to restrict the definition of culture and religion to the coherent answers to core existential questions (birth, sickness, death, love). Rather, we can take a wider definition of culture which will focus not only on formal religious institutions and movements but also those social processes and practices which generate and regenerate sacred symbols, be it the ceremonies of the state, rock concerts or the little sacred rituals which convey solidarity in small groups, or between friends and lovers. Hence we need to move away from approaches which read off consumption as a derivative of production and seek to dismiss it as 'mass' consumption. Instead we have to acknowledge that while consumerism results in an inflation in the quantity of goods in circulation, this does not result in a general eclipse of the sacred, something which is evident if we focus on the symbolism which goods have in practice.

Postmodernism and cultural disorder

In this final section we will inquire into some of the changes that have been taking place since the 1960s in Western societies which encourage some commentators to suggest that the beginning of a shift is taking place towards a postmodern culture. We will examine the relationship of these tendencies to consumer culture in general, and more specifically examine those changes taking place within intellectual and artistic circles, and their relation to other groups which are altering the means of transmission, circulation and reception of symbolic goods. In short, if a postmodern culture is emerging we need not just ask the question 'What is postmodern culture?' but 'Where is postmodern culture?' and 'Which groups have an interest in making it a reality?' through building upon more general sensibilities that may be emerging to educate and create larger audiences. We also, in a more speculative vein, need to relate these changes to wider shifts in the global order, to shifts in the balance of power between nation-states taking place on an intersocietal level. The notion of a postmodern culture is clearly derived from a Western context with the assumption that it represents a non-positive transcendence, a dramatic break with what was long regarded as the developmental trajectory of Western modernity. We need to ask the questions how far and in what ways will this alleged sensitivity to polyculturalism, to the integrity and 'otherness' of different cultural traditions, meet imminent tendencies in these other traditions halfway, to produce a more open and pluralistic global circumstance with some tendencies towards cultural disorder; and how far this is merely a temporary pause or relaxation in the struggle for dominance, with the possibility of an intensification of the power struggle and economic elimination contests taking place between states, holding out the prospect of changing trajectories for different cultural traditions and new orders of cultural dominance.

If we ask the question 'Who are the producers and carriers of postmodern cultural goods?' our attention is first drawn to changes which have taken place within various artistic and intellectual fields: the fields of art, literature, architecture, music, criticism and the academy. It was within such fields that the term was first used in the 1960s and 1970s to suggest a movement beyond the literary and artistic modernism, which was seen as having reached both its formal exhaustion as well as the end of its oppositional and avant-gardist impulse through its canonization by academics, museums and galleries, which in turn made it acceptable and a part of the syllabus in higher education institutions. The problem with attempting to define postmodernism is that it means different things within each particular field. Yet the role of critics and cultural intermediaries in circulating information between fields is in the process of creating a common sense of what the term means. This furthers its usage by various specialists in symbolic production such as artists, novelists, intellectual and academic commentators and researchers who use the term to interpret and frame a particular set of everyday experiences and cultural artefacts and modalities. From this perspective it is possible to isolate a number of features of postmodernism.

First, postmodernism involves an attack on autonomous, institutionalized art to deny its grounds and purpose. Art cannot be seen as a higher form of experience deriving from the creative genius or special qualities of the artist. Everything is already seen and written, the artist cannot achieve uniqueness but is doomed to make repetitions, which he/she should do without pretension. This move beyond the creative work of art, the artwork, or master text which becomes iconified in the museum, entails a blurring of the distinction between art and everyday life. In effect, art is everywhere: in the street, the refuse, the body, the happening. There is no longer a valid distinction possible between high or serious art, and mass popular art and kitsch.

Second, postmodernism develops an aesthetic of sensation, an aesthetics of the body which emphasizes the immediacy and unreflexiveness of primary processes, what Lyotard refers to as the *figural*, as opposed to the *discursive* which has its basis in secondary processes (Lash, 1988). It is, therefore, legitimate to subvert narrative into a series of flows, to dwell on the sonority as opposed to the meaning of the spoken word (Artaud's theatre), to focus on the body (interior as well as exterior) as art.

Third, in the literary, critical and academic fields postmodernism implies an antifoundational critique of all metanarratives, be it in science, religion, philosophy, humanism, Marxism or other systematic body of knowledge. Instead of the *grands récits* (metanarratives), Lyotard (1977) emphasizes *petits récits*. Hence 'local' knowledge in terms of the *pagus*, the space inhabited by the 'pagan', which takes on the cast of an antitheological knowledge disputing its pretensions to global knowledge, is valorized (Doherty, 1987: 215). Knowledge henceforth should be nomadic and parodic. It should playfully emphasize the discontinuities, openness, randomness, ironies, reflexivity, incoherences and multiphrenic qualities of texts which can no longer be read with the intention of extracting a systematic interpretation. Our inner-worldly condition and entrapment in an opaque symbolic web means that we should not speak of the end of history or the end of society in an epochal sense; rather, there has always already been the end of history.

Fourth, on the level of everyday cultural experiences postmodernism implies the transformation of reality into images, and the fragmentation of time into a series of perpetual presents (Jameson, 1984a: 15). Postmodern everyday culture is therefore a culture of stylistic diversity and heterogeneity, of an overload of imagery and simulations which lead to a loss of the referent or sense of reality. The subsequent fragmentation of time into a series of presents through a lack of capacity to chain signs and images into narrative sequences leads to a schizophrenic emphasis on vivid, immediate, isolated, affect-charged experiences of the presentness of the world – of *intensities*. Here the channel-hopping MTV viewer's fragmented view of the world is presented as the paradigm form.

Fifth, postmodernism, then, favours an aestheticization of the mode of perception and the aestheticization of everyday life. Art and aesthetic experiences therefore become the master paradigms for knowledge, experience and sense of life-meaning.

Clearly, these features we have isolated can as yet only be regarded as tendencies within small sectors of the academic and intellectual fields. In the first place it should be emphasized that these features are not themselves historically new or unique to the post-1960s phase. To take the second and fifth factors, for example, it is clear that, as discussed in chapter 5 above, a sense of the figural aesthetic and the aestheticization of everyday life can be traced back as far as the carnivals, festivals and fairs of the Middle Ages. This tradition became a source of fascination for the middle classes, some of whom incorporated features of the carnivalesque and its transgressions into both the products and lifestyles of the artistic and literary bohemias which developed in the nineteenth century. This is, of course, the source of the artistic avant-garde which become concerned with constantly shifting the parameters of artistic modernism. What would appear to be different with the emergence of the postmodern is the extent and proliferation of these sensibilities: the carnivalesque in the Middle Ages was a relatively circumscribed liminal enclave of short duration. Today the numbers of symbolic specialists and potential audiences both via artistic and consumer culture markets is much larger. Yet there are therefore grounds for assuming that the development of these perceptions themselves may be indicators of more basic cultural changes taking place within society. If this is the case, then we need to look more closely at the constituency for the aestheticization of life, the basis for wider audiences who may become attuned and educated into postmodern sensibilities.

It can be argued that in recent years a new enlarged market has developed for intellectual, cultural and symbolic goods, which is manifest in the expansion in numbers of specialists in these areas engaged in production, circulation and transmission of these goods in the new middle class. There are long debates about the rise and composition of the new middle class which there isn't space to go into here (see chapter 3 above for a discussion), save to note the lack of agreement in terminology manifest in terms such as 'the knowledge class', 'the new class', 'the new petite bourgeoisie' and 'the service class'. What social scientists do agree upon is that in a phase of increased unemployment this has been an expanding stratum. The sectors of greatest interest for our particular concerns, as we have continually emphasized, are the intellectuals, artists, academics and what Bourdieu (1984) refers to as 'the new culture intermediaries'. The new cultural intermediaries actively promote and popularize the intellectuals' lifestyle to a larger audience as well as help to break down the exclusivity of intellectual knowledge and the range of pursuits and fields intellectuals can be induced to comment on. This helps to collapse some of the old barriers and symbolic hierarchies which were based on the high culture/mass culture distinction. It also helps to educate and create a larger audience for intellectual and artistic goods and experiences which are receptive to some of the sensibilities manifest in phenomena like postmodernism.

As I have suggested earlier, the origins of these sensibilities should be regarded as part of a long-term process of numeric growth and increase in the power potential of specialists in symbolic production which can be traced back to the Romantic movement. Artists in particular, and specialists in symbolic production and intermediaries in general, are more disposed to a greater emotional exploration both as part of their work and lifestyle. This aspect was particularly evident in the 1960s in which a large cohort moving into higher education and the expanding service occupations become identified as a 'counterculture' which attacked emotional restraint and favoured a more relaxed and informal style manifest in styles of dress and presentation. In effect, this process of informalization (Wouters, 1986), which becomes noticeable in the 1960s and 1970s, while presented as a dangerous and naïve emotional regression in some circles, in fact depended upon greater self- control – 'a de-controlled control of the emotions' which involved a relaxation and a higher level of control in being able to confront previously repressed emotions. It has also been presented as having danger-ous self-centred narcissistic implications in the 1970s (Lasch, 1979). Yet it can be argued that less strict canons of behaviour and the relaxation of codes which accompanied informalization and emotional exploration demanded that individuals show greater respect for each other (Wouters, 1979). This may well be the case in some of the new religious movements and awareness therapies. The more widespread changes in organizational structures towards less authoritarian modes of management through nego-tiation (most noticeable in education and the helping professions, but by no means absent from other industrial and administrative organizations) also furthered greater flexibility in role performance and command structure (de Swaan, 1981; Haferkamp, 1987).

Postmodernism, then, has to be understood against the background of a long-term process involving the growth of a consumer culture and expansion in the number of specialists and intermediaries engaged in the production and circulation of symbolic goods. It draws on tendencies in consumer culture which favour the aestheticization of life, the assumption that the aesthetic life is the ethically good life and that there is no human nature or true self, with the goal of life an endless pursuit of new experiences, values and vocabularies. While this may be a particularly threatening and restrictive paradigm for social science research, there are not the same grounds for making the same assertion about its role in everyday life. The aesthetic justification for life must be examined dispassionately, and if this is carried out it may show that the controlled de-control of emotions and absence of a centralized, coherent religious belief system does not lead to nihilism and social disintegration; rather, the shift to aesthetic criteria and local knowledge may just as possibly lead to mutually expected self-restraint and respect for the other.

This does not necessarily lead to the end of the sacred; indeed, as I have argued, the sacred is able to sustain itself outside of organized religion within consumer culture. There are, however, if we are to follow some theorists of the postmodern, tendencies which would threaten the sacred. Baudrillard (1983a), for example. in drawing attention to the overload of information, signs and images in the society where 'TV is the world' argues that this overload threatens our ability to chain signs into narrative sequences. Instead we gain aesthetic pleasure from the surface experience of the intensities of the flow of images: we do not seek coherent lasting meaning. This, then, would entail the end of the symbolic, as signs would be free to take on whatever associations and elisions of meaning the acci-dental and bizarre juxtapositions of consumer culture could throw up. In effect, we would move towards cultural disorder. Yet if we move away from notions such as 'TV is the world' (the closest example would be a twenty-four-hour monadic MTV view) where television is conceived as a sort of 'moving wallpaper' to the actual practices of watching television, we note a collapsing of the public and private. This is especially the case when we have collective viewing in which viewers far from being passive may actively participate in the religiosity of events, spectacles and ceremonies, and indeed may even ritualize watching by dressing up (Dayan and Katz, 1988: 162). Hence once we move away from such notions such as information overload, in which the form of information determines the content and reception, to considering active viewing by embodied persons, then the symbolic and sacred dimension of social life can be sustained. In effect, the practical aspect of cultural reproduction demands that people will attempt to stabilize signs into classificatory schemes which possess a practical coherence and symbolic dimension without, as I have stressed, seeking the logical and rational consistency and plausibility which is more central to the practices of symbol specialists.

Finally, there is the question of how consumer culture and postmodernism can be related to the global order. It is often assumed that consumer culture on a global scale parallels the expansion of the power of the United States over the world economic order (Mattelart, 1979). Here consumer culture is seen as destined to become a universal culture which destroys each country's own national culture. Yet studies of the effect of television reception emphasize the importance of national differences in reading and decoding messages. In effect, the message embedded in television programmes only makes sense to those socialized into the codes, so that different nationalities and social classes will view internationally popular television programmes through inappropriate codes. It can also be argued that the tendency we have referred to within consumer culture to produce an overload of information and signs would also work against any coherent integrated universal global belief on the level of content. However, the prevalence of images of 'the other', of different nations, previously unknown or only referred to through narrow stereotypes, may effectively help to put the other, and the sense of a global circumstance, on the agenda.

With reference to postmodernism, the loss of the sense of 'the other' as alien or exotic as a stereotype, flowing from a loss of faith in the metanarratives which underlay such interpretations – here one thinks of the work of Said on Orientalism – produces a further crisis in the authority of interpreting different cultures or traditions from a centre-point or foundation. This crisis is beginning to emerge in theorizations throughout the social sciences and can be related to changes in the perception of the global circumstance. The openness to otherness and the previously ignored or the once felt threatening disorder of different cultures itself represents a shift in the power-balances between nations. To seek to know the other in its own terms, to seek to glimpse behind the narrow and overbearing stereotypes, registers the hermeneutic turn in cultural methodology. This movement towards cultural declassification and the deconstruction of long-held symbolic hierarchies points to a world in which the chains of interdependencies between nations and cultures are lengthened and more densely interwoven. In anthropology, for example, the postmodern-induced acceptance of the particularity and integrity of various bodies of local knowledge has been taken a stage further in which the anthropological subjects not only dispute the authority and validity of anthropologist's interpretation, but seek to speak for themselves. The anthropologist is left to tell a story about his own experience (Friedman, 1987). These changes taking place on an intersocietal level, which push academics and intellectuals towards a polyculturist perspective, are compounded by changes on an intrasocietal level, some of which I have referred to, which have on the one hand reduced the power of the intellectuals' authority through inflation in the intellectual field resulting in greater numbers of new intellectuals and a de-monopolization of the power of established intellectuals to define symbolic hierarchies; and on the other hand there is a pull from the consumer marketplace with an increasing demand for symbolic goods on the part of new cultural intermediaries to cater for the thirst for new cultural experiences, sensations etc. Effectively, the intellectual is reduced to the role of an interpreter, packaging particularities and unable to offer legitimate universal knowledge with any prospect of a legislative or practical effect Bauman, 1985).

From one perspective, postmodernism can be understood as a cultural image, a talismanic concept that incorporates images of disorder, dissolution, relativism, and fragmentation, which opens up a space beyond the hypostatizations of the systematically and universalizing conceptual arsenal of the modern. Its proponents find attractive the reemergence of images of cultural disorder, which have themselves been an adversarial and transgressive subtheme within the Western tradition, yet which remained largely enclaved within the liminal carnivalesque and its artistic recuperations. Such images themselves may have a wider appeal, not only through intrasocietal changes in the class structure which push to the fore new markets for symbolic goods and new opportunities for symbolic specialists, but also in terms of intersocietal and global processes. Indeed there is a sense in which, given the identification of the modern with the universalizing project of Western culture, the use of the term 'postmodern' can act to orientate us to the changing circumstances in which the world is seen as one place in which different competing images of the globe come to the fore (Robertson, 1987).

9

Common Culture or Uncommon Cultures?

To refer to a 'common culture' immediately raises problems of interpretation. The word 'common' means something shared, but it also has the further meaning of something low, vulgar and unrefined. In this second sense the term can be related to the Latin *vulgus:* the common people (R. Williams, 1976: 61). We could therefore shorten the title of this chapter to 'common culture?' and play off the two meanings of the term 'common': a culture which is or should be shared and integrative, and a culture which is low, vulgar and unrefined, and apparently in need of some direction and guidance to make it elevated and refined. The term 'culture' is, of course, even more problematic and is an essentially contested concept covering a wide range of meanings. It has been variously used to refer to norms, ideas, beliefs, values, symbols, languages and codes. It can also point to the process of spiritual and intellectual development of the person, or to specialist intellectual and artis-tic enclaves and practices (the cultural sphere or high culture) and even the whole way of life of a group, people or society (the anthropological view). This last meaning, culture as a 'whole way of life', as we shall see implicitly assumes a common shared set of meanings, beliefs and values between peo-ple which somehow cohere into an integrated whole.

It is possible to link together two of the meanings of culture we have just referred to: culture as 'the process of the spiritual and intellectual develop-ment of the person' and culture as 'the products of artistic and intellectual practices'. This is because it is often the positive value placed upon the cul-tured or cultivated person by those people we might call symbol specialists, those engaged in artistic and intellectual practices, which leads to the notion that culture, in the sense of the formation of a common culture in *their* terms entailing the education of the populace into a superior and coherent set of values and tastes, is a worthwhile project.

Here there is a danger of confounding the question of whether there actually is a common culture with the question of whether there should be a common culture, and we need to separate these levels of analysis which are often elided. In the first place we need to consider the common culture thesis which is found in sociology and anthropology and assumes that a coherent culture, or dominant ideology, plays a crucial role in sustaining social order and integration. This needs to be separated from a second con-cern which has developed within the fields of literary theory and cultural studies, about the value or necessity of having a common culture. Here we get a typical range of positions which emphasize that a common culture has existed in the past but now is in the process of being destroyed by a mass consumer culture, so that ways must be found to revitalize the cultural tradition; or alternatively that a common culture can only be created in terms of the education project of a cultural elite who will ultimately achieve the elimination of the vulgar and brutal cultural residues; or finally that some less elitist solution is possible which will enable a truly common culture to be developed which blends together and incorporates the culture of the common people (now positively evaluated) with selected elements of the 'high' cultural tradition. Raymond Williams would be one of the major proponents of this last position.

It is worth adding one final prefatory remark before we examine more closely the approaches just outlined. Today within the humanities and social sciences the common culture issue arouses little passion. The issue which is very much alive, postmodernism, is in many ways the antithesis of the common culture question. We therefore need to regard the common culture as not somehow an eternally fixed value or statically conceived abstraction. Rather we need to inquire into the conditions of its production and formation. In particular this entails an analysis of the changing power-balances and interdependencies between symbol specialists (intellectuals, artists, academics and cultural intermediaries) and other groups. It is in terms of these wider processes which propel forward particular groups of symbol specialists and see the demise of others that we should seek to understand why certain conceptions of culture can be seen to gain or lose popularity. It has recently been asserted that we are currently entering a phase of 'cultural declassification' in the Western world (DiMaggio, 1987) in which long-established symbolic hierarchies are being deconstructed. If this is the case, we should not merely follow those who delight in the demise of the canon and welcome the possibility of cultural disorder which signals the end of commitment to a common culture in the value-formative sense, but rather attempt to understand the social and cultural processes which bring about these swings.

The common culture thesis

The upsurge of interest in culture within sociology, the other social sciences and the humanities over the past decade, which has been manifest in the formation of new study groups, symposia, journals and other publications on culture, points to a movement beyond culture narrowly conceived as either 'the arts' or as relatively stable, shared and hence unproblematic norms, values and beliefs: the fixing cement of social relationships (Robertson, 1988). It is therefore only recently then that a serious attempt has been made systematically to theorize about the various dimensions of culture, and the relationship between culture and society.

Margaret Archer (1988: 1) has recently argued that the conceptualization of culture 'has displayed the weakest analytical development of any key concept in sociology and it has played the most wildly vacillating role within sociological theory'. For Archer the myth of cultural integration in particular is one of the most deep-seated fallacies in social science. She traces back the origins of this myth to German historicism and romanticism, which both conceive culture as a set of tightly woven strands which cohere together into an aesthetic unity. This is captured in terms such as *Zeitgeist* and *Weltanschauung* which emphasize the epochal unity of the spirit of an age and world-view. This tradition was particularly influential in anthropology in which culture was credited with the central role in integrating and producing social order (see Archer, 1988; Schweder, 1984; Kuper, 1988). Here again we have an aesthetic perception of culture which we can break down into two elements. First, it presents culture as a perfectly integrated whole in which there is an inner balanced order of the parts which relate together in harmony. Second, there is the assumption that we need a particularly gifted interpretative sensibility, that of artistic intuition, to grasp its inner meaning.

This emphasis upon aesthetic unity is also evident in functionalism in sociology. Sorokin (1957: 9), for example, insists that we can discover the 'logico-meaningful integration', the pattern of uniformity which enables us to relate together the chaos of individual components.[1] This position became known as 'the common culture thesis' which reaches its most influential statement in the work of Talcott Parsons (1951; 1961). Parsons emphasized that a coherent set of central values (the cultural system) acted as patterned normative elements which guaranteed integration and regulated interaction. The assumption that a common set of values is functionally necessary to induce the normative consensus which is vital to ensure social order has of course been heavily criticized.[2] Yet one of the problems associated with some of the criticisms of Parsons from a Marxist perspective is that the notion of a common culture is retained, or, to be more accurate, transformed into the notion of a dominant ideology with the key change being that culture is now used in a manipulative way, as something imposed by one set of people on another (Archer, 1988: 34). This is the argument put forward by Abercrombie, Hill and Turner (1980) in their book *The Dominant Ideology Thesis*. Basically they argue that societies do not reproduce themselves through either a common culture or a dominant ideology. They find little evidence for either a shared value system or dominant ideology in three case studies: feudalism, nineteenth-century early capitalism and twentieth-century late capitalism.

Two points can be developed from their work. First, they criticize the developmental model which assumes that societies were more integrated in the past. In feudal times, while the dominant class may have believed in the dominant ideology of Christianity, communications were poor, which hindered the integration of societies by central states. There was also considerable migration of people throughout Europe (Le Goff, 1984). Hence much of pre-Christian magic and superstition persisted in the popular culture of the lower orders (B.S. Turner, 1990; Ladurie, 1981; Ginzburg, 1980). The 'merry England myth', like the myth of primitive societies as integrated *Gemeinschaften*, in which a common culture played the crucial role in forming communal bonds, was being laid to rest (see also Laslett, 1965). This myth had not only entered into sociological theory through a misreading of Tönnies' *Gemeinschaft und Gesellschaft* but had also derived considerable impetus from Durkheim, and in particular Parsons' reading of Durkheim. Durkheim (1964) emphasized that early societies possessed a strong *conscience collective* through religion which coupled with their low social differentiation produced a high degree of moral and social integration. Modern societies on the other hand exhibited a high level of social differentiation through a complex division of labour and hence moral integration became more problematic and demanded a different social structural basis. Yet when Parsons (1937) took up Durkheim's theories in addressing modern societies, the problematic nature of engineering a moral consensus and cohesive sense of the sacred, which preoccupied Durkheim in his later writings, becomes obscured (see Archer, 1988: 35). Rather we have the assumption by Parsons that common shared values exist in modern societies, whereas for Durkheim such a high degree of integration was only a characteristic of premodern societies.

The second point can also be derived from Durkheim and directs us to the question of the maintenance of a moral consensus, a sense of *communitas* over time. If the common values are hard to sustain in a complex differentiated society with a high degree of division of labour, is it possible that they can be revived on certain occasions in which the feeling that society has become a unified national community is generated? In his later writings Durkheim argued that the sacred did not disappear in modern society and that there are many instances outside strictly religious situations in which sacred symbols and rituals are used to generate intense emotional experiences which break down the social distances between people (see Alexander, 1988; Tiryakian, 1978). Such occasions by dint of their quality as sealed off from everyday life have been referred to as liminal moments (V.W. Turner, 1969). Hence Shils and Young (1953) wrote an article on 'The Meaning of the Coronation' in which they argued that it was an act of 'national communion' which integrated everyone, including the working class, into the moral order of society. Few contemporary sociologists would agree with Shils and Young's position. Although civic rituals such as Remembrance Day, a royal wedding or funeral can be said to endeavour to represent the nation to itself as an imagined community (Anderson, 1983; Cohen, 1985; Chaney, 1979; Thompson, 1986), the problem is the degree of the communality of the sentiments generated. Civic rituals such as the Watergate hearings in the United States have rarely achieved the reaffirmation of the national tradition and the complete unification of the nation sought (Alexander, 1988), and are best regarded as part of a process involving moral entrepreneurs who attempt to overcome social divisions and exclusions (Gusfield, 1963; Gusfield and Michalowicz, 1984). Rather than assume that cultural integration is actually achievable, we would do better to consider the power of the myth that it has been, or can be, achieved. In short this points to the process of the formation of *communitas*, and the struggle to manipulate and create sacred symbols. Hence traditions have to be constantly invented and reinvented (Hobsbawm and Ranger, 1983) by specialists in symbolic production (intellectuals, artists, academics, cultural intermediaries), who have an interest in constructing and deconstructing representations of community. That is, those who have an interest in presenting a common culture as having occurred in the past, or as occurring now, or as a value we should strive to achieve in the future.

The making of a common culture

It is now over thirty years since the publication of Raymond Williams' (1958) influential *Culture and Society*, a book that examines the historical development of the idea of a restricted minority culture in Britain which is counterposed to the potential to develop a genuinely common culture. In looking back on Williams' plea for the project of 'the good common culture', it is worth noting that while he links the idea of a common culture to the development of a participating democracy, which remains a central preoccupation, the actual term 'common culture' seldom appears in his writing after the later 1960s. In a retrospective comment on the book, Williams (1979) places the issues of a common culture in the context of the time in which the book was written and points to the need for us to address the issues of our time in which it may be assumed that the debate over a common culture is less relevant. Indeed Williams (1979: 110) castigates Terry Eagleton (1968) for mechanically reproducing the argument of *Culture and Society* some ten years after its publication.

For Williams the essential intention was to attack what he saw as a divided culture, an 'uncommunity'. He sees the argument about culture as important 'because everywhere, but very specifically in England, culture is one way in which class, the fact of major divisions between men, shows itself (Williams, 1958: 24). Here he is strongly against the views of those who saw a common culture as only possible through the intervention and guidance of a cultivated and educated elite from above, be it the ideas of a 'clerisy' (Coleridge, 1837/1974) or a minority of 'aliens' (Arnold, 1869/1932). Williams (1989) finds a similar elitism in the advocacy of a common culture on the part of T.S. Eliot and F.R. Leavis. Both share a nostalgia for an 'organic' society in the past in which art and the common life were better related. Both, in their different ways, emphasize that a fully developed conscious culture can only be the property of an elite, and that the majority of people are incapable of sharing consciously in the minority culture. For Eliot (1948) the best that could be achieved for the minority was to participate in a distilled version of the elite culture. This 'common culture' and the capacity to articulate and consciously participate in its central elements, the common language and religion, is seen as different for different social strata. Attempts to extend the conscious culture and beliefs to all through education would only dilute and destroy the meaning of culture.

According to Williams (1958), 'Much of what upper-class egalitarians dreamed up for him, the ordinary man does not want – especially literacy.' For Williams a common culture should not only involve the transmission of higher values but the respect and receptivity of the everyday culture of the common people. As he (1989: 35) remarks:

> In talking of a common culture, then, one was saying first that culture was the whole way of life of a people, as well as the vital and indispensable contributions of specially gifted and identifiable persons, and one was using the idea of the *common* element of the culture – its community – as a way of criticizing that divided and fragmented culture we actually have.

The use of the term 'community', Williams (1979: 114 ff.) is at pains to stress, is not to suggest a return to *Gemeinschaft*; rather, it was chosen as a contrast to the dominant individualistic culture – or 'uncommunity' – of the upper classes. The way in which Williams (1958: 318 ff.) struggles to define a common culture that allows for the social differentiation essential to a complex society, yet as capable of providing a sense of solidarity, as capable of 'achieving diversity without creating separation', is reminiscent of Durkheim.[3] Yet paradoxically, while Williams advocates the development of a common culture, he stresses that culture is essentially unplannable. Here the idea of culture rests upon the metaphor of the conscious tending of natural growth. In this sense a common culture is always an unplanned process and however much it depends upon an educated and participatory democracy, which for Williams were central features of socialism. these are merely elements which enrich and prepare the ground on which a common culture can flourish.

Williams is equally critical of the view that a subtopian or dystopian mass culture is the perverse outcome of the misguided quest for a common culture. For those who fear the dilution or engulfment of the cherished value or high culture by the vulgar masses Williams (1958: 287 ff.; 1976: 158 ff.) is at pains to unpack the notion of *the masses*. In a significant sense 'masses' refers to the multitude, implying that the most evident thing about the common people is that there are so many of them. The term also carries the associated meaning of the vulgar, the rabble and the mob (shortened from the Latin phrase *mobile vulgus*) – the unstable common people in the eighteenth century. In this latter sense the term masses became identified with the urban industrial lower orders and working people, the gullible, low herd, which formed a perpetual threat to culture. Technology and mass communications are often enlisted to suggest that society has become massified and an homogeneous tasteless mass culture produced which has destroyed the ideals of humanistic elite culture, a 'post-culture' (Steiner, 1971). This fear of the mass, through the sheer numbers and lowest common denominator effect, was often coupled with a feeling of revulsion and disgust on the part of the middle and upper classes, which close contact with working-class people in the new urban spaces and transportation systems encouraged under conditions of increased democratization and social mixing where social distance was difficult to maintain (Wouters, 1979). For those educated into the ideal of the civilized or cultivated person, the established elite, the fear of falling, of being dragged down or engulfed by the vulgar mass of outsiders and of losing the self-control which had been won with considerable personal investment was particularly strong. In this sense the discrimination and taste of the cultivated person which was affronted by the masses and their culture, entailed a distaste for the masses which was in part visceral or embodied a sense of disgust.

Williams (1958: 289) is technically correct to state that 'Masses are other people. There are in fact no masses; there are only ways of seeing people as masses.' Yet it can be argued that the capacity to apply the label is much more likely to occur in a top-down manner on the part of established groups who have attained education and high cultural values for whom outsiders can be regarded as undifferentiated others, whose capacity to speak back or be listened to on a relatively equal footing is seriously limited – although nevertheless perceived as threatening. Williams' statement is therefore more of an injunction than a statement of fact: certain groups were disposed to see the common people as masses to emphasize their low-ness and vulgarity as opposed to cultivated taste. The control of the emotions and the capacity to develop a taste for the good things in life in a measured, distanced manner – be they painting, books, music, food or drink – is the product of a lifelong education process and must itself be understood as part of a more general long-term civilizing process in which emotional controls are developed more systematically in the upper and middle classes than in the lower orders (Elias, 1978b, 1982). From the perspective of someone educated into high cultural tastes and able to manipulate the discrimination of fine distinctions, the tastes of the common people often appear too simple and easy, too closely linked to the palpable pleasures and sensual desire of animality (Bourdieu, 1984: 32). Pure taste, then, which Kant (1790/1952) regarded as distanced and disinterested, is oppositionally defined against vulgar taste, that which is facile, easy, childish, simple, shallow and cheap – easily decodable and culturally undemandable (Bourdieu, 1984: 486). Pure taste entails a refusal, a disgust of simple enjoyment and pleasures. The disgust can be related to a horror for the vulgar on the part of those who have had to achieve painfully the discipline and respect for cultural tastes which are difficult. To such people the horror relates to the danger of loss of control which the surrender to sensation, to losing distance and reflection entails. The disgust relates to the reduction of enjoyment 'to animality, corporeality, the belly and sex, that is to what is common and therefore vulgar, removing any difference between those who resist with all their might and those who wallow in pleasure, who enjoy enjoyment' (Bourdieu, 1984: 489). Hence Bourdieu (1984: 490) comments 'The antithesis between culture and bodily pleasure (or nature) is rooted in the opposition between the cultivated bourgeoisie and the people.'

What is interesting about Bourdieu's remarks (written in the late 1970s with reference to French culture) is the way in which this 'vulgar critique of "pure" critiques of taste' chimes closely with what has become practically the orthodox position among those who study popular culture. If the issue of a common culture in the manner posed by Williams is dead, then the sympathy for critics of the growth of mass culture such as Arnold, Ortega, Dwight McDonald or Adorno has practically vanished. We therefore have had a double displacement in the attempt to theorize the making of a common culture. The first by Williams demands less elitism, it argues for a respect for the nonliterary tradition of ordinary people, the recognition of the dignity of labour and that trade unions and other aspects of working-class life are important cultural institutions in the formation of a common culture based upon participatory democracy. The second displacement is to recover the undignified culture of the common people. It seeks to gain equal acknowledgement for and even glorify the vulgar: the popular pleasures and transgressions of the carnivalesque tradition of the common people. Here there is no dignity, no humanistic ideals, no cultivation and improvement, no *Bildungsprozess*, sweetness or light, only the egalitarian right to be different – of otherness, to remain the other in its own inchoate terms. It is to a consideration of this tendency in the analysis of culture which is manifest in the growing interest in popular culture and postmodernism, that we will now turn: to the celebration of uncommon cultures.

Popular culture and the turn to postmodernism

The popular tradition of carnivals, festivals and fairs was disturbing for those who sought to educate the common people into better tastes. It celebrated symbolic inversions and transgressions of the official culture as well as the excitement, untamed emotions and direct bodily pleasures of fattening food, intoxicating drink and sexual promiscuity (Bakhtin, 1968; Stallybrass and White, 1986). Of course these carnivalesque occasions when 'the world was turned upside down' were very much enclaved liminal moments of 'ordered disorder' in contrast to the dull routines of everyday life. Nevertheless they represent a tradition now accorded increasing importance by commentators on popular culture. This carnivalesque tradition, which can be traced back to the Middle Ages, underwent numerous transformations. It can be found in the music halls of the nineteenth century (Bailey, 1986a, 1986b) and the seaside outing (Walvin, 1978) with the cheeky seaside postcards, fun fair and naughty belly-laugh humour of end-of-the-pier comedians like Max Miller and Frank Randall. We are now asked not to frown on the mass pleasures of Blackpool but smile knowingly at the populace rightly enjoying their pleasures (Mercer, 1983). It can also be found in the disordered vulgar bric-a-brac of the tasteless working-class popular culture described in books like Nuttall and Carmichael's (1977) *Common Factors/Vulgar Factions*.

It is of course wrong to see this culture as totally sealed off from the middle classes. Elements of the carnivalesque were displaced into literature, something which we find particularly noticeable from the late eighteenth century onwards. The romantic revolt against classicism generated an interest in the particularity and diversity of the folk and primitive culture of the ordinary people (Burke, 1978). Hence the culture of the lower orders remained a source of fascination and the symbolism of this tradition found its way into literature through writers such as Wordsworth, Rousseau and Herder. A further strand of the carnivalesque tradition became taken up in the artistic and literary bohemias and avant-garde which began to develop in Paris and subsequently other large cities after the 1830s (Seigel, 1986). In effect it can be argued that the portion expelled from those who sought, like Arnold, to generate and use what we now refer to as high culture as part of a civilizing process to produce cultivated persons, still remained a source of fascination for the middle classes. Hence the attractions of the 'otherness' of the forest, fair, theatre, circus, slum and savage for the middle classes and their endless representation and duplication in fiction, film and other media.

This tradition represents an important minor tradition within the formation of the culture of Western modernity, and is directly critical of the latter's global universalism and civilizing pretensions. It plays a central role in the upsurge of interest in popular culture since the 1970s which is manifest in a number of ways, not least the relativistic egalitarian spirit we have referred to and the desire to take apart the long-established symbolic hierarchies within higher education which have been based upon the canon of classic great works of literature to the exclusion of popular culture. For example a study of nineteenth-century Boston by DiMaggio (1982) shows the way in which in the early part of the century symphony music (which we would now regard as 'classical' music) was played at the same concert alongside popular songs, freak-show exhibitions and music-hall turns. It was only by the 1870s that sponsoring middle-class literati had managed to separate out the strand which they wished to tend exclusively and conserve into something which we would now regard as high culture. Lawrence Levine (1989) in his recent book *Highbrow/Lowbrow: The Emergence of Cultural Hierarchy in America* uses many a similar argument which he reinforces with a personal anecdote about a conversation with a colleague after watching several Buster Keaton films. Levine said '"Yes", I agreed, "Keaton was a great artist."' The 'colleague appeared puzzled for a moment and then came back with the familiar adjective correction: "A great popular artist"' (Levine, 1989: 1). Another example can be taken from the back cover of Craig McGregor's (1984) book *Pop Goes the Culture* which reads (in multicoloured, multitypefaced format which assaults the eyes):

> *Pop Goes the Culture* ranges over jazz, rock music, Australia, suburban living and equality. Its central theme is the creation of popular culture. For Craig McGregor, Culture is not something neatly sold to 'the masses' by transnational packagers. Rather culture is formed by working people in their everyday

experiences at work, at play and in their communities. The essays in *Pop Goes the Culture* violate the polite norms of 'high' culture. A 'new journalist' Craig McGregor brings a radical populist commitment to his subjects – the jazz of Harlem and New Orleans, the 'Awfulville' suburbs of Australia's cities, the humour of Barry Humphries. His engagement is a bracing antidote to the refined detachment of our cultural establishment.

A further example of the growing audience for popular culture both inside and outside the academy is the American-based Popular Culture Association. The Association held their eighteenth annual meeting in New Orleans in 1988 attended by over 8000 people. This prompted a man who has made his living out of popular culture, Ronald Reagan, to seek out the national media to complain about the waste of money. In the 250 plus pages of the programme one finds papers on 'The Hard-boiled Crime Novel', 'College Basketball', 'Madness in Literature and Poetry', 'Hairweaving: An Example of Material Culture', 'Writing Television History', 'Arthurian Legends', 'Women in the Ministry', 'Gravestones as Indicators of Social Trends', 'Cajun Cooking', 'Andrew Lloyd Webber and Postmodernism', 'How Deep Is Deep Ecology', 'Sex in Rogers and Hammerstein', and in a session on Psychology and Culture two papers coupled together entitled 'Freud and Nietzsche: Death, Desire and Myths of the Origin of Culture' and 'Jung at Heart, Sinatra and His Music 1939–1954'. The puns and catchy titles abound. What is staggering is the sheer range of subjects: almost anything can be included under popular culture and linked to almost any theoretical framework. Looking through the institutional affiliations of the papers given one again finds a very broad range of people from departments of history, cultural studies, politics, literature, English, sociology, popular culture, modern languages, commerce, economics, geography, anthropology – in fact the full range of the humanities and the social sciences. Apart from a sense of the impossibility of grasping the sheer range of subjects and orientations on view, we have to face the implications of this shift, which is also taking place in Britain, Europe and other countries, for the structure of higher education.

In this context it is worth quoting Michael Schudson's (1987) remark in his state of the art article 'The New Validation of Popular Culture' that 'the new study of popular culture now offers a serious challenge to the identity of the modern university'. This statement can be taken to prompt a number of points. First, the study of popular culture has been usually excluded from higher education – or given a very minor role within history courses. It was at best regarded in the same way as we have long regarded folklore in Britain: something for the interested amateur but not really worthy of systematic study – certainly not to be seen as something which develops minds. Its inclusion raises questions about the principles of construction of higher education in the humanities and social sciences. It makes implicit hierarchies explicit. It questions the received tradition and canon.

Second, it represents an attack on the notion of ordered unity and systemicity from the perspective of diversity and disorder. To take two examples of this process which entails the spatialization out and deconstruction of symbolic hierarchies: the study of Sinatra songs or Gothic gravestones carries as much weight as the French Revolution or Tolstoy. The second example comes to mind from an article by Elizabeth Wilson (1985) in which she argued that knitting is a valid art form whose exclusion discriminated against women and that it should take its place in fine art courses and exhibitions.

Third, this egalitarian and democratic spirit not only means that educationalists have to decentre their enterprise to recognize a wide diversity of regional and local alternative cultures and practices, but this could be achieved both in terms of the diversity of the content taught and in terms of a plurality of educational forms employing different media.

Fourth, from this perspective with its tendency to globalize diversity, a common culture in terms of shared values, or a common culture as a project to be made, becomes impossible. Even the definition of a common culture as a shared language becomes retainable only at the deepest civilizational level, as attempts are made to rediscover and resurrect traditions, local and regional variations – the babble of different tongues which have been suppressed.

Fifth, in terms of content (and in some cases the form of presentation), with the absence of an agreed cultural hierarchy or developmental notion of history. the study of popular culture can become influenced by 'the interesting', 'the current', or 'the fascinating' and can be seen as similar to the experience of watching television. The academic becomes an interpreter of the exotic and banal. Relativism becomes the watchword in an 'anything goes' attitude, which according to one of the leading American anthropologists. Clifford Geertz (1983: 275) means that anthropologists should conceive their role as 'merchants of astonishment' (see Friedman, 1987: 43). Here we move into André Malraux's (1967) imaginary 'museum without walls' in which all the styles, traditions and cultural forms of the past can be represented (Roberts, 1988). But not in a developmental sequence; rather, the principle of organization becomes montage and eclecticism, with the nearest juxtaposed to the most distant (see also Bann, 1984).

We are now in the familiar territory of postmodernism. The term 'postmodernism' and the associated term 'postmodernity' are frequently used in a confusing range of ways to suggest: a movement in the arts and architecture which has transcended modernism; a new epoch; a new range of cultural sensibilities involving the effacement of the boundary between art and everyday life; an antifoundational mode of theorizing. This last aspect is developed by Lyotard (1984) in his influential book *The Postmodern Condition*. Lyotard argues that the major foundational theories, or in his terminology *meta-narratives*, of Western modernity – science, humanism, socialism and Marxism – are essentially flawed, as they are unable to ground their own authority in a claim to universality. Rather, for Lyotard, we should accept the bounded, limited nature of knowledge. In effect we should accept the scaled-down claims and tolerance of diversity in local knowledge.

The implications of this shift are particularly marked with respect to the role of the intellectuals. Contemporary intellectuals, according to Lyotard (1988), should accept a more limited definition of this vocation and be less willing to pronounce on humanity; and recognize the limited nature of their claims. Hence it is argued that one central feature of postmodernism can be related to the changing function of the role of intellectuals. In effect they have lost their confident role as prospective and potential *legislators* for society and humankind to take on the more restricted role of *interpreters*, who are able to ransack the vast array of cultural traditions in order to produce interesting and exotic material for wider audiences (Bauman, 1988). The role shifts from confident educator, who possesses confidence in his judgement of taste and the need to mould society in terms of it, to that of the commentator, who represents and de codes the minutiae of cultural objects and traditions without judging them or hierarchizing them. Indeed the intention of the intellectual may cease to be guided by notions of objectivity, that an accurate interpretation is possible and desirable (as for example in Dilthey's hermeneutics), and become more one in which immersion into the experience of the culture is sought. In short some intellectuals may seek to 'go native'.

The loss of confidence in the projects of Western modernity and modernization which the interest in postmodernism points to is not only found among Western intellectuals, it is also occurring in the newly industrializing countries and the Third World. Here we can make explicit the link between postmodernism and popular culture which we have been developing, for it is clear that postmodernism celebrates the multifaceted nature, and bewildering and nonhierarchical disorder of popular cultures. In discussing the position of the intellectual in Brazil, Osiel (1984: 249) writes:

> The shift in intellectual sensibility from the fifties to the present could be crudely summarized as one from a negative to a positive view of popular culture. The intellectual once perceived, in the religious and recreational practices of the poor, the very antithesis of what they sought for their country's future. The theologians saw doctrine, deviation and paganism. The liberal politicians saw illogic and unreason. The Marxists saw alienation and false consciousness. The social scientists saw particularism and ascriptiveness. All four saw superstition.

Now the Brazilian intellectuals find spontaneity, communality and authenticity in the culture of the poor, values which should not be sacrificed for the falsely found universalism of (Western) modernity. This appreciation of the common people and what in the past were seen as their vulgar, primitive, superstitious and disordered culture contrasts with the rational world-ordering stance which we find in much of intellectual culture. Collins (1988a: 152) draws attention to the ways in which Weber saw religious intellectuals and other symbol specialists as propelled by the drive towards intellectual consistency in an endeavour to achieve logical and rational coherence in systems of both belief and conduct. In effect they have an interest in presenting to lay audiences a vision of the world as coherent, as rationally ordered and orderable. The concept of a common culture in both its manifestations within the social sciences and cultural studies can be understood in this way.

The broader question of why this project should be abandoned and the incoherence and the diversity of uncommon cultures embraced, is difficult to answer. In the first place we should be cautious about taking postmodernism as a wholly unique theoretical stance. A similar evaluation of the culture of the common people occurred in the late eighteenth century with the discovery of popular culture on the part of Herder and others in the movement which became known as Romanticism (Burke, 1978). It may be possible to understand such swings towards discovery and identifying with the culture of the populace in terms of the changing power-balances and interdependencies between classes and class fractions. In particular the emergence of large numbers of educated members of the middle class in the form of a distinctive cohort which has the self-consciousness to regard itself as a 'generation' may threaten existing culture establishments. Outsider groups who are faced with a monopoly situation, in which knowledge in the form of a stable symbolic hierarchy and canon is transmitted to initiates through a patronage and sponsorship system operated by a stable establishment, may have to adopt usurpatory tactics. Phases of intense competition, it can be argued, tend to be transitional between more stable phases of ordered exclusion and monopolization (see Murphy, 1989). There is every reason to believe that this will be the case with the present phase of cultural declassification, and that there will be a return to a more stable symbolic hierarchy and canon. There are, however, a number of points which can be mentioned which suggest that the current phase of cultural declassification might be more sustained.

In the first place, there exists a tradition of cultural declassification among those engaged in cultural production. While this may be a minor or lesser tradition within the culture of Western modernity, there is a significant line of continuity in Romanticism, the artistic bohemias and avant-gardes, modernism and postmodernism with an emphasis upon transgression. the popular and the quest for newness and innovation. This countercultural tradition has periodically gained greater prominence within the mainstream of cultural production and consumption (for example, in the 1960s).

Second, the long-term process of functional democratization has meant that the balance of power between dominant and less powerful groups has narrowed to the extent that it is less feasible to regard established groups as able to monopolize definitions of culture and civilized behaviour. The extension of higher education to outsider groups in the post-war era coupled with the expansion of the numbers of cultural intermediaries in the mass media has made it more difficult for established groups to retain a monopoly. In effect nationalism, the tendency towards centralization that accompanied the state formation process, in which attempts were made to eliminate differences in order to create a unified integrating culture for the nation, has given way to decentralization and the acknowledgement of local, regional and subcultural differences in the Western world. This process has been accompanied by the emergence of larger numbers of outsider cultural intermediaries who are predisposed to seek out and let be heard those popular and uncommon cultures via an expanding range of mass media for an expanding audience of people interested in the full range of cultural matters.

Third, if we consider the relations between nation-states and power blocs on the global level, it can be argued that a shift is taking place away from the West. As we have already mentioned, dimensions of this process can be found in anthropology with the 'other' speaking back and disputing the anthropologist's interpretative authority, and in the Third World intellectuals' rejection of commitment to Western modernity and modernization in favour of a recuperation of their own popular cultures and traditions. This points to a situation in which other nations are able to resist the various oversimplifying cultural labels which Western nations have attached to them, such as 'savage', barbaric', 'native', 'backward', 'exotic', 'colourful', 'simple', and through a shift in their relative power force the West to take notice of their own alternative formulations of cultural identity. Said (1978) has drawn attention to this process with regard to the Western transference of their own repressed otherness' in the construction of the Orient as exotic.

Conclusion

It should therefore be clear that we cannot attempt to understand the notion of a common culture without asking the question 'Who is speaking about it?' This directs us to the important role of symbol specialists in formulating the idea of a common culture. This is as much the case for sociologists and anthropologists who seek to persuade us that there is a coherent common culture 'out there' in the social world as it is for literary theorists and critics who are committed to bringing a 'genuine', integrated common culture into being. It has been argued that there has been a shift away from both these positions in recent years and that the discovery and celebration of the vulgar and the popular – uncommon cultures – should be linked to changes in the nature of intellectual production and in the relationship between intellectuals and other groups. Finally, we should mention that one definition of a common culture is a common language. While advocates of popular culture might point to the wide range of regional, local and subcultural languages and vernacular forms which adherents of a common language have to suppress in the very act of its formulation and codification, the notion of a language can also refer to a deeper cultural level. Here one thinks of the figures, tropes and recurrent forms which may be common to a particular language at a point in time (Bann, 1984) and which underpin our particular sense of the order or ambiguity inherent in social life (Levine, 1985). That such deeply coded formal features underpin families of languages and civilizational complexes is also apparent. Here then we are pointing to a notion of a common culture not on the level of *content* – the possession of an integrated set of beliefs and values – but more on the level of form – the underlying formal generative possibilities for a recognizable set of variations. In this context we might close with a reference to Durkheim (1964) who drew attention to the noncontractual elements of contract, the culturally embedded and taken-for-granted set of common moral assumptions which underlie economic transactions. In this sense it is possible to speak of the order underlying conflict as in, for example, the case of strikes in which both parties, although often engaged in a bitter conflict, play it out according to an implicitly acknowledged set of ground rules, which are nevertheless common while never having been overtly agreed. It is perhaps the generative formal articulation of the meaning of a common culture, in which communality entails the capacity to recognize differences as legitimate and valid, which forms a thread uniting the conception of a common culture from Eliot and Williams down to the contemporary students of popular culture.

Notes

My understanding of multiculturalism has benefited a great deal from discussions with Roland Robertson and Bryan S. Turner and I am grateful to acknowledge this support.

1 It should be stated that Sorokin found an empirical lack of integration with widespread incoherent mixtures the most frequent type.

2 See Lockwood, 1964: Dahrendorf, 1968: Gouldner, 1971: Giddens, 1984: Elias, 1971. What some of these critics miss is the shift in conceptions of culture Parsons employs over time. In short it may do him an injustice to focus solely on *The Social System* (1951) phase to the neglect of the notion of culture as a 'code' found in his later writings (see Schmidt, 1988).

3 Although it is evident that, in contrast to Durkheim, Williams works within an English tradition, which Lepenies (1988: 155 ff.) refers to as 'concealed sociology', with its characteristic lack of theoretical systemicity and shifting and, at times, rambling argumentation.

10

The Globalization of Diversity

Each sees what is in his own heart.

(Max Weber, 1949: 107)

We live now amidst the ruins of a civilization, but most of these ruins are in our minds.

(John Lukács, *The Passing of the Modern Age*,
quoted in Kramer, 1982: 36)

In focusing attention on the postmodern one of the central concerns has been to raise the questions 'Why this question?' and 'Why and how has postmodernism become a central issue in cultural life today?' If postmodernism is from the point of view of modernism a sign and symptom of cultural disorder, then modernism, with its increasingly popular associated term modernity, is from the perspective of postmodernism a constant which highlights images of order, unity and coherence. Both terms feed off each other and often seem propelled by a binary logic of opposition which sharpens the differentiation as the process of conceptualization runs ahead of social and cultural realities. It has been argued that many of the characteristic features listed under postmodernism can be found within the modern, and indeed the premodern. The aestheticization of everyday life, the tendency for a figural culture of shifting images and the controlled or playful de-control of the emotions have all been discussed as examples. Given this, how far can it be argued that what is labelled the postmodern' has always existed. and it is only now that we are granting it significance? And if this is the case how far can we attempt to understand the social process which led to this particular conceptional frame (1) becoming adopted within particular institutional practices and by particular sets of cultural specialists and (2) being proliferated and accepted by particular audiences and publics?

To investigate this process is not to fall for the banality that postmodernism is a social construction, or a deliberate and conscious power-move in the prestige economy of cultural specialists, or cultural intermediaries and entrepreneurs in the middle classes. Such interpretations have the danger of reducing postmodernism to strategic action and miss the ways in which it offers and acts as relevant means of orientation for particular cultural specialists (artists, intellectuals, academics) and their various audiences. To focus on postmodernism as a means of orientation is to emphasize its place within the processes which form and deform the cultural sphere and give rise to distinctive artistic and intellectual life orders. These life orders have long sustained subcurrents and subcultures which have displayed a fascination with the popular, the carnivalesque, the wild, the savage, the undomesticated, the part which the order-establishing drive of civilizing processes has sought to contain and exclude both on the social and individual levels. The democratic, populist impulses, the fascination with 'the other', the tolerance of popular pleasures, the interest in intense, disconnected affect-charge experiences which are associated with postmodernism, can be located within this tradition. The associated references to the 'end of the social', 'the end of normativity', 'the end of the intellectuals', 'the end of the avant-garde' and general 'fin-de-millennium' pathos which are often linked to postmodernism, may then not indicate an abandonment of all the old frames, but rather the development of more flexible modes of classification. A new frame which entails a more flexible generative structure within which a wider range of differences can be recognized and tolerated. This can occur without the previous rigid reaction of exclusion and repression of what we are perceived as emotionally overwhelming, embarrassing or self-threatening encounters.

This focus upon the development of a more flexible habitus on the part of cultural specialists, intermediaries and audiences can be related to the discussion of the problem of a common culture in 'Common Culture or Uncommon Cultures?' In that context Durkheim's notion of the non-contractual basis of contract, and the underlying cultural consensus within which strikes and industrial disputes take place, were given as illustrations of the notion of a taken-for-granted, flexible generative structure which permits differences to exist, and this was taken as the model for a common culture. Durkheim also employed this theoretical framework in his argument about the religion of humanity. For Durkheim, as societies became more complex this social and cultural differentiation increased to the extent that the only thing individuals were able to retain in common was their humanity (Lukes, 1973: 338 ff.). In effect the 'idea of the human person became a powerful symbol, one of the few examples of the sacred which had potential for universal appeal in the modern world. This conceptualization of unity through diversity, or a unity permitting differences, is becoming more acceptable today as part of some of the changes which have given rise to, or are associated with, postmodernism that are undermining the cultural integration project of the nation-state. At the same time, and an important part of this process, we have both the incorporation of states into larger units and the transformative effects of global economic and cultural flows. Both point to larger and necessarily more abstract units: the unity within which diversity can take place. An example of the former is the current efforts to create a

European identity sponsored by the European Community (see Schlesinger, 1987) in such a way as to allow cultural variation and unity through diversity. Yet to talk about a common European culture in the abstract is problematic; rather, it is much more useful to observe and refer to specific sequences and practices. In this context it is instructive to note that the current efforts to create an 'imagined community' for Europe, to generate unifying symbols which differentiate Europeans from others, draw sustenance from areas of cultural conflict. The greater Europeanization of television services becomes one such rallying call in relation to the perceived threat posed by the United States (Schlesinger, 1987). To know who you are, you need to know who you are not: the potential for conflict with outside bodies allows for the construction of the other as threatening rather than fascinating and exotic and increases the potential for discovering self-identifying features.

The task for those cultural specialists who construct the 'imagined communities' (Anderson, 1983) and police the boundaries of a common culture is made that much easier if there exists a common *ethnie*. The notion of *ethnie*, the set of symbols, myths, memories, heroes, events, landscapes and traditions woven together in popular consciousness (Smith, 1990), is the ground for a common culture. But whereas intellectuals were able to mobilize the various *ethnie* as part of the state-formation processes in Europe in the late eighteenth century and help create national cultures, the parallel case for the emerging European superstate and its potential supernational culture is, needless to say, more problematic. The danger of the rhetoric of modernism (in the sense of modernity) is to assume that all cultures can be reconstructed, that under the impetus of capitalism or state-formation processes 'all that is solid melts into air'. As we move towards the end of the twentieth century we are discovering that the *ethnie* has much greater resilience than many commentators and politicians ever imagined. Yet if we move our frame of reference from the supernational state to the transnational or global, the 'highest' level of possible synthesis, we can discuss a number of problems which throw light not only on these issues of a common culture and unity in diversity, but also illuminate the rise of postmodernism with which we began.

I have argued throughout against those who would wish to present the tendency on the global level to be one of cultural integration and homogenization – for example those notions of multinational capitalism, Americanization, media imperialism and consumer culture which assume that local differences are being obliterated via these universal forces. Yet, if we accept that there will always be misreadings, ambiguities and the resistance of the *ethnie* and popular traditions to such forces, does this mean that we should abandon the concept of a global culture altogether? The increased international flows of money, goods, people, images and information have given rise to 'third cultures', which are transnational and mediate between national cultures; the global financial markets, international law, and various international agencies and institutions are examples (Gessner and Schade, 1990). They point to a level beyond interstate exchanges. Yet there is a further sense in which we can talk about a global culture: the process of global compression whereby the world becomes united to the extent that it is regarded as one place (Robertson, 1990). The globalization process thus leads to the acceptance of the view that the world is a singular place, which acts as a form capable of generating and sustaining various images of what the world is, or should be. From this perspective a global culture does not point to homogeneity, or a common culture, but rather it can be argued that the increased sense that we all share the same small planet and are daily involved in an increasing range of cultural contacts with others could increase the range of conflicting definitions of the world with which we are brought into contact. This coming together of competing national cultures engaged in global cultural prestige contests is one possibility for a global culture.

The other possibility is linked to postmodernism. It has been argued that one of the state's central aims since its formation has been to produce a common culture in which local differences have been homogenized and strangers within the state boundaries have been assimilated (Bauman, 1990). The abandonment of such state-led cultural crusades and nationalist assimilation projects which were central to modernity is one symptom of the move towards postmodernity. This offers the prospect of a greater chance of tolerance as we enter an era in which national and cultural boundaries are more easily crossed and redrawn. This second possibility suggests that postmodernism offers the prospect of a unity through diversity which might lead to the realization of the dream of a secular ecumene, one which was based upon some notion of humanity as we discussed in relation to Durkheim. It should be added that the only way (without the emergence of a world state) we can imagine global cultural homogeneity and identity being generated would be in terms of some pan-global threat. To date this cultural possibility is only to be found in the pages of science fiction books.

Whichever of these two – or other – historical possibilities becomes actualized it can be argued that the movement in either direction, or the swings between the two, cannot but help to raise the general profile of culture and bring cultural questions to the fore. Crosscultural encounters tend to problematize the taken-for-granted everyday cultural habits and dispositions which have sedimented into social life. On the global level postmodernism not only signifies a revival of the neo-romantic interest in the exotic other, but the fact that the other now speaks back and disputes the claims of what were once assumed to be the universal cultural centres of the world and are now increasingly seen merely as centres of the limited Western project of modernity. We are only now – prompted by the rise of Japan – starting to think of what it might entail to translate our culture into the classificatory schemes and symbolic hierarchies of a potentially world-dominant non-Western civilizational bloc with its own self-confident global cultural project. This suggests that in the last analysis, if we are to conceptualize the problems of the globalization of cultural diversity and postmodernism it is vital that we consider the shifting power-balances and interdependencies that exist between nation-states and civilizational blocs which increasingly bind them together in the emerging global order.

11

Modernity and the Cultural Question

> We are past the time of generally applicable forms.
>
> (Novalis, Fragment 2167, cited in Luhmann, 1998: 21)

Modernity is a concept which continues to fascinate. Yet like its associated terms in the conceptual set deriving from the modern, the more the term is interrogated the more it seems to evaporate into a series of contradictory definitions. The continuing interest in modernity is all the more surprising, at a time when the mood in the social sciences and humanities has swung away from higher level categories of knowledge which claim universal authority towards a greater sense of diversity, difference and singularity. Apart from society, nature or humanity, it is hard to find a higher level and more general concept than modernity. On one level this continued interest is reproductive, given that many major figures in the social sciences and humanities such as Habermas, Lyotard, Giddens, Therborn, Hall, Appadurai, Beck, Bauman and Chakrabarty, have all written on modernity and its associated terms in the last twenty years and the ripples are still spreading out with the secondary literature and accounts of the debates continuing to grow. A noted event was the Habermas paper 'Modernity: An Incomplete Project', which he gave on receiving the Adorno prize in 1980 (Habermas, 1985a). Habermas's depiction of Foucault and Derrida as young conservatives raised the tempo of a debate about the value of the modern and the emergent postmodern. Despite their pleas about the inappropriateness of the term, Foucault and Derrida became associated with the postmodern and labelled postmodernists.

The Habermas confrontation with the postmodern linked into a number of high profile debates which had started in the 1970s, drawing on artistic postmodernism which had flourished in the 1960s. Not only artistic modernism was assumed to have become exhausted, but also the modern project itself in all its various manifestations: hence opening up a space in which the challenge was to think beyond the modern. This transference from an artistic and intellectual to epochal usage seemed to trouble few people in the social sciences when they took up the debates and began to search social life and cultural forms for evidence of the postmodern. The modern and postmodern and the associated family of terms, were batted back and forth between Europe and the United States with a range of major figures involved and invoked, such as Bell, Baudrillard, Deleuze, Derrida, Foucault, Habermas, Jameson, Lyotard and Vattimo (see this book, chapter 1).

In the post-war era, up until the mid-1970s in sociology, it was capitalism which was the dominant term. The influential *Introduction to the History of Sociology* (Barnes, 1966) has no place for modernity in the index, although it had a large number of references to capitalism. Anthony Giddens' (1973) influential early work *Capitalism and Modern Social Theory* foregrounds capitalism, also prominent in the index, but has no place for modern or modernity. Yet by the early 1990s the focus for Giddens was more directly on spelling out the contours of modernity in books with titles such as *The Consequences of Modernity* and *Modernity and Self-Identity*. In cultural studies, it may well be possible to chart a similar shift with Stuart Hall and his associates producing the influential Open University volume *Formations of Modernity* in 1991. When terminology shifts it is possible to see this renaming process as a strategic move in the field of academic and intellectual cultural production (Bourdieu, 1984). A new generation of scholars can confine a previous one to history and make them appear outdated if they succeed in imposing a new, allegedly superior set of concepts.

In the late 1970s and 1980s the interest in postmodernism, then, helped to stimulate an interest in revisiting and defending the modern. Nietzsche remarked that what has a history cannot be defined. There is clearly a plurality of genealogical lines, with breaks and stoppages as we look back into the histories of the terminology around 'the modern.' According to Habermas (1985b, who follows Hans Robert Jauss), one of the earliest usages of the term modern in the western tradition is the Latin term *modernus*, first used in the late fifth century in order to distinguish the officially Christian present, from the Roman and pagan past. Here the emphasis is on the consciousness of a new time, a break with the past, the start of a new epoch (cf. the Renaissance, or the Quarrel between the Ancients and Moderns in France in the late seventeenth century).

It could be argued that in the 1980s there was a similar sense that we were on the edge of a shift to new times. This had been prefaced by the so-called 'cultural revolution' of the 1960s generation, the disputes about the movement into 'post-industrial society' (Bell, Touraine et al.), the new emergent information society, the decline of United States' power with the Vietnam War defeat, the 1973 oil crisis and predicted limits to growth which signalled the end of the vision of permanent accumulation and abundance. There was a clear searching for new terminology to better account for these changes allegedly signalling the move towards a new social order, or even epoch: postmodernity. This led to a good deal of inventiveness in rethinking and expanding the set of terms deriving from the modern: modernity, modernization, postmodernization, high modernity, late modernity, reflexive modernity, transmodernity, liquid modernity, postmodernity, modernism, postmodernism, global modernity, global modernities, multiple modernities, alternative modernities, hypermodernity and countermodernity.

The focus of this chapter is on the relationship of modernity to culture. It can be argued that the cultural dimension is important in the literature on modernity for a number of reasons. First, culture is often invoked in the accounts which see modernity as having its exclusive origins in Western Europe. There is also the related sociological argument about the transition from traditional to modern societies, and 'take off' growth factors leading to modernization. Second, there is the question of the culture of modernity in the sense of whether this is a particular generic experience of modern life which leads to certain common expressions and cultural forms. Third, there is the global aspect to the question, whether there are multiple or alternative modernities. There is also a key dimension to the process of conceptualization linking it to the shifting balance of global power. As Western power declines relatively, it can be argued that we will see the emergence of a range of different definitions and solutions to the modern condition: complexes of interests will emerge as the new powerful players on the global stage seek to retell the origins of modernity. The shifting global balance of power, manifest in economic and cultural power shifts, is also accompanied by changes in the production and circulation of knowledge. Finally, this relates back to the questions Max Weber raised about values and modern life: what are the constraints, parameters and dilemmas of modern experience? Is there any sense in which they can be regarded as having hardened into a common fate? Can we in any sense still talk about a modern or postmodern condition?[1] How do we understand the cultural possibilities of modern or contemporary life for innovation and invention in a globalizing and interconnected world?

In this chapter I will seek to address a number of aspects of these questions. A central focus will be on the commonly held assumption that it was the unique cultural complex of the West that gave rise to modernity, through the way it provided the generative source, which could be transmitted into economic and socially structured forces. The case of China provides an interesting counterexample to the orthodox sociological views which tend to depict Western societies as dynamic and protomodern and China and Asia as tradition bound and reproductive. The current wave of scholarship, doubtless spurred by China's rise since the 1990s, is restructuring the archive to discover a much more significant and central role for China in world history and pointing to many similarities in terms of economic growth with Western societies up until the early nineteenth century. If these assumptions are correct, it is to be expected that there would be evidence of the emergence of an expanding literate cultural sphere and consumer culture in parts of Asia and this is discussed through the examples of Ming Dynasty China and Tokugawa Japan. The interesting development of a cultural aesthetic sphere, or series of enclaved public spheres, is also discussed through the case of Japan, in its alleged protomodern phase. The emphasis upon aesthetic perceptions, civility and identity-switching, are contrasted to Habermas's theory of the bourgeois public sphere's more overt political function as a key outcome of European modernity. The relevance of these questions in terms of the building of a global public sphere today, is also discussed. At the same time, the series of depictions of Tokugawa Japan by twentieth-century Japanese scholars as modern, protomodern or traditional, highlight one of the central problems in research on modernity: the modern as harbinger of the new is endlessly subject to recasting in each succeeding historical phase, as new generations address their present value concerns to reconstruct the lens through which they illuminate the past. Tradition and modern can all too easily operate as praise-words and blame-words from a present-day perspective primarily interested in constructing its own historical uniqueness, communality or difference from the past. In the final sections, the chapter returns to a discussion of the different views of culture in relation to modernity and argues against the assumption of spatially separated, integrated 'deep structured' cultures, to discuss the questions of cultural invention within modernity. For some this inventiveness provides the basis in the contemporary world for the generation of a range of alternative modernities.

The modern in the Western conceptual order

Sociology has long worked off a dichotomous model in which the modern, scientific, rational, industrial stage is contrasted with dogmatic, irrational traditional knowledge. This distinction between tradition and modern societies, often conceived in ideal-type terms, became established as the disciplinary conventional wisdom. The dynamic for the transition between the two types was often located in the West's unique cultural constellation. In the influential Weberian formulation, the 'spirit of capitalism' behind the success of Western modernity was linked to a particular world-changing ethic, 'inner-worldly asceticism,' with its purest form found in the Protestant sects of the European Reformation. Max Weber's sociology of religion, involving studies of the religions of China and India, was seen as providing further evidence for the thesis, by arguing that these other world religions lacked this inner-worldly ascetic ethic with its transformative potential.

Max Weber's whole intellectual endeavour, started from the acceptance of the limited and perspectival nature of our knowledge (see Weber, 1949). Weber was well aware that although he tackled major questions such as the origins of capitalism and 'the fate of modernity,' these questions could only be formulated through values. In effect these issues were selected because they were relevant to his own values and the values of his age. Indeed, Weber emphasises that history was not only coloured anew from the point of view of each age, but that the potential for cumulative scientific knowledge was strictly limited. He was pulled towards a radical historicist position, and at the same time towards delineating the emergent historical universals which gathered force and effectively became our human fate, as in his theory of rationalization and disenchantment of the world, which is central to his view of modernity. He was well aware of the limited nature of the answers we get to the questions we ask from history.[2] Today, a century after Weber (1930) first formulated his Protestant Ethic thesis, other relevant questions have necessarily emerged. Today, people are no longer speculating about a potential 'decline of the West' in the large civilizational brush strokes in the manner of Spengler who wrote in the wake of World War I, but concretely witnessing 'the rise of the East,' the dramatic gains in power of Asia over the last quarter of century.[3]

The rise of Asia could also see a shift in knowledge formation which could well redefine the way we conceive questions such as modernity and modern society. Globalization processes not only mean the intensification of flows of goods, people, information, data, money, but also academic knowledge too (Featherstone, 2006a). The predominant form of academic knowledge flow, markedly in the social sciences and humanities, has entailed the export of theory from Western centres to the peripheries, with raw data moving the other way (Sakai, 2001). The conceptual order and classification system of disciplines such as sociology formed in the West is assumed to have supplied universal categories. There has been minimal interest in utilizing theoretical formulations or classification systems arising outside of the West.[4] For those outside the West who wish to have their ideas taken seriously in the global field, the English-language dominated academic investment curve is steep. It is difficult to shift the existing power balances and patronage networks in the production and dissemination of global knowledge, although clearly postmodernism, poststructuralism and postcolonial theory have had some intellectual impact, yet their impact on mainstream disciplinary structures and modes of classification and method-ology has been limited.

It is possible to envisage some of the conditions which could produce a shift in this balance of power away from the West. There are of course many complicating factors, not least the shibboleth terms West and East, which conceal internal heterogeneity: in knowledge terms there is a West in the East, as well as many people moving from the East for education in the West. Yet, the rise of China and East Asia could also be accompanied by, not only the broadening of the type of content taught, but to a greater questioning of some of the categories and classificatory terms used. This could lead to the investigation of alternative genealogies of global history, along with the expansion of the canon to take in Asian figures. With some predicting the parity of China with the United States in economic terms by 2030, some of these shifts in knowledge formation could well be underway and become manifest within a generation.[5] It is also to be expected that such changes would be uneven: those parts of higher education which are tied more directly to the global economy such as business and management education and training could well continue to produce skilled system analysts, who work with more abstract forms of knowledge (Reich, 2006).

In the social sciences and the humanities, theory could well continue to be exported from the Western centres, but in the longer term we can assume there would be an expansion in the horizons of Western theorists not only to take into account the 'abstract non-Western other', but to rethink the scope of their concepts and delve into concrete historical and cultural detail. Especially so when some of the critics of Western knowledge classifications who contest the claim to universality, now speak from within the West, or are in a process of constant movement between the West and other parts of the world. Here we think of books such as *Provincializing Europe* (Chakrabarty, 2000) and *On the Postcolony* (Mbembe, 2001) both of which take a critical stance on the concept of modernity as used in Western intellectual thought, to show its inherent deficiency when applied to Indian or African contexts. Hence, the range of postcolonial and other critical writings following on from the influential work of Said (Venn, 2006), suggests the start of the process of excavation and reordering of the knowledge archive (see Featherstone, 2000, 2006b). This, of course, is not the archive Weber knew, but an expanding archive in which new questions and angles of research are leading to the rediscovery and reclassification of material driven by a new sense of value relevance (see Featherstone and Venn, 2006). With the shift in the global balance of power towards Asia, we are starting to see a rejection of some of the 'orientalist' categories and assumptions about the ossified unchanging East contrasted to the dynamic West. This binary was easily fed into the tradition–modernity dichotomy with temporal and spatial dimensions. Tradition not only seen as the past of the West, but as central to cultural reproduction in non-Western societies, which would have allegedly remained confined to tradition without West intervention.

China modern and the question of tradition

As China continues to return growth figures of more than 10 per cent GDP in recent years and is becoming increasingly central to the global economy, it is now on a trajectory which will see it resume a position as one of the dominant world powers. It is no accident that the scholarly interest in China increases and the number of book series, texts, journals and university courses devoted to China rises. China assumes a growing position on the horizon of knowledge and not only its present geopolitical potential, but its role as the centre of the world economy up until the end of the eighteenth century (Pomeranz, 2000; Gunder Frank, 1998) is currently under scrutiny, casting doubts on previous depictions of China as ossified and stagnant. This suggests the reconstruction of the China archive, the re-assemblage of material which became scattered around the world in the wake of the twentieth-century China wars and diaspora. The reconstituted archive will doubtless form the basis for a revaluation of the role of China in world history, a process which will potentially emphasise the many occluded and obscured contributions made by Chinese people to the stock of knowledge of humanity.[6]

China, clearly is becoming increasingly relevant for our values, for the values of our age. Yet a century ago, when Max Weber, was developing his Protestant Ethic thesis, China occupied the category of the counterexample. Weber (1930) sought to link Protestantism to the greater rationalization and systematization of conduct in daily life, laying the ground for the development of the voracious modernizing capitalist spirit. For Weber, this ethos was unique to Western Europe with its base in Christianity (although he did trace back the origins of the rational conduct back to Ancient Judaism and Biblical prophecy). For Weber, the other major civilizations and world religions, specifically the religions of China and India, did not have a similar basis for the generation of an inner-worldly ethic which had world transformative potential. Rather, they were generally 'other-worldly' religions or 'world accommodating' in relation to conduct. The logic of Weber's argument is to focus on the impediments for the growth of capitalism provided by Buddhism, Taoism and Confucianism, Hinduism and Islam. Key elements of Weber's argument are that capitalist modernity is based upon the separation of the public and the private which permits the extensive development of formal rationality, stimulating the process of rationalization which penetrates into all the various spheres of life. This was seen as a condition which occurred uniquely in the West. It was the extension of this rationality, which helped produce capitalism – along with industrialization, urbanization, rational state governmental administration, secularization, individualism, science and technology, the various dimensions of social life which make up modernity.

In contrast, the rest of the world, especially when viewed through the prism of late nineteenth- and early twentieth-century colonialism, was seen as static and subject to the reproduction of tradition.[7] The operation of the binary tradition–modernity within sociology tended always to cast Asia on the wrong side of the divide, forever subjected to constraining tradition, or more recently in the twentieth century as trying to catch up, to modernize. Tradition, as Elias and others have pointed out, often operates as a blameword, suggesting the domination of habit and fixed everyday routines. Modern people in contrast are presented as engaging in rational calculation of courses of action and exercising individual choice. Traditional culture is presented as integrated, normative and involving inflexible social bonds and belief systems. By contrast modern culture is seen as dynamic, innovative and inventive; as obsessed with 'the new' and the excitement of transformation. We will return to these two depictions of culture later. But it is also important to note that once we have societies depicted as traditional it is very hard to see any immanent means of change. Change has to come from the outside: traditional Asian societies are seen as having to wait for the West to liberate them from tradition and open the door to modernity.

Tradition and modern are terms, then, that tend to cast societies on either side of the binary. But if we look at the history of China and Japan it is clear that the terminology is inadequate. Recent research has started to show that many of the preconceptions previously held in the West about the lack of commercial enterprise, absence of merchant groups, individualism or market freedom, do not stand up to scrutiny. The evidence about China is compelling. The world economy prior to 1800 has been described as 'Sinocentric' (Hobson, 2004: 61). Pomeranz (2000: 17) remarks that core regions in China and Japan circa 1750 seem to resemble the most advanced parts of Western Europe, combining sophisticated agriculture, commerce, and non-mechanized industry in similar, arguably even more fully realized ways.

Indeed, Hobson (2004: 77) further tells us that Chinese share of world manufacturing output outstripped Britain's until 1860 and that 'the Indian share was higher than the whole of Europe's in 1750 and was 85 percent higher than Britain's as late as 1830'. In addition it is argued that it is mistaken to claim that after the withdrawal of Admiral Zheng He's 'great ships' in the Ming Dynasty in 1434, China remained closed to foreign trade (Pieterse, 2006: 412). It is argued that China experienced not only proto-industrial development, but industrial development (in ceramics and later cotton). As Goody (2004: 104) remarks China enjoyed

> ... an age of astonishing creativity and transformation during the Song (960–1279) and the Yuan (1279–1368) dynasties ... the period 1000–1500 CE witnessed an economic revolution such as the world had never seen. Cities grew, mainly in the south-east, agriculture was transformed, commerce flourished. Gunpowder, the magnetic compass and printing – the three inventions that Francis Bacon named in 1605 as the foundation of the modern order in Europe – had all come into common use in China in Song times.

After 1492, with the opening up of trade with the Americas to Western European nations, the access to gold and silver, the development of slave plantation agriculture, begins to move the global balance of economic power away from China towards Europe. For economic historians such as Gunder Frank (1998) or Blaut (1993, 2000) the only way in which European nations could gain admission to the China dominated global economy and open up trade relations with China was through the forceful acquisition of silver through the conquest of the Americas.[8] Silver was the only commodity China valued from the West and needed it in order to replenish its treasury. Gunder Frank emphasizes the interrelatedness of the world economy, and the way in which precious metals, trade, technology and knowledge moved around through an opportunity–cost logic. Hence it is not surprising that many of the Chinese inventions documented by Needham (1980) found their way to Europe, even if their origins were obscured, or that Arab medicine along with Greek philosophy came into Europe via the Moors in Spain (see discussion of Averroes by Venn, 2007).

Yet against Gunder Frank's assumption that it was only the American bullion that permitted Europeans to gain entry to the China-dominated world economy, Goody (2004: 77) emphasises the importance of seapower and weaponry: the means of destruction. The epic voyages of Columbus and the Portuguese navigators occurred in and after the 1490s, much later than the exploratory voyages to Africa and various parts of Asia by the Chinese navy under Zheng He in the period 1405–33 (Levathes, 1994). The Ming Court's decision to lay up the massive treasure ship fleet, meant that the European powers were able to dominate at sea and gradually develop sophisticated military maritime technology.[9]

To cite the title of the book by Cipolla (1965), it was *Guns and Sails* that enabled European powers like the English, Dutch, Spanish, French and Portuguese to control sea routes and force open ports of entry around the world. Even when they were unable to conquer and colonize, most notably in China and Japan, it was not for want of trying with numerous military incursions made.[10] The memories of these wars, raids and punitive actions, plus the subsequent humiliating unequal treaties which were imposed, stoked the sense of injustice and desire to be modern. They increased the desire to counter the arrogant and violent uninvited Westerners. For Asian countries to seek to develop equivalent economic, technological and military power should not therefore be interpreted in the same way as the reasons for the expansion of Western modernity. Indeed, it was often motivated by the desire to be able to control and shut the door that the West forced open. As Shintaro Ishihara (1991) put it, in the title of his bestselling book written at the time of the Japanese bubble economy, it meant *The Japan that Can Say No*. The threat and reality of violence and military humiliation gives an important insight into the dynamics of modernity. As Chua Beng Huat (2006: 469) writing about Singapore's modernity remarks:

> Humiliation at the military prowess of the West caused a rethinking of the local culture as 'backward', 'traditional' against the 'modernity' of the West. The desire to be 'modern' was as much driven by the need to erase the humiliation as a people, as it was by the need to catch up with the West technologically; the latter being itself a means to the former. Western modernity was therefore never totally taken on board, there has always been an insistence that local, historical cultural resource can provide the necessary concepts for the organization of a new society that will embrace Western science within Asian culture; the latter as essence of the culture, of society and of self, with Western science and technology for economic development. The genealogy of this line of reasoning stretches from the early 19th century to the attempt to develop an 'Asian Value' discourse in the late 20th century.

Indeed it is the economic success of China and Japan and the Chinese diaspora scattered through East and South-east Asia, which can lead to the rethinking of the Weber thesis and notions of East as tradition in contrast to the West as modernity (Cheah, 2007). Certainly there does not seem to be an absence of entrepreneurial spirit, commercialism and capacity for economic accumulation in East Asia. Gunder Frank and others regard this as a return to the Asian domination of the world system, after a brief century and a half of 'Western interlude'.

It is the intertwining of military and economic power which was important in producing a Western modernity which had world changing impact. Important here was the particular condition of Western Europe with its jumble of small nation-states drawn together in an increasingly competitive figuration, in which colonial conquest became an important resource base for inter-European political rivalries (Elias, 1994). This unstable situation can be contrasted to East Asia; certainly in the role of overseas colonies, although this is not to underemphasize the number of internal regional conflicts and peasants revolts and attempts at conquest by Japan and China around their peripheries. Yet it is also, the realisation of military force and economic power through a range of technologies which was important. This entails the capacity to improve the design of ships to increase efficiency and accuracy and speed of navigation, and also the design of weaponry and military tactics. Knowledge is of crucial importance, then, for the development of the means of destruction.[11] Science and technology develop within literate cultures, which in turn are associates with urbanism and the success of merchants.

As Goody (2004: 61–2) points out, Eurocentric historians are reluctant to grant that there could have been 'bourgeois revolutions' led by merchants and professionals in other parts of the world. He cites Goiten (1967) who wrote of a 'bourgeois revolution' marked by the presence of scholar-merchants in the medieval Jewish communities of the Geniza in eighth- and ninth-century Cairo. He also refers to Zafrani's (1996) study of the bourgeois revolution which took place in Islam manifest in the intellectual effervesce in knowledge, poetry and artistic activities involving Jews, Muslims and Christians in tenth-century Cordoba and Granada. The library of Cordoba at that time possessed some 400,000 books, whereas the library of the monastery of St Gall in Switzerland had around 400 (Goody, 2004: 74). A period followed two to three centuries later by the extraordinary activity of a school of translators, largely Jewish, who translated works of philosophy, medicine, astronomy and mathematics from Arabic into Latin and other vernacular languages. The key role of the Arabs in Spain as the 'postmen' redelivering the Greek knowledge which they had long preserved and guarded is well known (Sayyid, 2006). It was this phase, involving the birth of the university in Europe, which formed the basis for the weakening of the authority of religious knowledge in Europe and the revival of secular enquiry, which culminated in the Enlightenment and the expansion of cumulative independent learning.

But less well known, is the connection and flows of knowledge from China to the Arab World and the general 'criss-cross diffusion' which occurred. The West clearly had no monopoly on merchant and bourgeois activities and there are similarities in the pattern of the merchant groups and their specialist professional and artisanal middle-class associates, who produced an expanding urban commercial sphere with concomitant knowledge, communication, consumption, and leisure practices in both the East and the West (Goody, 2004: 71). Likewise it is possible to see economic 'individualism' and entrepreneurial orientations, innovation, exploration and rationality, as accompanying merchants' activities everywhere. Yet it is hard to see commercial activity, monetization of the economy, banking systems, use of paper money, calculation of interest rates, and even rice future markets which occurred in China and Japan at various times up to the seventeenth and eighteenth centuries, as not involving rational calculation and practical rationality.[12] In addition, Habib (1990: 398–9) argues that Indian trade was little different from commerce in Western Europe and that it enjoyed commercial institutions such as brokerage, deposit banking, bill money and insurance, adding that perhaps

> The European triumph over Indian (and Asian) merchants was not, then, one of size and techniques, of companies over peddlers, of joint stock over atomized capital, of seamen over landsmen. Might it not have been more a matter of men-of-war and gun and shot, to which arithmetic and brokerage could provide no answer, whether in the earlier 'Age of Partnership,' or after Plassey?[13] (cited in Goody, 2004: 152)

Prior to the rise of the military power of European nations in the second half of the eighteenth and the nineteenth centuries, with their capacity to colonize, set up the slave trade and systems of indentured labour, and force open unequal treaty ports through firearms and gunboat diplomacy, there were multiple trade circuits within Asia as well as links between Europe and Asia through the development of merchant cultures.[14] The rigidities of the social structures of China and Japan with their alleged impediments to merchants could well have been exaggerated (Goody, 2004: 106). Ming China after 1434 and Tokugawa Japan were by no means closed to overseas trade as is often assumed. Gunder Frank (1998) estimates that overseas trade still made up over 10 per cent of the Japanese GNP at this time based on a network of overseas settlements of Japanese merchants in Vietnam, the Philippines and other places. In Ming China Confucian doctrine may have been hostile to trade and consumption, but there was a good deal of ambivalence in practice. In addition the Ming state left the economy pretty much alone to expand. In Japan, the *baku-han* system which places samurai at the top of the four groups, above farmers, tradesmen and merchants, formally placed all power in the hands of the samurai. Yet in practice, especially in the expanding cities such as Osaka and Edo, merchants enjoyed a lot of power and influence along with access to cultural participation (Ikegami, 2005). Hostility to merchants under imperial and monarchical forms was pretty much the rule. But in many different parts of the world, those in power had also to rely on merchants, as the global economy began to emerge and grow under its own impetus, certainly from the Song Dynasty (tenth century) onwards.

The rise of consumer culture in China and Japan

If the orthodox view of the exclusive rise of modernity in the West tends to depict culture as a set of deep-rooted stable background factors which demarcate peoples, nations, civilizations, then this view of culture has difficulty accounting for cultural innovation and interchange. Yet modernity is generally presented as involving cultural innovation in a wide range of areas: in literate forms of knowledge such as science and technology, but also the development of a literate cultural sphere based on the circulation of books and innovation and discussion of the arts. In addition, there is an emergent consumer culture in which new goods circulate, in which taste hierarchies and classifications become important. The mastery of the new world of goods and fashion systems in turn help to create new forms of experience, with a greater sense of individual authorship and reflexivity. The people who are caught up in this expanding world, along with those who hover on the margins and seek to enter, require pedagogies, practical guides to help them cope with the new bodily controls and interactional forms, given their need to cultivate and 'naturalize' the new sensibilities. If capitalism, seen as the development of production geared to the market along with the use of money to purchase an expanding range of goods and experiences, is seen as central to modernity, the nature of the new world of goods and experiences becomes the subject of cultural accounting, both practically (the guide books and encyclopedias designed to outline pedagogies of lifestyle and consumption) and theoretically (the novels, artistic and other forms designed to explain, interpret and speculate on the larger significance of the experience of these shifts). Indeed, one might speculate that the development of a modern culture should not just be conceived as a sudden break, the emergence of the modern urban man who seeks to invent himself à la Baudelaire, but as a long-term process of accumulation of sensibilities. A process of cultural accumulation which took place, not just in Western Europe but in many parts of the world, where there was the development of markets, trade and merchant communities. The cities of East Asia, especially China and Japan, therefore, can be seen as having many of the characteristics which we associate exclusively with Western modernity, not just the infrastructure of trade and manufacturing, but culture too.

The development of a world economy did not only mean the rise in the power potential of economic specialists (merchants, financiers et al.), but in the cities which expanded through trade and manufacturing we also see the rise of other specialists in knowledge and culture, along with various intermediaries. Merchant cultures, then, are more than the cultures of merchants, being larger urban cultures, taking in the whole urban network involving the manufacture and supply of goods for exchange, as well as the groups of lawyers, doctors, and professionals, plus the artisans and craftsmen needed to operate the system (Goody, 2004: 152). There are similarities between merchants in East Asia, the Near East with merchants in the West in their common organizational problems and difficulties, along with their cosmopolitan orientation and seeking of prestige and cultural influence. There was also a consumption side to this dynamic. This is particularly noticeable in China and Japan. Commercialization can be traced back to the late Song Dynasty with its flourishing market culture and production of luxury goods in cities such as the Song capital Kaifeng, it is the Ming Dynasty (1368–1644) that commodification becomes widespread and an urban consumer culture began to develop. This became particularly marked in the late Ming dynasty (1368–1644), with the increase in trade in luxury goods and the development of interest in connoisseurship. Books with titles such as *Eight Discourses in the Art of Living* and *Treatise on Superfluous Things* were available in the marketplace which outlined principles of appreciating and collecting art and fashionable luxury goods (Clunas, 1991). As Norbert Elias

(1994) argued in his discussion of European 'civilizing processes', changes in patterns of conduct meant new forms of bodily and emotional restraint, which created a market for 'how to' handbooks and manners books. It can be argued that in Ming China there was an increase in handbooks, almanacs and 'encyclopaedias for daily use' (Goody, 2004: 113), effectively guidebooks to the new forms of consumption and lifestyles. The same can be said for pre-Tokugawa and early Tokugawa Japan, where an increase in literacy and book publishing provided a wide range of guide books, handbooks and practical encyclopedias (Ikegami, 2005). This would seem to have been more than an elite-based form of conspicuous consumption, or the court society system of good manners and fine distinctions, but forms of consumption of goods involving a more fluid supply of goods along with new fashions, which could permeate the expanding middle classes in large cities.

The rise of a consumer culture is a long-term process and like modernity, it is difficult to chart and fix a point of origin. There are many genealogies of consumer culture and we can note the confluence between the restricted fine-graded distinctions of court consumption (one of the clearest depictions of the European accounts of court society being Norbert Elias's (1983) account of Louis XIV's Versailles in the seventeenth century) and middle-class patterns of consumption. In Elizabethan England with the increase in wealth and influx of new goods from the Americas, along with the stimulus from the Italian Renaissance, there were also changes in consumption patterns with new fashions and tastes not only in court society, but in the middle classes and through the trickle-down effect via servants to other groups in large cities (McCracken, 1988). Clunas (1991: 148) emphasises that an examination of 'the situation in China and Europe in the century or so from 1550 to 1650 reveals a strikingly similar picture, with an increasing lack of regard paid by consumers to the state's attempts to intervene in their behaviour.' As sumptuary laws, designed to rigidly fix the access to certain goods and styles of dress to particular social groups, gave way to fashion systems, in which new goods and tastes were introduced from the outside or through the innovation of cultural specialists on the inside, cultural intermediaries and brokers within particular societies were able to circulate information on how to consumer and experience the new sensations, especially for literate rising groups in the middle classes.[15] Not only how to eat, consumer and deport oneself through bodily regimes and controls, but also the governance of the household: the furnishing of rooms, the display of luxury items in the right setting became important not just for aristocrats and the lesser nobility, but for merchants and others. Also important in the process in addition to connoisseurship, was the transformation of luxuries into everyday goods for the middle classes and eventually the poor. What Sidney Mintz (1995) called 'the drug foods', sugar, cocoa, tobacco, coffee and tea, were all luxuries in sixteenth-century Europe, but became widespread in much of western Europe by the late nineteenth century (Pomeranz, 2000: 115). But this was also the case in China and to some extent Japan.

What is interesting here is the emergence of a fashion system, which means people will throw away goods and purchase new ones, thus increasing demand and stimulating the economy. The attempts to apply sumptuary laws were clearly attempts to fix status signifiers and restrict access to goods. Yet they frequently failed with people in the middle and lower orders seeking to acquire fashionable goods. The story of indigo, the blue dye which is familiar to us in denim jeans, has a long history before it became workwear for the inhabitants of Nîmes and the fashionable vernacular of post-1960s youth around the world. Indigo, became a more valuable commodity than sugar, through being a prized fabric colour, which tells us something about the fashion priorities in early modern culture (see Taussig, 2007). Fashion, then as Simmel (1997a) pointed out involves both imitation and distinction, with the denigration of outdated goods. It can be argued that it is a key dynamic of modern culture. A fashion system requires an increase in the variety of goods deemed socially significant as well as an increase in the velocity of turnover. It also requires an increase in the range of the people allowed to possess the goods and the degree they can be acquired from strangers. Additionally, it points to the need for an increase in imitative consumption, and the circulation of information – either by word of mouth (gossip) in private and public spaces or in the form of printed paper (handbills, broadsheets, magazines, handbooks, home encyclopedias etc.), to provide advice on not only the 'latest', and 'tasteful', but also advice on use. Ideally this should occur in urban settings where there is the opportunity to see the new fashions, observe people wearing new clothing, or glimpse new interiors and artefacts. Pomeranz (2000: 129) tells us that 'these phenomena are *best* documented for various urbanized regions of western Europe: Renaissance (northern) Italy; Golden Age Spain; Holland; some parts of France; and England'. Yet the upper-class households and merchant homes of Ming Dynasty China and Momoyama and Tokugawa Japan also became crammed with luxury goods, paintings, sculptures, fine furniture etc.

What is notable in China and Japan of this period is the conspicuous consumption strategies of *nouveau riches* groups, who not only indulged in extravagance and luxury, eating and drinking to excess, but also engaged in lavish patronage of the arts (Burke, 1993). This meant not only the need for guidebooks and manners books to help the new urban public, who lacked the traditional education in the Confucian classics, but also the demand for the educative novel. Notable here is the early seventeenth-century novel *Jin Ping Mei*, described as the first novel of manners, and the mid-eighteenth-century *Hong Lou Meng*, or *Dream of the Red Chamber* (also known as *The Story of the Stone*). The *Jin Ping Mei* tells the story of a rich merchant from Shandong, who is a connoisseur of *objets d'art* and a great drinker and womanizer to boot, and is 'a novel absolutely stuffed with descriptions of expensive furnishings' (Burke, 1993: 152). The *Hong Lou Meng* is referred to by Burke as a kind of eighteenth-century *Buddenbrooks*, a nostalgic chronicle of the decline of a great merchant family, the Jias, doomed because, as an outsider puts it, 'Both masters and servants ... lead a life of luxury and magnificence ... they can't bring themselves to economise'.

He goes on to tell us that

The contents of different rooms in the family mansions are described with living care, so that the novel sometimes reads like an inventory of *objets d'art*, often antiques: paintings, calligraphic scrolls, mirrors, low tables of coloured lacquer, brocade curtains, yellow cedar-wood armchairs ...' (Burke, 1993: 152).

It is interesting to note that in French literature, like Chinese literature, the novel of manners also appeared in the seventeenth century, with Antoine Furetière's *Roman Bourgeois* (1666), a story about the attempts of the professional bourgeoisie to pass as nobility. There are interesting comments on interiors (antiques, furniture and curiosities) and the concern for clothes and language.

A similar trend towards display and conspicuous consumption is apparent in the Momoyama period in sixteenth-century Japan. The trend continued in under the Tokugawa Shogunate, with not only a cycle of ruinous lavish court consumption as the shogun forced daimyo and nobility with their retinue to attend court in the new rapidly growing capital Edo and engage in a cycle of ruinous lavish consumption through the construction of great houses with fine decorations and furnishing and ceremonial spaces. This was a gilded-cage court-society existence under the watchful eye of the shogun and his spies, similar to that described by Norbert Elias (1983) in Louis XIV's Versailles occurring at approximately the same time in seventeenth-century France. Although nominally at the bottom of the four-scale social ladder in Japan, merchants prospered in the cities and *the chonin* turned to the arts and urban entertainments. In practice in the cities there was a good deal of mixing in the new urban leisure spaces and the pleasure quarters. As Burke (1993: 154) remarks:

A new society was producing a new culture. There was a trend towards the commercialization of leisure, at much the same time as in the great cities of the west, Paris, Rome and Madrid as well as London. In Edo, Kyoto and Osaka it took the form of tea houses rather than coffee houses, sumo wrestling rather than boxing or bull-fights, but the role of courtesans, the theatre and cheap print was remarkably similar in east and west. In practice, as one might have guessed, the separation between social groups and cultural genres was very much less clear cut than it was in principle. The boundaries were transgressed on both sides. The *daimyo* could not keep away from the pleasure quarters. Lower-status groups also appropriated or imitated high culture. Wood-block prints or kimono patterns associated with noble ladies allowed townswomen to imitate them.

A number of points can be made. First, neither in Japan nor China did the luxury culture go uncriticized or unopposed. Although Ming merchants were not impeded institutionally, culturally or politically to the extent often assumed in the West, conspicuous consumption did not sit easily with Confucianism. The emphasis on connoisseurship and gentility, or gentlemanly conduct, was also accompanied by a valuation of the amateur as against the professional, and the scholar against the dilettante. Clunas (1991) empha-sises that the distinction between professional and amateur painters was still of great importance in the Ming Dynasty.

In Japan the development of the *za* arts, the multiplicity of cultural circles of *haiku* and *waka* poetry, painting, the tea ceremony, cookery, kimono making and performing arts, formed a networked aesthetic public sphere which drew in merchants, samurai, tradesmen and other groups from the Momoyama period onwards. These enclaved public spheres were hobby groups and voluntary associations which had a high level of active participation. They could swing between phases of luxury connoisseurship, austerity and purity, as well as commercialisation (the handbooks, advice manuals etc. fed off and stimulated an active book print industry). One famous example of the pull to purity and simplicity is the case of Sen no Rikyu, the inventor of the tea ceremony and his various struggles and implicit critiques of the luxurious excesses of the Shogun, Toyotomi Hideyoshi. Sen no Rikyu (1521–91) developed the tea ceremony into a highly refined aesthetic ritual, the *wabi-cha*, or 'poverty' tea ceremony with its zen-inspired emphasis on minimalism and simple bamboo and pottery utensils, contrasted with the vulgar display of Hideyoshi, who in 1587 had a gold tea room built (Ikegami, 2005: 120 ff.). Sen no Rikyu's spirited artis-tic intransigence, along with his fame, eventually cost him his life as he was ordered to commit suicide by Hideyoshi. The Rikyu case offers an interest-ing illustration of the dynamics between high and low, vulgar and refined taste, stoical self-control and excess, individuality and obligation to author-ity, the struggles between nobles, merchants and artists, between cultural capital and economic capital. This suggests that these dynamics, which are assumed to be more marked in the development of the European cultural sphere and autonomous art, are by no means unique to the West.

Second, according to Pomeranz there is good reason to think that 'luxury' demand was as dispersed among the various classes of Chinese and Japanese as it was among Europeans. In terms of the role of 'free labour' and markets in the economy, Europe was not ahead of China and Japan; indeed, Pomeranz (2000: 165) tells us it may have lagged behind China and concludes 'At the very least, all three of these societies resembled each other in these matters far more than any of them resembled India, the Ottoman Empire, or southeast Asia.' If a modern culture took a good deal of impetus from the market to generate the flows of new goods and expe-riences, the beginnings of the fashion and information systems associated with the beginnings of consumer culture, it also required forms of account-ing and administration which depended on widening literacy, which in turn helped to stimulate print culture, handbooks, novels, broadsheets (in Japan, *kawaraban*) which advised the middle-class initiates on the appropriate desires, dreams and conduct.

It has been argued that the focus in Western theories of modernity on the transition from feudalism to capitalism in Europe and the depiction of

Asian societies as oriental despotisms, obscures the way that both were variants of a 'tributary' system (Wolf, 1982; Goody, 2004: 132). In any case the concentration on feudalism would seem to have not only obscured the common origins, but played down the role of towns in the West. Unlike Western European towns which suffered a decline in continuity in the Middle Ages ('Dark Ages,') after the fall of the Roman Empire, the towns in Eurasia, such as Damascus and Baghdad as well as the cities of China and India continued to develop trade and knowledge networks. Changes in patterns of consumption took place incrementally over a long period of time and were necessarily linked to changes in production. These were changes which increased the power potential of merchants and traders and the literate bourgeoisie, the cultural and knowledge specialists in the middle classes. The similarities in levels of production and consumption between China, Japan and England we have mentioned, suggests that the alleged antipathy towards trade and economic matters in Asia, was far from the whole picture. Goody (2004: 136) sees the assumed difference between European and Asian cities as highly questionable, especially the assumption that Western towns which emerged in the Middle Ages developed a fundamentally different form. It relied on an alleged historical difference constructed to show that only the Western towns were capable of producing the necessary entrepreneurs: 'the freedom–loving bourgeoisie that could form the basis of a capitalist system'.

Here again the assumptions of European exceptionalism, in this instance that of the democratic commune, following the thesis of Pirenne and others which guaranteed the legal system and structures for commercial enterprise, is not the whole story. The analysis of Hankow by Rowe (1984) and Hunan by Perdue (1987) make the case that such features, emphasised by Max Weber in his study of the city, were also to be found in the Asiatic city.[16] This could also suggest that although the public sphere, generally assumed to be excusive to Europe, might not be totally absent from the Asian context. The linking of the public sphere to deliberative democracy, discourses on human rights and political change, as described by Habermas (1989) and others, would seem undisputable in the European context.[17] Yet there could well have been other public sphere variants in Asia, which instead of having an overt political dimension, had a cultural one. This is the argument of Ikegami (2005), who in her analysis of Tokugawa Japan seeks to interrogate and broaden the notions of public and civil society.

Protomodern civility in Tokugawa Japan

Ikegami (2005) argues that in the Tokugawa era (1603–1867) Japan experienced 'civility without civil society', not a form of civility linked to the emergence of a new type of public supported by associations of citizens seeking political rights, as was the case in Europe, but certainly a form of civility associated with good manners and polite modes of conduct. Rather than a single integrated public sphere as emerged in Europe, through freedom of the press and public discussion in the piazza or coffee house (long the source of contestation, struggles and re-monopolization processes), in Japan there emerged a range of enclaved public spheres formed around voluntary associations in the arts – associations which were not perceived as a political threat to the powerful Tokugawa state rule. These enclaved publics and even counter-publics in the form of the plea-sure quarters, the *ukyo* (floating world), provided relatively free discursive spheres for aesthetic sociability, which made possible forms of experimen-tation and creativity, cultural diversity and identity play. People enjoyed participating in various cultural circles and learning the skills of poetry, flower arranging, the tea ceremony, painting, the various *za* arts, in enclaved interactional spaces within which there occurred a good deal of public mixing.[18]

It is also important to consider the degree of urbanization which took place in Tokugawa Japan, with Edo (Tokyo) rapidly rising from a fishing village in the early 1600s to the largest city in the world in the eighteenth century (McClain et al., 1994). The urban economy not only meant the rise of the fortunes of merchants, the development of luxury goods, entertainments and pastimes as mentioned above, but also the development of a strong print industry with relatively cheap availability of novels (via bookshops and book peddlers), such as Iharu Saikaku's depictions of the rise and fall of people in the urban life of consumption (Burke, 1993: 154), poetry books, handbooks, manners books, guidebooks, encyclopedic dictionaries (*setsuyo-shu*) and home encyclopedias (many of which catalogued material and summarized knowledge without express editorial principles) and the *kawaraban* (broadsheets with advertisements, and lurid accounts and pictures of disasters, murders etc.). It also meant a literate public in the process of development, a public in which some women also read *kana* novels, and reading aloud to groups of people was not uncommon.

Tokugawa Japan contained many of the sensibilities and forms of cultural life we associate with modernity. Not just the means of production, but the means of consumption and the means of information too, which encour-aged the development of discriminating publics interested in fine distinc-tions and experiencing creative aesthetic sensibilities and sensations. This involved the training of not just the eye, but the body: the development of a sense of *iki*, or sense of style and aesthetics in body movement, presenta-tion of self and demeanour. This was coupled with a fashion system featur-ing changing styles and concern for high quality cotton, silk and linen fabrics with subtle patterns and dyeing techniques (Ikegami, 2005: 245 ff.). The capacity for stylized aestheticized interactions on the part of city-dwellers, especially in the enclaved aesthetic publics necessitated a capac-ity to manage a more fluid and situational (context dependent) sense of identity. People developed the capacity to temporarily decouple themselves from the *baku-han* chains of interdependencies, responsibilities and power balances as they explored different modes of sociability and playful (although seriously framed) imaginative work while engaging in voluntary associational activities. Ikegami (2005: 368) remarks that:

> Although it is difficult to define the distinctive quality of modern social life in any precise way, the possibility of multiple affiliational identities made on the basis of individual choice seems to be an important index of modernity. Any society that does not allow individuals associational ties other than those they are born with – whether territorial or religious affiliations or kin ties – cannot be called modern. Although Tokugawa Japan was deliberately organized as a segmented society in which individuals were destined to live within structurally separate components, its aesthetic networks nevertheless facilitated individual choices regarding associational ties. Yet, having developed a domain of voluntary association ties on the plane of private aesthetic socializing, this society truly deserves the name of proto-modern as far as its civic culture is concerned.

Ikegami (2005: 374), goes on to remark that this new model of civility and enclaved pubic spheres revolving around poetry and the performing arts, should make us conclude that 'Japan was moving towards its own versions of "proto-modernity", or "modernity before modernization", in the dimension of cultures of sociability'. Ikegami adds that the guidebook image of Japan as a land dedicated to beauty emerged from this cultural communicative sphere, and that the aesthetic socialization connected people with the common culture of Japan. This experience of a commonality formed through shared aesthetic experiences laid the ground for the construction of the modern nation-state. This was not a deliberate attempt on the part of the Tokugawa state but rather the result of people's networking and the market forces which created new channels of communication. But after the Meiji restoration of 1868 these pre-existing images of Japan as an aesthetic nation, the sense that people already had a clear cognitive map of their own culture through the aesthetic sensibility and the articulation through commercial publications, were rapidly exploited to shape Japanese cultural identities as a modern nation ready to compete in the global power struggle.

Although, Ikegami (2005: 290) only makes one passing reference to Benedict Anderson's (1991) study of the role of print capitalism in the creation of imagined communities, it can be argued that this construction of nation provides the sense of being networked together, through newspapers and other media, is the other side of the coin of culture. On the one side we have the Habermasian public sphere and its various transformations, the aesthetic enclaved public spheres Ikegami speaks of, but on the other side and certainly occupying the same time–space framework or chronotope, we have the attempted construction of nation as *Gemeinschaft* as an 'organic community' (Cheah, 2006). The latter depends on some sense of *ethnie*, common language, myths, sentiments and is not just an invention (see Smith, 1998) on the part of rulers, who seek to exploit the dynamics of in-group/out-group, insider/outsider conflicts.

Tokugawa Japan could be drafted in to provide images of aesthetic Japan, particularly relevant at certain points in its history, such as in the wake of the 1945 defeat by the United States, when Japan sought to step aside from politics and war, to promote an image of its peaceful past, of Japan as a cultured nation, the land of beauty and politeness, of skilled craftsman and refined sensibilities. In contrast, in World War II, powerful symbols of the cultural tradition of beauty, such as the cherry blossom, had been used to mobilize people's patriotic sacrifice for the Japanese homeland. Top-down nation-building, the project to be modern to establish Japan's place in the world (the 'strong army, rich nation' doctrine), to become civilized on Western terms, had meant the eclipse of culture in the German sense of *kultur*, the *za* arts and the aesthetic tradition, a particular definition of Japaneseness. Culture (Japanese) gave way to civilization (western), to meet the demands of the day. Or better, culture (the resilient different Japanese, with their own distinctive range of aesthetic sensibilities which had beautified Japan), became pushed into the back room, to be used as a repository of difference, with items to be wheeled out when necessary, as the frenzied activity of building the façade and substance of a competitive modern state which could escape the clutches of subordinate neo-colonialism, continued up front.

Ikegami has discovered a particular Japan relevant to her values and the values of the current age. The searchlight of her value question, the reevaluation of the arts and aesthetic publics, has helped illuminate a particular image of Japan, the benefits of 'civility without civil society', the 'strength of weak ties', linked together in 'the proto-modern network revolution', with its 'cultural innovation and vitality', an image which could be useful in contemporary global politics as a counter to other more dialogical (clashing of reason) constructions of the public sphere. Indeed, there is much to be said for this particular genealogy both for Japan and for the nascent global public sphere in the current wave of market-led, finance-capital and transnational corporate-dominated globalization with its range of powerful global institutions such as the WTO, World Bank, WEF etc. But it also raises questions about the designation of Tokugawa Japan as proto-modern and the invention of genealogies.

Reading Edo as tradition and modernity

To know you are modern, to know this moment is new and impose this image on the future, also involves knowing it is substantially different (not just a difference of degree as one moves through a regular series of known moments), from the past (Koselleck, 1993). In effect the past has to be constructed as tradition, as repetitive, ossified and static, dominated by ritual cycles. As Carol Gluck (1998: 262) remarks:

> Modernity, by definition saw the future by setting itself off from the past. Newness was all, but it could only be grasped by juxtaposition to what was old. In France the ancien régime came to represent the whole of the old order; the very antithesis of the new revolutionary age ... In Japan the Edo period became just this sort of historical imaginary. 'Edo' (meaning the Tokugawa era, not the city later named Tokyo) was the invented other in relation to which modernity

positioned itself. From early Meiji times, Japan's before-the-modern was imagined largely in terms of an Edo identified as Japanese 'tradition'.

The Meiji reformers preoccupied with constructing their own image of Japanese newness, Meiji as civilization (*bunmei*), as national and progressing, depicted Edo as oldness, as feudal, a hindrance (Gluck, 1998: 265). But once this Euro-American inspired modernity had become a reality in the early 1920s (Japan's GNP surpassed those of England, France and Germany, after is 'de-shackling' from the Meiji unequal treaties and economic boom from being on the right side in World War I), the attitude to Edo shifted. For when the new Western-inspired modernity disappointed, the disappointment became attached to the West. As Gluck (1998: 272) tellingly puts it: 'A syllogism had formed: Modernity is Westernization. Japan is now modern. Therefore, Japan is Westernized: Japan is no longer Japan'. This was the background for Japan to begin the adventure of developing an alternative modernity, a Japan purified of its Westernized materialism and find a more spiritualized and militarized Japanese modernity. This became the basis of Japanese fascism, leading to war in the 1930s. Its intellectual side became explored by members of the Kyoto School in the 1930s and 1940s (Nishida, Tanabe, Nishitani et al.) who sought to think through the basis for an alternative globalization with a different basis than Western colonialism (see Heisig, 1996; Sakai, 1993). And this was the Japan which according to Harootunian (2000) was *Overcome by Modernity* in World War II.

After the war, a period of disenchantment with 'feudal' Edo as the closed country, which should have been opened to give the Japanese chance to develop a 'scientific spirit' followed, as Japan sought to tie itself to a reformed and revamped modernity drawing its inspiration from the Meiji reformers.[19] Edo again became premodernity and tradition, impediments to the modern. In the 1980s, with the expansion and success of the Japanese economy which produced scare stories in the United States captured in the media in titles such as *Japan in the Passing Lane* (Kamata, 1983) and movies such as *Rising Sun* (see Raz and Raz, 1996), in Japan itself there was an Edo boom with the image of 'happy feudalism'. This was accompanied by the discovery of the superior balanced 'ecological' Edo, with its floating world, simulations and sign play etc., which had allegedly reached the postmodern before the modern: in effect 'Japan's premodern was in fact already post-' (Gluck, 1998: 275). Then after the fall of the postmodern fashion in the 1990s and with it the fading of postmodern Edo, there briefly emerged an interest in Edo as somehow 'transmodern,' as the term modern itself became fluid and lost its referents. This was followed in the early 1990s by a more positive, protomodern view of Edo, with Bito Masahide (1992; Gluck, 1998: 275) asking 'What is Edo?' and answering 'Japanese modernity.' Everything before Edo for him became ancient, everything after Edo became modern. Other civilization theorists in the 1990s found in Edo 'a kind of socialist paradise based upon policies of economic equality', as having experienced an industrial revolution and peace, a lesson for the world in a time of diminishing resources. A modernity not just for Japan, but for the world (Gluck, 1998: 276). Enter Ikegami.

Once we have engaged in this sociology of knowledge exercise and started to sift through the genealogies of the modern, the world becomes a different place. It is no longer possible to start to narrate the world in forward mode, innocently jumping from one event to another. A central feature of our modernity is our expectation of change and a different future: that modernity amounts to this constant colonization of the past by the future. Each new time can mean a new time in academic fashions, not just driven by institutional and disciplinary processes of knowledge monopolization, or insider and outsider struggles with their avant-garde dynamics, but through the attempt to respond to the complexities of a changing sociocultural world with its shifting political struggles, which propels upward or downward particular nations, social groups and strata, predisposing them to develop an affinity for particular progressive or fateful narratives.

One aspect of the culture of modernity, then, could well be this 'condition' in cultural and knowledge production. Not driven only by a market dynamic (economic capital driving cultural production), but also by various cultural dynamics which are manifest in popular culture, consumer culture and artistic, intellectual and academic cultural production (fashion dynamics, avant-gardism, invention and preservation of classics and canons, hybridization and fusions etc.) within the field of cultural production.[20]

If we seek to understand the relationship between modernity and culture, then, we cannot avoid being conscious of the changing meanings attributed to particular ages, variously designated as the seedbed of modernity or the enduring source of tradition. The conditions of possibility of these designations, as Gluck argues, lie in the present, in the responses to contemporary issues, and shifting value complexes in response to larger socioeconomic and political events. But this is not just a question of writing history, in recoding Edo through an expanding range of tropes. It is also a question of the cultural archive that makes it possible. This entails an archive of cultural material, especially texts, but in the case of Edo also visual images (*ukiyo* and other paintings and drawings), which drew from popular culture and the market. As we mentioned above, in the discussion of Ming novels and handbooks, this needed a literate public, which in turn depended on the institutions and markets of cultural production and consumption. The *za* arts and enclaved publics, along with the market for novels, handbooks and home encyclopedias, discussed by Ikegami, provided this basis in Tokugawa Japan. Hence, the literate popular culture provided an Edo repository, an archive which could be explored and reformatted to provide significant material to meet the needs of a particular age.

In 1920s Japan, Edo again became fashionable with the explosion of mass culture at a time when the Japanese economy was strong and the Meiji westernization which had previously confined Edo to backward feudal tradition, was rejected. Now the Edo 'cultural storehouse' could be reopened to show Edo in a more positive light, as the source not just of pro-tomodern tendencies, but a uniquely Japanese past which had produced its own form of ecological stable efficiency, the potential source of a Japanese modern. Edo provided material for popular entertainment not only in cheap books, novels, magazines, newspapers, but also in the new radio broadcasts and movies. What is of particular interest here is that this embracing of the Edo past, the reconstitution of Edo as a positive source of popular Japanese tradition, occurred at the same time as 'the modern' was being celebrated in the nascent consumer culture. In 1920s Tokyo the modern girl, or *moga*, emerged in the Ginza and the downtown city streets, the department stores, the *sakariba* entertainment areas of dance halls, cinemas and cafés. The modern girl, with her flapper style, expressed a vitality, freedom of movement and independent spirit, in marked contrast to the Meiji reinvented tradition of the modest 'good wife and wise mother' (see Tamari, 2006). The *moga*, was assumed to be the epitome of the modern embrace of the new, a largely media-invented new woman, whose impact was all the more heightened in Japan. The modern girl can be contrasted to the *jokyû*, the café waitress, who manifested a fusion of modern styles with elements drawn from the long history of female sex work (Silverberg, 1998). As Chakrabarty (1998: 292) remarks, the term *jokyū* was only intelligible as part of the new culture of the inter-war period with its importation of foreign words and media images, which only proved intelligible when combined with, and differentiated from, other Japanese words referring to women in public such as *meshimori onna, yūjo, inbaita*, etc. The modernity of the *jokyū*, then, only took its meaning from a sign chain and field of differences in which old and new lay alongside each other without strict hierarchy. Chakrabarty, concludes that 'The erection of polarities such as tradition and modernity has to ignore these carry-overs between categories. The modern like any other historically evolved structure, is hybrid. It contains polysemy ...'. Various founding taxonomies, such as tradition/modernity, feudalism/capitalism, are binaries which become transformed into hierarchies. They are based on progressive, developmentalist metanarratives of history which are kept in place by the various discourses and practices of institutional power. But in saying this, it does not mean that it is possible to go back to the field of differences, beneath these founding classificatory acts, in which the answer to the question 'what was Japanese tradition' can clearly emerge. Rather, there is the play of ambiguities and polysemy in the constitution of the categories of Japanese modernity and tradition, which points to the contingent space in which the two interdependent categories were invented and continue to be reinvented. Contingent, because as Gluck shows there is a continual process of reworking the Japanese historical cultural archive in terms of the present contingent events, which propel the trajectory of the nation-state forwards through history. These events mean that it is inevitable that historians and the public will continually be drawn to reevaluate, reinscribe and reinflect the past as tradition and modern, to fit in with the 'demands of the day'. This involves a continual process of declassification and reclassification.

Multiple and alternative modernities

The relationship of culture to modernity is complex. As we have mentioned culture often is perceived as bifurcating: an unchanging set of values, beliefs and assumptions which ensures the coherent reproduction of social life as tradition. At the same time some cultures are seen as carrying within them the seeds of world transformation. So while often regarded as something fundamental, fixed and persistent, particular cultures or subcultures, such as the Protestantism addressed by Weber (1930), embody a powerful generative force: the Protestant ethic not only was conducive for the spirit of capitalism, but the process of rationalization and valuation of transformative inner worldly conduct which produced modernity and the modern life. Weber's argument, although couched in ideal-type terms, has the merit of not just working a cultural logic through a reading of texts (cultural logic being a not unproblematic notion – see ch. 4 of this book) but of seeking to link the discussion to conduct and life transformative experience.

As mentioned earlier in relation to the discussion of modernity, the key question as Jack Goody (2004: 29) states it is 'If culture changes, as surely it must, how then is it an explanatory variable?' The problem is that culture becomes a meaningless variable as it is generally used in an all-inclusive way, which does not permit the focus on particular features. Culture is presented as outside and resistant to economics, as designating 'inner values and attitudes', as an enduring set of background variables. If it is everything outside economics – that which hinders or helps the economy take off into modernity – then culture also includes the social.

There is a further problem in terms of identifying the unit of cultural specificity. In discussions of modernity, especially those which argue for multiple modernities, there is the tendency to reify cultures as well-bounded integrated entities which have inner coherence that persists over time. Effectively cultures are presented as islands, with the units of culture generally seen as civilizations or nation-states. Yet the definition of civilizations and the construction of the culture of the nation-state as an 'imagined community', or 'invented tradition', as we have discussed in the case of Japan, is itself a product of modernity. Only in modernity do we have cultural specialists and intermediaries directed by politicians, state functionaries and powerful economic interests, given the latitude to reorder the cultural archive in coherent and affectively-binding ways to produce all the paraphernalia – the folklore, stories, heroes, myths, rituals, ceremonies, memorials – which function to pull together the nation. A reordering process which has an important exterior dimension in international politics, taking place within the figuration of competing nation-states, as nations sought to mobilise their populations as economic and military resources designed to maximise 'biopower', and construct the nation as a 'sacred community' through cultural education processes.

The concept of multiple modernities suggests that what modernity supposedly left behind stubbornly persists, blurring the boundaries between the modern and the premodern (Dirlik, 2003: 287). It suggests a readily demarcatable global multiculturalism with coherent manageable units of culture, ready for comparison and plays down internal conflicts and diversity. In addition, it neglects the continual process of intercultural exchange, the movement of knowledge and culture around the world by merchants, religious movements which points to a high level of internal cultural complexity. As Sakai (1998) points out the project of the construction of the national society as a homolingual community, which forms the basis for assumptions of a common culture, depends upon a process of imposed language standardization. This entails the suppression of the heterolingual nonaggregate linguistic community of foreigners, in which people engaged in polyglot discourse, with the assumption that their addressees formed a mixed audience and that translation would always be incomplete and imperfect, but workable.

Multiple modernities, then, suggests cultural differences that are themselves structured around 'spatialities' such as civilizations, nation-states, cultures and ethnicities which are themselves the product of modernity, or the modernization process. The focus on culture as the main or decisive source of difference, relegates to the background social and political differences which cut across the background of these various spatial boundaries (Dirlik, 2003: 285). This focus on spatial separation, not only misses intercommunication between the various structured units (societies), it also tends to lead to the playing down of the differences over time. In the case of Japan the construction of *Nihonjinron*, Japanese uniqueness, as a national ideology, plays down the societal family resemblances between modern, or modernizing societies. As Schmidt (2006: 81) puts it 'Is Japan significantly *more* different from Spain than Denmark or Britain or Greece are? And does contemporary Japan have more in common with *pre-modern* Japan than with, say, *contemporary* Canada or Germany?' The multiple modernities perspective is based upon the assumption that there must be greater differences across civilizational lines and cultures than across time (Lee, 2006).

Multiple modernities and the related concept 'alternative modernities' are of course discovered after the event and it is legitimate to ask, in the way Carol Gluck dissected the shifting Japanese historical presentation of Edo as tradition or modernity, what is at stake in such designations. Alternative modernities can legitimately be applied to the various projects to construct a different cultural programme and alternative institutional framework for modern societies. Here we think of the projects of soviet socialist and communist party dominated societies, such as the USSR or China, or fascist and national socialist societies such as Germany and Italy (see Arnason, 2000, 2001; Arnason, Eisenstadt and Wittrock, 2004; Herf, 1986). Or Japan in the Asia and Pacific Wars, 1930–45. In all these cases alternative modernity was an active project conceived by a party structure with its own ideological apparatus and institutional structures designed for the total mobilization of the population to serve the state/national aims. What is clear is that, after various military and economic defeats in 1945, 1989 and 1991, all these projects have failed, with the ambiguous case of China remaining to be played out.

If the notion of alternative modernity in the sense of a cultural project for wholesale social transformation, given these defeats, no longer makes sense today, there are those who emphasize a more restricted project of producing differences within the cultural spheres of modern society. Gaonkar (1999), for example, argues that once modernity has expanded from its origins in the West to become established globally, non-Western people are able to critically engage to produce their own hybrid modernities. Alternative modernity, then, is in this sense used to argue that with the decline of Western master-narratives of modernity there is no longer a governing centre and hence 'modernity today is global and multiple' (Gaonkar, 1999: 13). What has travelled to the rest from the West is not only modernity in the sense of institutional arrangements, social practices and cultural forms, but also modernity in the sense of a critical discourse which interrogates the present. Different sites around the world do not mimic the Western institutional order of modernity, nor generate and adversarial modern culture with its preoccupation with self-realization and self-expression as discussed by Daniel Bell (1976) and others. Rather they engage in a unique contingent culturally-specific reading of the two strands of modernity (societal modernization and cultural modernity) to pluralize the experience of modernity; following Charles Taylor (1999), it is argued we need both to 'recognize *and* problematize the unavoidable dialectic of convergence and divergence'. Convergence usually thought of in terns of institutional frameworks (market economy, state administration etc.). Divergence primarily thought of in terms of lived experience and cultural expressions filtered through the habitus and social imaginary of a particular set of people. The alternative modernity perspective focuses on site-specific variations, the 'creative adaptations' to societal modernization. The site-based analyses according to Gaonkar (1999: 17) enable us to see 'creative adaptation' as an interminable process of questioning the present, which is the attitude of modernity. Precisely in this sense, 'modernity is an incomplete project and necessarily so'.

The connection of the cultural dimension of modernity to experience echoes the concerns of Koselleck (1993) who endeavours to answer the question: what kind of experience is opened up by the emergence of modernity? He focuses on the categories experience and expectation, arguing that the distance between them expands in *Neuezeit*, with expectations distancing themselves more from previous experience. A new horizon of expectations is opened up, with history conceived as a long-term process of growing fulfilment, subject to active human intervention, later to be conceived as progress. Koselleck (1993: 267) goes on to tell us that Kant, may well have been the originator of the term *Fortschritt* (progress), in his strenuous opposition to the thesis that things would always remain the same and belief that new experiences, such as the French revolution, could be accumulated to sustain an 'advance to the better'. History became formulated and experienced as unique, as open to human intervention, with the need to bridge the increase in the gap between experience and expectation.

In his essay 'What is Enlightenment?' Foucault (1984: 39) remarks that modernity should not be seen as an epoch, but rather following Kant as an attitude, a distinctive way of acting and behaving, 'an *ethos*'. Kant's work is important because it involves a reflection on the moment he is writing, on history, on the conditions of possibility of knowledge. This modern attitude, is 'one that simultaneously problematizes man's relation to the present, man's historical mode of being, and the constitution of the self as an autonomous subject' (Foucault, 1984: 42). This is the basis of the European Enlightenment spirit of critique. Something which can also open up a new horizon of expectations for political practice, which Kant hoped would lead to a new republican *Bund* (league of associations), of 'self-organizing peoples', to produce a cosmopolitan new international politics. Yet if modernity as conceived by Kant involved an attitude of critique, of problematizing the present, and emphasized a new attitude or ethos, involving a voluntary way of thinking and feeling, of acting and behaving, then this new form of consciousness could occur in art too.

For Baudelaire this new modern attitude involves an ironic heroicization of the present, but not that of the *flâneur* who drifts through the city as a spectator, more that of the *dandy* who seeks to extract from fashion the quality of the new or modernity, to grasp, imagine and transform the highly valued present. To be modern for Baudelaire, Foucault (1984: 41) comments, involves a *dandyisme* which not only involves a surrender to the flux of the present moment, but a deliberate asceticism, through seeking to make one's body, conduct, feelings and passions a work of art. Modern man, for Baudelaire, is a man who tries to invent himself, who forces himself to face the constant task of producing himself anew. As Maffesoli (1991) has argued, this involves an 'ethic of aesthetic', not just an aesthetic attitude to life, the aestheticization of everyday life, but the concern to aestheticize one's persona, conduct and life, to create an ordered life (Featherstone, 1995: chs 3, 4; see also ch. 4 of this book).

This attitude of questioning the present, of invention of the self, involves an attitude of taking the emergent, the flux of material thrown up by the present moment along with the reworking of the experience in the fashions of art and consumer culture seriously. Baudelaire's perceptions developed in mid-nineteenth-century Paris and it is this experience of city which gave rise to the new aesthetic sensibility which is seen as the founding moment of modernism by Benjamin (1999) and others (Berman, 1982). It is possible to write the history of modernism as the counterculture of modernity, involving a constant critical artistic dialogue attempting to grapple with the transformations of modern life, the technological, industrial and business changes which restructured and remodelled the fabric of urban life into the experience of metropolis which Simmel (1997b) spoke about in his famous essay. Notable here is the affective response to modern life, the dizzying visual, aural and proprioceptive bodily sensations of shock, speed, movement, intensity, not just produced by the crowd, but the trams, motor cars, buses, trains with their attendant dangers producing new stresses, anxieties and fears, to be theorised and clinically diagnosed as neurasthenia, psychasthenia and other 'new' illnesses. Not only did this different present produce new historical memories, which were recorded, recreated and narrated by new twentieth-century media such as the gramophone, radio and movies which sought to capture the pace of modern life, they also produced the longing for the opposite: the reassuring images of harmonious rural life and the 'timeless folk'. As Chakrabarty (1998: 294) reminds us in his discussion of invented tradition in Japanese modernity:

> In effect, 'anxiety,' 'shock,' and 'fear' circulated … as the most uninterrogated categories, while serving, most usefully, to remind us that no 'invention of tradition' is effective without a simultaneous invocation of affect, of sentiments, emotions and other embodied practices.

What is interesting here is the dual response to this modern condition: both modernism driven by the avant-garde dynamic quest for 'the new,' and the retreat to the imagined reassuring images of tradition, both place a high premium on invention.[21] This dynamic of invention, according to Gaonkar (1999: 13) was played out around the world in different sites, as various peoples encountered the experience of modernity, as the institutional parameters, social practices, cultural forms and intellectual discourses of Western modernity became circulated. Alternative modernities, then, for Gaonkar, unlike Eisenstadt's notion of multiple modernities, is not written in a strong sense to indicate persistent civilizational or cultural forces which endure to shape long durée differences. In addition, it is not a societally mobilized project, but rather smaller-scale, mediated cultural responses to the spread of Western modernity, in the wake of the dominance of western techno-economic modernization. These responses were not premised on robust persistent cultural differences which marked different ways into modernity, nor do they retain the promise of different routes out of modernity, as for example the Soviet Union after the Russian Revolution of 1917, or the 1930s and 1940s German or Japanese modernity sought. Rather, alternative modernities points to the view that modernity today offers people around the world the opportunity to engage critically with their own hybrid modernities. Not the end of a single master narrative for modernity, the end of modernity or coming of postmodernity, but instead the absence of a governing centre produces latitude for multiple variation and 'creative adaptation' in a range of sites.

This reading of the culture of modernity as invention is premised upon the cultural resources, the availability of means of cultural production, circulation and consumption. Yet as we have shown in the example of Ming

China and Tokugawa Japan, the evidence of these resources themselves gives rise to the search for similarities with Western modernity and endless discussions about protomodern potentials. What it does is broaden the range of phenomena, which can be considered as relevant for modernity and take us away from models which stress the replication of the allegedly key Western cultural ingredient. In relation to the cultural dimension of modernity, clearly the expansion of the cultural sphere is a crucial process, whereby people discover through various literary and artistic cultural forms and institutions that they are modern (Featherstone, 1995: ch. 2). If the experience of the modern points to the expectation of a different present, then, the expansion of the market for cultural goods produced by cultural specialists, certainly helped to cater for it. If a change in the rhythm of movement in lived time and space creates the potential for new experiences, reflections and expectations, then travel itself could be considered as ushering in something which presaged the experience of modernity (Featherstone, 1995: 152). There are, then, complex genealogies of the modern, which are in the process of being uncovered.

In addition, ambivalent attitudes towards the modern are manifest in the characteristic ways of dealing with the new sense of temporality seen as accompanying, or defining the emergence of the modern. The move towards modern consumption should not be seen as a move from Puritanism to hedonism as Bell (1976) Campbell (1987) and others have argued, but more of a 'calculating hedonism', as people sought to experience and cope with, not necessarily resolve, the dilemmas of both. As Simon Sharma (1987) indicates, in his discussion of the emergence of modern consumption in seventeenth-century Amsterdam, the seemingly contradictory impulses of calculative rationality and abstraction and hedonism existed alongside each other. Attending to both church and tavern in everyday life, may have involved people in a moral ambivalence, but according to Sharma (1987: 371; cited in Miller, 1994: 79) in many

> departments of Dutch culture, opposite impulses were harmoniously reconciled in practice ... Nor did it take any lofty wisdom to see that the world was not torn asunder between abstinence and indulgence. Any fool could see that the *same people* embodied, at different times, in different places, the values appropriate to their impermanent role.

The demands of a radical sense of the present, along with the demands of the day and eternity, helped to produce the experience of modernity as a dilemma. As Miller (1994: 79) puts it

> The core dilemma of modernity lies in the consequences of the new temporality: that is a distinct sense of present, future and past, which leads to an increasing concern with the knowledge of self-construction of the criteria by which we live.

This ambivalence has departed from the conventional sociological accounts of modernity, which can be too quick to set out from the neat ideal-type dichotomies of tradition and modern societies. Certainly secularization does not fit neatly into the process, although it was clearly central to the eighteenth-century European philosophical discourse of modernity as progress and enlightened escape from religious dogma and deception.[22] Chakrabarty (2000: 14–16, 101–4), for example, in discussing India mentions two logics of power in modernity, one secular and based upon European institutional rule and the other continuing to bring gods and spirits into the domain of the political, suggesting a pluralization of power within global modernity. Chakrabarty goes on to contest the authority of secular historicizing western forms of knowledge which seek to define modernity in a singular way which draws from European experience.

Conclusion: culture, civility and the global public

As mentioned earlier, a further dimension of modernity which is often seen as definitive of modern societies is the question of the right to speak and participate in the public arena: democratization. Habermas (1989) focused on the emergence of the bourgeois public sphere in eighteenth-century Europe, the rise of what he was later to call 'communicative rationality', modes of critical debate and argumentation which had political potential for democratization. Ikegami (2005: 25), on the other hand, argues that Tokugawa Japan in the seventeenth and eighteenth centuries, like Europe, produced hierarchical civility (good manners with a stress on politeness and the 'mask of courtesy'). But whereas the European civility opened up into a civil society to help produce spaces in which a public sphere and the Enlightenment could develop, Japan in contrast produced a form of 'civility without civil society', due to the Tokugawa system of social segregation and restricted formal public world with its hierarchical civility. Yet, according to Ikegami (2005: 39), 'wide enclaves of free discursive spheres emerged outside the boundaries of the formal public world'. These 'enclaved publics', the za arts, the arts and literature associations, were not seen as challenging to the Tokugawa Shogunate, and were allowed to form a network of communicative spheres in which people could experience sociability, identity switching and cultural mobility.

The Tokugawa aesthetic publics contrasted with the critical-rational European publics in the way in which the former valued more implicit tacit modes of communication and the latter assumed more explicit articulation of differences through argumentation. Yet Ikegami (2005: 383) is reluctant to let go of the potential of the aesthetic-cultural sphere and argues for its relevance in the modern world in which 'we participate in multiple publics in society and are constantly switching connections from one to the other'. The Japanese za arts and use of the ritual logic of the mu'en (no relation) spaces, encouraged horizontal fellowship and the acceptance of differences. Ikegami (2005: 384) adds:

> The current world situation with its communicative demands and challenges is in many ways structurally similar to the situation in the Tokugawa era. The normative implications of the Japanese aesthetic publics this resides, paradoxically, in underscoring the human ability to create connectivity by means of decoupling into a 'no relation' mode within relational networks.

Ikegami sees this as a potential step forward from the difficulties associated with the paralysis of democracy in multiethnic and multireligious societies and in a world in which we increasingly have to interact with others either directly or through mediate systems such as email, whose communicative styles often differ radically from our own. Ikegami (2005: 384) adds that the modern world could need 'a new form of global civility for effective communication', and that the pluralism of communicative styles and switching of identities and capacity to handle diversity needed, could well learn from the Japanese example.[23]

If, as Norbert Elias (1994) argues, there is a link between civility and violence control, this relationship is being severely tested today in a time of increasing belligerency and warfare, based on the United States' 'state of exception' views of its sovereignty (Malik, 2006; Dirlik, 2003; Ugarteche, 2007).[24] If a global public sphere is to emerge, then it could well need to explore more flexible modes of communication, as Ikegami suggests. Max Weber's vision of modernity emphasizes a sort of Darwinist struggle between nation-states bent on winning in an elimination contest. The nation-state with its sense of singular purpose and national destiny, was one, albeit problematic, outcome of modernity. Certainly a glance at international politics today, with the growing instabilities of the so-called *Pax Americana* and end of 'the American Century', offers the prospect of a new cycle of global political and economic struggles with the potential for military conflicts, as power balances shift with the rise of Asian powers (notably China, India, Pakistan and Iran) with their own agendas. Yet modernity is also associated with the development of a range of counter-institutions and public spaces. If modernity in its various manifestations has bequeathed us a public and cultural sphere, which has the potential to reach from transnational to even global scope, then this space has to be relational and expansive enough to work through a plurality of communicative styles and modalities.

****

Modernity is generally associated with a heightened intellectual impulse for reflexivity, for rethinking the grounds of knowledge in a shifting context of rapid social change. In Europe the assumption was that universal knowledge was not only possible, but the scope of the rational scientific method could be extended from the analysis of nature to the human domain. Yet the quest for universality in the human and social sciences has been fraught with difficulties in terms of the historical and praxiological dimensions of human existence, on the one hand, and on the other, the active discovery and construction of cultural differences alongside the development of the nation-state in which culture became synonymous with national cultures. The dangers of the emphasis on culture is to promote and essentialize national differences. At the same time, while this invention of national cultures is to be seen as part of modern culture, the culture of modernity clearly means more: pointing to the invention of an active cultural sphere based both upon print and commodity production, along with a range of interstitial quasi-public spaces. As we have argued, the roots of this cultural sphere go back a long way and cannot be regarded as the exclusive province of a particular area, such as Europe. A consumer culture and a print culture have the potential to alter the nature or public life. Yet increasingly we are becoming aware that the public sphere, as described by Habermas in terms of European development and associated with rational argumentation and democratization, may not necessarily be the only outcome. Habermas of course was aware of the deformation of the public sphere related to the mass media monopolization processes; also significant were the active policies of authoritarian states, analyzed by Horkheimer and other critical theorists, which are still with us. A globalized public sphere in the positive sense, is still only a potential. In this context, Ikegami's investigation of an alternative genealogy of public life and civility provides an interesting counterexample.

There is a lesson here in terms of the increasingly globalizing archive which stands behind all scholarship. We can no longer assume this to be located within the West, nor can we clearly presume that Western developments were somehow benign, or superior prototypes for the development of the world as a whole. Global knowledge is an impossible ambition, yet it is an ambition written into the authority claims of many forms of knowledge, especially those which sought scientific and rational legitimation as they emerged within modern societies. If our intention has increasingly become one in which we subject these claims to critique, and uncover alternative genealogies, then the classification of knowledge also becomes subjected to critique; certainly in terms of scope and level of generality. Postmodernism and postcolonial theory point to the difficulties of existing authority claims, along with those things which have been misplaced, forgotten and occluded from authoritative accounts. In many ways there has always been a crisis in modern thought, in adjusting to a world in which new knowledge and social experimentation became more prevalent and officially sanctioned, throwing doubts on the grounds and legitimacy of knowledge. Today we face a further crisis in this process, one in which Western-based claims to global knowledge have become problematized.[25] To construct adequate knowledge and to think through the ways in which it could work in relation to a nascent global public sphere, along with the modes of sociability and civility that ground that sphere, is one of our pressing tasks.

Notes

1 For some the concern with modern experience and the quality of modern life (*modernité*), can be traced back to Baudelaire and the Paris of the 1840s (see Berman, 1982). The artistic movement modernism is often located in the first decades of the twentieth century (cf. Virginia Woolf's oft-quoted remark made in 1924, that 'on or about December 1910, human

character changed'. Certainly this period was also the focus in the work of Georg Simmel, characterized as 'the first sociologist of modernity' (Frisby, 1985a) in his analyses of the metropolis, money and the concern with style and experience in the emergent consumer culture. As can Max Weber's influential account of the differentiation and rationalization of the value spheres, the dilemmas of modern existence in terms of how to live a meaningful ordered life in a post-religious world (see Featherstone, 1995: ch. 3).

2 There are of course many interpretations of Weber's work, some which emphasize the ideal-type method as used in *Economy and Society* as a step towards the development of general universal categories of knowledge. The interpretation here emphasizes the centrality of the value questions and the life orders along with a strong historical sense of the development of knowledge and the categories of the social sciences (see Featherstone, 1995: chs 3 and 4).

3 Some commentators are now talking not only about the eclipse of US hegemony, but the coming World War III between the West and Islam, with China and India the gainers (see Chan Akya, 'China and India in World War 111', *Asia Times*, 25 July 2006). *Asia Times* contains regular articles on the decline of US power and the rise of Asia. Critiques of the Weber thesis from an Asian point of view are more evident; see, for example, the cleverly titled 'The Protestant *Ethnic* and the Spirit of Capitalism', Chow (2002). Weber was of course himself aware of the rise of Japan in his day and also predicted that the Chinese would adapt well to modern capitalism in his *Religion of China*.

4 There are clear problems with trying to use enthnophilosophy and African philosophy as a basis for alternative sociology or forms of knowledge, as Paulin Hountondji (1983, 2002) identifies. Not least do they rely on models of static isolated islands of culture which misses the long process of movements of knowledge and culture. As Eric Wolf (1982) has also shown local knowledge is a relative concept within all societies and different groups depend in different ways on horizons of limited and local knowledge. More powerful groups have always had greater access to regional and globally circulating forms of knowledge.

5 See *The Economist* special issue on the China revival, 16–22 September 2006.

6 A process of *rediscovery* because of the positive reception Ming advances had in seventeenth- and eighteenth-century Europe (see Leibniz, Adam Smith and other evaluations).

7 Marx's theory of the Asiatic mode of production is also well known for its negative depiction of the East. Another influential theoretical concept was Wittfogel's theory of 'oriental despotism', which depicted Asian societies as unchanging, authoritarian and reproductive.

8 One indication of China's dominance was the role it enjoyed in the imagination of writers, scientists and philosophers in the seventeenth and eighteenth centuries. Not only did Adam Smith and others admire the efficiency of Chinese bureaucracy, the free-market notion in economics was also taken from China. In fact it was Quesnay, not Adam Smith, who was the first European to criticize mercantilism, with his doctrine of Physiocracy (rule of nature). As J. J. Clark (1997: 49) remarks 'Quesnay's revolutionary ideas amounted to a liberation from the economic orthodoxy of ... mercantilism ... and his influence on the free market theories of Adam Smith was profound. What is often omitted in accounts of Quesnay's place in modern thought which emphasises his role in developing economics as a scientific method, is his debt to China – unlike in his own day when we was widely known as "the European Confucius". One of his key influential ideas which he imported from Chinese political economy was *we-wei*, which was translated into French as *laissez-faire* (Hobson, 2004: 196). In addition it has also been argued by Pomeranz (2000) that China and to a lesser degree Japan in the eighteenth century, more closely resembled the neoclassical ideal of a *laissez-faire* market economy than Western Europe. For an insight into the major influence of China on another central figure in Western mathematical and scientific thought, Leibniz, see Perkins (2004).

9 This was especially the case after China abandoned the naval expansion policy with the triumph of the land party over the seas party within the Imperial Court which led to the laying up of the Chinese junks (which dwarfed Vasco de Gama's Portuguese caravels) in Admiral He's fleet which some held sailed not only to East Africa, but rounded the Cape and reached Portugal and some speculate even sailed the Pacific to Mexico (see Levathes, 1994). Yet the impact of the strengthening of the army in face of threats from the north, and the laying up of the great ships and the imperial ban on foreign commerce of 1434 has been argued by

Hobson (2004: 62) in no way amounted to isolationism, indeed along with the continued importing of silver, international trade remained vibrant as did internal trade and economic infrastructure building.

10 Just to take two examples. First, the infamous Opium Wars (1834–43 and 1856–60), in which England bombarded the coast of China and made numerous raids into the interior), were caused by British affront at Chinese resistance to the extension of the British East India Company run opium trade into China. These events resulted in a humiliating Chinese defeat, the doubling of the number of opium addicts and the opening-up of a series of treaty ports. It stamped the decline of China and the rise of Europe, and opened up the argument that the only response to Western domination was for China to modernize. In Japan, after the increased incursions from Western powers in the wake of the US Admiral Perry's 'black ships' visit of 1853, a British warship bombarded the Satsuma port of Kagoshima in Kyushu. The pretext for the Satsuma–British 'War' of 1862–3 was the execution by the Japanese of a British sailor who stole a cow.

11 Knowledge, as Todorov argues, was central to the conquest of Mexico, and Cortez used a wide array of tactics, propaganda and ruses to triumph over the Aztecs and Montezuma (Todorov, 1992: ch. 4).

12 Indeed, it is also possible to see forms of individualism and rational calculation as important at particular times in Japanese history, despite all the commonly held Western stereotypes of 'groupism', 'group mind', emotional intuitionism and differently wired brains, which frequently resurface in popular and academic accounts of Japan. On honorific individualism in Samurai culture prior to Tokugawa Japan see Ikegami (1995).

13 Ha-Joon Chang (2002) has argued that in the nineteenth century free trade was used as a means to de-industrialize colonial economies, in a similar way that WTO policies which favour the intellectual property rights of transnational corporations, further exploitation today in the contemporary South (see Pieterse, 2006).

14 The process of taking in first silk goods from the East, then Chinese knowledge and machinery for silk production in Northern Italy over a number of centuries from the thirteenth century onwards – a long-term process of import substitution and then the development of an export market is one example (see Goody, 2004). The cotton and ceramics trades provide others. Notable is the attempts to breakdown the monopolies of production techniques and knowledge through observation and industrial espionage, not just the creative imagination of the lone inventor or entrepreneur of popular mythology.

15 On sumptuary laws see Appadurai (1986) and also Pomeranz (2000). The latter argues that in England, Holland, China and Japan sumptuary laws lessened in influence earlier than in Spain and Italy. Pomeranz (2000: 131) remarks that in Ming China, while the early Ming state passed various sumptuary laws to regulate dress, tableware etc., they had little effect and soon became hopelessly outdated and irrelevant. At the same time there were periodic attempts in seventeenth century England and the Netherlands and also Japan to reintroduce them. In Japan, sumptuary laws became enforced with the rise of the Tokugawa state in 1604 (the same time as they were ending in England), but they were difficult to impose and the burgeoning fashion system and use of fine silks flourished, especially in the cities (Ikegami, 2005: 257 ff.).

16 In Japan not only the independence and fluidity of the enclave publics in Edo should be mentioned, but the rise of independent towns, such as the city of Sakai, the home of Sen no Rikyu. The city was one of the few places in Japan to achieve a degree of autonomy, and was protected by gates and moats resembling the European free cities. It was governed by a board of merchant councillors and the arts flourished. But it was conquered by Oda Nobunaga in 1568 (Ikegami, 2005: 122).

17 Current interest revolves around the global or transnational public sphere and the potential to extend the notion of public beyond the nation-state and the potential new types of public will formation (see Fraser, 2007).

18 The term public has a complex set of genealogies in Japan, with a range of terms such as *kogi, ko and oyake* used (Ikegami, 2005: 366). For a discussion of the relevance of *mu'en* spaces in the context of the development of equivalent public spheres in Japan see Hanada (2006) and Hayashi (2006).

19 It should also be added that the image of modern society in the post-war era was influenced a good deal by the American social science 'oversocialized' view of culture as integrative and orderly, with works such as Ruth Benedict's *The Chrysanthemum and the Sword* (1946) highly influential. This assumption that Japan enjoyed a persistent cultural identity beneath the flux of modernization became not only a truism of area studies, but also fed back into Japanese social science (Silberman, 2002).

20 I am conscious that a similar analysis of the construction of China Modern could be made in the same way as Carol Gluck performs on Japan. Important here are the ways in which, in the 1990s, postmodernism has been varyingly embraced and challenged within Chinese academic and intellectual circles seeking to define itself in relation to the Maoist communist past and a present in which an emergent consumer culture gained major significance. See the discussions by Chen Xiaoming on postmodernism (2006) also Dirlik and Zhang (2000).

21 1920s Japan, especially with the rebuilding of Tokyo after the 1923 earthquake and the expanding consumer culture, as Harootunian (1998, 2000) points out, played this out. Not only exhibiting the intellectual and artistic fascination with modern life, the *modan*, but the retreat from it into the invented tradition with its talk of harmony, beauty and spirit, the alleged categories of the 'timeless folk'.

22 The secular nature of the public sphere is often overestimated; a strong impetus for reform continued within the public sphere in the West from Unitarian Church and other non-conformist religious groups (Venn and Featherstone, 2006).

23 There is not the space here to address the question of the intimate or affective public sphere (Berlant and Warner, 1998) and neo-vitalist attempts by Lazaratto and others to rethink public life as a site of expression and invention (see Terranova, 2007; Featherstone and Venn, 2006). There are also interesting parallels between Ikegami's view of Edo and Sennett's (1976) discussion of the functionality of 'masking' and playfulness in eighteenth-century French public life, prior to the fall of public man through our over-concern with revelatory intimacy in public and 'destructive Gemeinschaft'.

24 There are considerable debates among Elias scholars about the relationship between civilizing and de-civilizing processes and the switching between modes of civility and violence control in the metropolitan centres and violent excesses in the colonial peripheries (see Mennell, 1989).

25 The investigation of this process and the attempts to rethink knowledge in the light of the processes of globalization and digitalization is one of the aims of the *Theory, Culture & Society* New Encyclopaedia Project – see the *Theory, Culture & Society* 'Problematizing Global Knowledge' special issue – especially introduction by Featherstone and Venn (2006).

Bibliography

Abercrombie, N., Hill, S. and Turner, B.S. (1980) *The Dominant Ideology Thesis*. London: Allen & Unwin.

Abrams, P. and McCulloch, A. (1975) *Communes, Sociology and Society*. Cambridge: Cambridge University Press.

Adorno, T. (1967) 'Veblen's Attack on Culture', *Prisms*, trans. S. and S. Weber. London: Spearman.

Alexander, J.C. (1988) 'Culture and Political Crisis: Watergate and Durkheimian Sociology', in J.C. Alexander (ed.), *Durkheimian Sociology: Cultural Studies*. Cambridge: Cambridge University Press.

Allen, J.S. (1983) *The Romance of Commerce and Culture*. Chicago: Chicago University Press.

Anderson, B. (1983) *Imagined Communities*. London: New Left Books.

Anderson, B. (1991) *Imagined Communities*. Revised edition, London: Verso.

Anderson, P. (1987) 'The Figures of Descent', *New Left Review*, 161.

Andre, L. (1984) 'The Politics of Postmodern Photography', *Minnesota Review*, 23.

Appadurai, A. (1986) 'Introduction: Commodities and the Politics of Value,' in A. Appadurai (ed.), *The Social Life of Things: Commodities in Cultural Perspective*. Cambridge: Cambridge University Press.

Arac, J. (1986) *Postmodernism and Politics*. Minneapolis: Minnesota University Press.

Archer, M.S. (1988) *Culture and Agency*. Cambridge: Cambridge University Press.

Arnason, J. (2000) 'Communism and Modernity', in S.N. Eisenstadt (ed.), 'Multiple Modernities', *Daedalus* 129(1).

Arnason, J. (2001) 'The Multiplication of Modernity', in Eliezer Ben-Rafael and Yitzhak Sternberg (eds), *Identity, Culture and Globalization*. Leiden: International Institute of Sociology and Brill Academic Press.

Arnason, J., Eisenstadt, S.N. and Wittrock, B. (ed.) (2004) *Axial Civilizations and World History*. Leiden: Brill.

Arnold, M. (1869/1932) *Culture and Anarchy*. Cambridge: Cambridge University Press.

Bailey, P. (1978) *Leisure and Class in Victorian England*. London: Routledge & Kegan Paul.

Bailey, P. (1986a) *Music Hall: The Business of Pleasure*. Milton Keynes: Open University Press.

Bailey, P. (1986b) 'Champagne Charlie', in J.S. Bratton (ed.), *Music Hall: Performance and Style*. Milton Keynes: Open University Press.

Bakhtin, M.M. (1968) *Rabelais and His World*. Cambridge, MA: MIT Press.

Bann, S. (1984) *The Clothing of Clio: A Study of Representations of History in Nineteenth Century Britain and France*. Cambridge: Cambridge University Press.

Barbalet, J. (1986) 'Limitations of Class Theory and the Disappearance of Status: The Problem of the New Middle Class', *Sociology*, 20(4).

Barnes, H.E. (ed.) (1966) *Introduction to the History of Sociology*. Chicago: University of Chicago Press.

Bataille, G. (1988) *The Accursed Share*, Volume I. New York: Zone Books.

Baudelaire, C. (1964) *The Painter of Modern Life and Other Essays*. Oxford: Phaidon Press.

Baudrillard, J. (1970) *La Société de consommation*. Paris: Gallimard.

Baudrillard, J. (1975) *The Mirror of Production*. St Louis, MO: Telos Press.

Baudrillard, J. (1981) *For a Critique of the Political Economy of the Sign*. St Louis, MO: Telos Press.

Baudrillard, J. (1982) 'The Beaubourg Effect: Implosion and Deterrence', *October* 20.

Baudrillard, J. (1983a) *Simulations*. New York: Semiotext(e).

Baudrillard, J. (1983b) *In the Shadow of the Silent Majorities*. New York: Semiotext(e).

Bauman, Z. (1985) 'On the Origins of Civilization', *Theory, Culture & Society*, 2(3).

Bauman, Z. (1988) 'Is There a Postmodern Sociology?' *Theory, Culture & Society*, 5(2–3).

Bauman, Z. (1990) 'Modernity and Ambivalence', *Theory, Culture & Society*, 7(2–3).

Bauman, Z. (2000) *Liquid Modernity*. Cambridge: Polity Press.

Bayley, S. (1979) *In Good Shape: Style in Industrial Products*. London: Van Nostrand Reinhold.

Beck, U. (1993) *Risk Society*. London: Sage.

Beck, U. (1996) 'World Risk Society', *Theory, Culture & Society* 13(4).

Beckford, J. (1985) 'The Insulation and Isolation of the Sociology of Religion', *Sociological Analysis*, 46(4).

Belk, W. (2004) 'The Human Consequences of Consumer Culture', in K.M. Ekstrom and H. Brembeck (eds), *Elusive Consumption*. Oxford: Berg.

Bell, D. (1976) *The Cultural Contradictions of Capitalism*. London: Heinemann.

Bell, D. (1980) 'Beyond Modernism, Beyond Self', in *Sociological Journeys*. London: Heinemann.

Bellah, R., Madsen, R., Sullivan, W.M., Swidler, A. and Tipton, S. (1985) *Habits of the Heart*. Berkeley: University of California Press.

Bender, D.E. and Greenwald, R.E. (2003) *Sweatshop USA: The American Sweatshop in Historical and Global Perspective*. London: Routledge.

Bendix, R. (1959) *Max Weber: An Intellectual Portrait*. London: Methuen.

Bendix, R. (1970) 'Culture, Social Structure and Change', in *Embattled Reason: Essays on Social Knowledge*. New York: Oxford University Press,

Benedict, R. (1946) *The Chrysanthemum and the Sword*. Boston, MA: Houghton Mifflin.

Benjamin, W. (1973) *Charles Baudelaire: A Lyric Poet in the Era of High Capitalism*. London: New Left Books.

Benjamin, W. (1979) 'Berlin Chronicle', in *One Way Street and Other Writings*. London: New Left Books.

Benjamin, W. (1982a) 'On Some Motifs in Baudelaire', in *Illuminations*. London: Cape.

Benjamin, W. (1982b) *Das Passagen-Werk*, 2 vols, ed. R. Tiedermann. Frankfurt: Suhrkamp.

Benjamin, W. (1999) *The Arcades Project*. Cambridge, MA: Harvard University Press.

Bennett, T., (1988) 'The Exhibitionary Complex', *New Formations*, 4.

Bennett, T., et al. (1977) *The Study of Culture I*. Milton Keynes: Open University Press.

Bennett, T., Martin, G., Mercer, C. and Woollacott, T. (eds) (1981) *Culture, Ideology and Social Process*. London: Batsford.

Bennett, T., et al. (1983) *Formations of Pleasure*. London: Routledge & Kegan Paul.

Berg, M. and Clifford, H. (eds) (1999) *Consumers and Luxury: Consumer Culture in Europe 1650–1850*. Manchester: Manchester University Press.

Berger, P. (1969) *The Social Reality of Religion*. London: Faber.

Berlant, L. and Warner, M. (1998) 'Sex in Public', *Critical Inquiry* (winter).

Berman, M. (1982) *All that Is Solid Melts Into Air*. New York: Simon and Schuster.

Bernstein, R.J. (ed.) (1985) *Habermas and Modernity*. Oxford: Polity Press.

Berry, C. J. (1994) *The Idea of Luxury*. Cambridge: Cambridge University Press.

Bertens, H. (1995) *The Idea of the Postmodern: A History*. London: Routledge.

Bito, M. (1992) *Edo jidai to wa nani ka: Nihonshijō no kinsei to kindai*. Tokyo: Iwanami no Shoten.

Blaut, J.M. (1993) *The Colonizer's Model of the World: Geographical Diffusionism and Eurocentric History*. New York: Guilford.

Blaut, J.M. (2000) *Eight Eurocentric Historians*. New York: Guilford.

Bourdieu, P. (1971) 'Intellectual Field and Creative Project', in M. Young (ed.), *Knowledge and Control*. London: Collier-Macmillan.

Bourdieu, P. (1977) *Outline of a Theory of Practice*, trans. Richard Nice. Cambridge: Cambridge University Press.

Bourdieu, P. (1979) 'The Production of Belief: Contribution to an Economy of Symbolic Goods', *Media, Culture and Society*, 2.

Bourdieu, P. (1983a) 'The Field of Cultural Production', *Poetics*, 12.

Bourdieu, P. (1983b) 'The Philosophical Institution', in A. Montefiore (ed.), *Philosophy in France Today*. Cambridge: Cambridge University Press.

Bourdieu, P. (1984) *Distinction: A Social Critique of the Judgment of Taste*, trans. R. Nice. London: Routledge & Kegan Paul.

Bourdieu, P. (1986) 'Interview', *Theory, Culture & Society*, 3(3).

Bourdieu, P. (1987) 'The Forms of Capital', in J .G. Richardson (ed.), *Handbook of Theory and Research for the Sociology of Education*. New York: Greenwood Press.

Bourdieu, P., Boltanski, L., Castel, R. and Chamboredon, J.C. (1965) *Un Art Moyen*. Paris: Minuit.

Bourdieu, P. and Passeron, J.C. (1990) *Reproduction in Education, Society and Culture*. 2nd edn. London: Sage (1st edn 1977).

Boyer, M.C. (1988) 'The Return of Aesthetics to City Planning', *Society*, 25(4).

Bradbury, M. (1983) 'Modernisms/Postmodernisms', in I. Hassan and S. Hassan (eds), *Innovation/Renovation*. Madison: Wisconsin University Press.

Bradbury, M. and McFarlane, J. (eds) (1976) *Modernism 1980–1930*. Harmondsworth: Penguin.

Braidotti, R. (2006) 'Posthuman. All too Human: Towards a New Process Ontology,' *Theory, Culture & Society Annual Review* 23(7–8).

Brecher, J. and Costello, T. (1994) *Global Village or Global Pillage: Economic Reconstruction from the Bottom Up*. Boston, MA: South End Press.

Brewer, J. and Porter, R. (eds) (1994) *Consumption and the World of Goods*. London: Routledge.

Bruce-Briggs. B. (ed.) (1979) *The New Class*. New York: McGraw-Hill.

Buck-Morss, S. (1983) 'Benjamin's *Passagen-Werk*', *New German Critique*, 29.

Buck-Morss, S. (1986) 'The *Flâneur*, the Sandwichman and the Whore: The Politics of Loitering', *New German Critique*, 39.

Bürger, P. (1984) *Theory of the Avant-Garde*. Manchester: Manchester University Press.

Burglin, V. (1985/6) 'Some Thoughts on Outsiderism and Postmodernism', *Block*, 11.

Burke, P. (1978) *Popular Culture in Early Modern Europe*. London: Temple Smith.

Burke, P. (1993) '*Res e Verba*: Conspicuous Consumption in the Early Modern World', in J. Brewer and R. Porter (eds), *Consumption and the World of Goods*. London: Routledge.

Burnett, J. and Bush, A. (1986) 'Profiling the Yuppie', *Journal of Advertising Research*, April.

Burris, V. (1986) 'The Discovery of the New Middle Class', *Theory and Society*, 15.

Calefato, P. (1988) 'Fashion, the Passage, the Body', *Cultural Studies*, 2(2).

Campbell, C. (1987) *The Romantic Ethic and the Spirit of Modern Consumerism*. Oxford: Basil Blackwell.

Carter, R. (1985) *Capitalism, Class Conflict and the New Middle Class*. London: Routledge & Kegan Paul.

Chakrabarty, D. (1998) 'Afterword', in S. Vlastos (ed.), *Mirror of Modernity: Invention of Tradition in Modern Japan*. Berkeley: University of California Press.

Chakrabarty, D. (2000) *Provincializing Europe*. Princeton, NJ: Princeton University Press.

Chambers, I. (1986) *Popular Culture: The Metropolitan Experience*. London: Methuen.

Chambers, I. (1987) 'Maps for the Metropolis: A Possible Guide to the Postmodern', *Cultural Studies*, 1(1).

Chaney, D. (1979) *Fictions and Ceremonies*. London: Arnold.

Chaney, D. (1983) 'The Department Store as a Cultural Form', *Theory, Culture & Society*, 1(3).

Chaney, D. (1990) 'Dystopia in Gateshead: The Metrocentre as a Cultural Form', *Theory, Culture & Society*, 7(4).

Chang, Ha-Joon (2002) *Kicking Away the Ladder*. London: Anthem.

Cheah, P. (2007) *Inhuman Conditions. On Cosmopolitanism and Human Rights*. Cambridge, MA: Harvard University Press.

Chen, K.H. (1987) 'Baudrillard's Implosive Postmodernism', *Theory, Culture & Society*, 4(1).

Chen, Xiaoming (2006) 'The Development of Postmodernism in China', New Encyclopaedia Project Megacities Workshop, Beijing Languages and Culture University, September.

Chow, R. (2002) *The Protestant Ethnic & The Spirit of Capitalism*. New York: Columbia University Press.

Chua, Beng Huat (2006) 'Singapore's Routes to Modernity', in special issue on Problematizing Global Knowledge, *Theory, Culture and Society*, 23(2–3).

Cipolla, C.M. (1965) *Guns and Sails in the Early Phase of European Expansion, 1400–1700*. London: Collins.

Clark J.J. (1997) *Oriental Enlightenment: The Encounter between Asian and Western Thought*. London: Routledge.

Clark, T.J. (1985) *The Painting of Modern Life*. London: Thames & Hudson.

Clunas, C. (1991) *Superfluous Things: Material Culture and Social Status in Early Modern China*. Oxford: Polity Press.

Cohen, A.P. (1985) *The Symbolic Construction of Community*. London: Tavistock.

Cohen, I. (1986) 'The Status of Structuration Theory: A Reply to McLennan', *Theory, Culture & Society*, 3(1).

Cohen, I. (1987) 'Structuration Theory and Social Praxis', in A. Giddens and J. Turner (eds), *Social Theory Today*. Oxford: Polity Press.

Cohen, L. (2004) *A Consumers' Republic. The Politics of Mass Consumption in Postwar America*. New York: Vintage.

Coleridge, S.T. (1837/1974) *On the Constitution of Church and State*. London: Dent.

Collins, R. (1988a) 'Review of Lash and Whimster (eds). *Max Weber, Rationality and Modernity*', *Theory, Culture & Society*, 5(1).

Collins, R. (1988b) 'The Durkheimian Tradition in Conflict Sociology', in J.C. Alexander (ed.), *Durkheimian Sociology: Cultural Studies*. Cambridge: Cambridge University Press.

Connolly, William E. (2007) 'The Christo-Capitalist Assemblage', *Theory, Culture & Society*, 24(7–8).

Cooke, P. (1988) 'Modernity, Postmodernity and the City', *Theory, Culture & Society*, 5(2–3).

Cooke, P. and Onufrijchuk, I. (1987) 'Space the Final Frontier ...', unpublished paper.

Cooper, M. (2006) 'Pre-emptive Emergence: The Biological Turn in the War on Terror', *Theory, Culture & Society*, 23(4).

Corrigan, P. and Sayer, D. (1985) *The Great Arch: English State Formation as Cultural Revolution*. Oxford: Basil Blackwell.

Cowley, M. (1951) *Exiles Return*. New York: Viking.

Crane, D. (1987) *The Transformation of the Avant-Garde*. Chicago: Chicago University Press.

Crary, J. (1984) 'The Eclipse of the Spectacle', in B. Wallis (ed.), *Art after Modernism*. New York: New Museum Press.

Cross, G. (2000) *An All-Consuming Century: Why Commercialism Won in Modern America*. New York: Columbia University Press.

Dahrendorf, R. (1968) 'Out of Utopia', in *Essays in the Theory of Society*. London: Routledge & Kegan Paul.

Davis, M. (1985) 'Urban Renaissance and Spatial Postmodernism', *New Left Review*, 151.

Davis, M. (2006) *Planet of Slums*. London: Verso.

Dayan, D. and Katz, E. (1988) 'Articulating Consensus: The Ritual and Rhetoric of Media Events', in J.C. Alexander (ed.), *Durkheimian Sociology: Cultural Studies*. Cambridge: Cambridge University Press.

De Landa, M. (2006) *New Philosophy of Society: Assemblage Theory and Social Complexity*. London: Continuum.

de Swaan, A. (1981) 'The Politics of Agoraphobia', *Theory and Society*, 10(3).

Del Sapio, M. (1988) 'The Question Is Whether You Make Words Mean so Many Different Things: Notes on Art and Metropolitan Languages', *Cultural Studies*, 2(2).

Denzin, N. (1984) *On Understanding Emotion*. San Francisco: Jossey-Bass.

DiMaggio, P. (1982) 'Culture Entrepreneurship in 19th Century Boston', Parts I and II, *Media, Culture and Society*, 4.

DiMaggio, P. (1986) 'Can Culture Survive the Marketplace?', in *Non-Profit Enterprise in the Arts*. Oxford: Oxford University Press.

DiMaggio, P. (1987) 'Classification in Art', *American Sociological Review*, 52(4).

DiMaggio, P. and Useem, M. (1978) 'Cultural Property and Public Policy', *Social Research*, 45(2).

Dirlik, A. (2003) 'Global Modernity? Modernity in an Age of Global Capitalism', *European Journal of Social Theory* 6(3): 275–92.

Dirlik, A. and Zhang, X. (eds), (2000) *Postmodernism and China*. Durham, NC: Duke University Press.

Doherty, T. (1987) 'Theory, Enlightenment and Violence: Postmodern Hermeneutics as a Comedy of Errors', *Textual Practice*, 1(2).

Douglas, M. (1982) 'The Effects of Modernization on Religious Change', *Daedalus.*, 111(1).

Douglas, M. and Isherwood, B. (1980) *The World of Goods*. Harmondsworth: Penguin.

During, S. (1987) 'Postmodernism or Post-colonialism Today', *Textual Practice*, 1(1).

Durkheim, E. (1964) *The Division of Labour in Society*. New York: Free Press.

Durkheim, E. (1974) Value Judgments and Judgments of Reality', in *Sociology and Philosophy*. New York: Free Press.

Eagleton, T. (1968) 'The Idea of a Common Culture', in T. Eagleton and B. Wicher (eds), *From Culture to Revolution*. London.

Easton, S., Hawkins, A., Laing, S. and Walker, H. (1988) *Disorder and Discipline: Popular Culture from 1550 to the Present*. London: Temple Smith.

Ehrenreich, B. and Hochschild, A. (eds), (2003) *Global Women: Nannies, Maids and Sex Workers in the New Economy*. London: Granta.

Eisenstadt, S.N. (2000) 'Multiple Modernities', in S.N. Eisenstadt (ed.), *Multiple Modernities* special issue. *Daedalus* 129(1).

Elias, N. (1971) 'Sociology of Knowledge: New Perspectives. Part I', *Sociology*, 5.

Elias, N. (1972) 'Theory of Science and History of Science', *Economy and Society*. 1(2).

Elias, N. (1978a) *What is Sociology?* London: Hutchinson.

Elias, N. (1978b) *The Civilizing Process*. Volume I: *The History of Manners*. Oxford: Basil Blackwell.

Elias. N. (1982) *The Civilizing Process*. Volume II: *State Formation and Civilization*. Oxford: Basil Blackwell.

Elias, N. (1983) *The Court Society*. Oxford: Basil Blackwell.

Elias, N. (1984a) 'On the Sociogenesis of Sociology', *Sociologisch Tijdschrift*, 11(1).

Elias, N. (1984b) 'Knowledge and Power: An Interview by Peter Ludes', in N. Stehr and V. Meja (eds), *Society and Knowledge*. New Brunswick, NJ: Transaction Books.

Elias, N. (1987a) 'The Changing Balance of Power between the Sexes', *Theory, Culture & Society*, 4(2–3).

Elias, N. (1987b) 'The Retreat of Sociologists into the Present', *Theory, Culture & Society*, 4(2–3).

Elias, N. (1987c) *Involvement and Detachment*. Oxford: Basil Blackwell.

Elias, N. (1987d) 'On Human Beings and Their Emotions', *Theory, Culture & Society*, 4(2–3).

Elias, N. (1994) *The Civilizing Process*. Single vol. edn. Oxford: Blackwell.

Elias, N. and Scotson, J. (1965) *The Established and the Outsiders*. London: Cass.

Eliot, T.S. (1948) *Notes towards the Definition of Culture*. London: Faber.

Elwert, G. (1984) 'Markets, Venality and Moral Economy', mimeo; conference on Civilizations and Theories of Civilizing Processes: Comparative Perspective, University of Bielefeld.

Ewen, S. (1976) *Captains of Consciousness: Advertising and the Social Roots of the Consumer Culture*. New York: McGraw-Hill.

Ewen. S. (1988) *All Consuming Images*. New York: Basic Books.

Ewen, S. and Ewen, E. (1982) *Channels of Desire*. New York: McGraw-Hill.

Featherstone, M. (1982) 'The Body in Consumer Culture', *Theory, Culture & Society*, 1(2) reprinted in M. Featherstone, M. Hepworth and B.S. Turner (eds), *The Body*. London: Sage, 1991.

Featherstone, M. (1983) 'Consumer Culture: An Introduction', *Theory, Culture & Society*, 1(3).

Featherstone, M. (1986) 'French Social Theory: An Introduction', *Theory, Culture and Society*, 3(3).

Featherstone, M. (1987a) 'Consumer Culture, Symbolic Power and Universalism', in G. Stauth and S. Zubaida (eds), *Mass Culture, Popular Culture and Lifeworlds in the Middle East*. Frankfurt: Campus Verlag.

Featherstone, M. (1987b) 'Leisure, Symbolic Power and the Life Course', in D. Jary, D. Horne and A. Tomlinson (eds), *Sport, Leisure and Social Relations*. London: Routledge.

Featherstone, M. (1988) 'Cultural Production, Consumption and the Development of the Cultural Sphere', paper presented at the Third German–American Sociological Theory Group Conference, Bremen.

Featherstone, M. (ed.) (1990) *Global Culture, Theory, Culture & Society* special issue. Reprinted in 1990 as *Global Culture: Nationalism, Globalization and Modernity*. London: Sage.

Featherstone, M. (1992) 'The Heroic Life and Everyday Life', *Theory, Culture & Society*, 9(1). Reprinted in M. Featherstone (1995).

Featherstone, M. (1995) *Undoing Culture: Globalization, Postmodernism and Identity*. London: Sage.

Featherstone, M. (1998) 'Love and Eroticism: An Introduction', *Theory, Culture & Society* special issue on Love & Eroticism, 15(3–4).

Featherstone, M. (1999) 'Body Modification: An Introduction', *Body & Society*, special issue on Body Modification, 4(2–3). Reprinted as a *Theory, Culture & Society* Book Series title; London: Sage, 2000.

Featherstone, M. (2000) 'Archiving Cultures', special issue on Sociology Facing the Next Millennium, *British Journal of Sociology*, 51(1).

Featherstone, M. (2001a) 'Consumer Culture', in *International Encyclopaedia of the Social and Behavioral Sciences*. Oxford: Elsevier, 2001.

Featherstone, M. (2001b) 'Globalization Processes: Postnational Flows, Identity Formation and Cultural Space', in Eliezer Ben-Rafael and Yitzhak Sternberg (eds), *Identity, Culture and Globalization*. Leiden: International Institute of Sociology and Brill Academic Press.

Featherstone, M. (2002) 'Cosmopolis: An Introduction', Special issue on Cosmopolis, *Theory, Culture & Society*, 19(1–2).

Featherstone, M. (2004) 'Automobilities: An Introduction', Special issue on Automobilities, *Theory, Culture & Society*, 21(4–5). Also reprinted as a *TCS* Book Series title, London: Sage, 2005.

Featherstone, M. (2006a) 'Genealogies of the Global', in special issue on Problematizing Global Knowledge (ed. M. Featherstone, C. Venn, R. Bishop and J. Phillips), *Theory, Culture & Society*, 23(2–3).

Featherstone, M. (2006b) 'Archive', in special issue on Problematizing Global Knowledge (ed. M. Featherstone, C. Venn, R. Bishop and J. Phillips), *Theory, Culture & Society*, 23(2–3).

Featherstone, M. (2007) 'Transformations: Body, Image and Affect in Consumer Culture', *Body & Society*, forthcoming.

Featherstone, M. and Hepworth, M. (1982) 'Ageing and Inequality: Consumer Culture and the New Middle Age', in D. Robbins et al. (eds), *Rethinking Social Inequality*. Aldershot: Gower.

Featherstone, M. and Hepworth. M. (1983) 'The Midlifestyle of George and Lynne', *Theory, Culture & Society*, 1(3).

Featherstone, M. and Hepworth, M. (1991) 'The Mask of Ageing and the Postmodern Life Course', in M. Featherstone, M. Hepworth and B.S. Turner (eds), *The Body: Social Process and Cultural Theory*. London: Sage.

Featherstone, M., Hepworth, M. and Turner, B.S. (eds) (1991) *The Body: Social Process and Cultural Theory*. London: Sage.

Featherstone, M. and Venn, C. (2006) 'Problematizing Global Knowledge: An Introduction', in special issue on Problematizing Global Knowledge (ed. M. Featherstone, C. Venn, R. Bishop and J. Phillips), *Theory, Culture & Society*, 23(2–3).

Feifer, M. (1985) *Going Places*. London: Macmillan.

Fenn, R.K. (1982) 'The Sociology of Religion: A Critical Survey', in T. Bottomore, S. Nowak and M. Sokolowska (eds), *Sociology: The State of the Art*. London.

Finch, J. and Vidal, J. (2007) 'You've checked the price and calorie count, now here's the carbon cost: Supermarket giant to introduce emission labels; Tesco promises 'green consumption revolution,' *Guardian*, 19 January.

Fisher, M., Bianchini, F., Montgomery, J. and Warpole, K. (1987) *Cities and City Cultures*, Birmingham: Birmingham Film and Television Festival.

Fisher, W.F. and Ponniah, T. (eds) (2003) *Another World Is Possible: Popular Alternatives to Globalization at the World Social Forum*. London: Zed Books.

Fiske, J. and Hartley, J. (1978) *Reading Television*. London: Methuen.

Forty, A. (1986) *Objects of Desire*. London: Thames and Hudson.

Foster, H. (ed.) (1984) *Postmodern Culture*. London: Pluto Press.

Foucault, M. (1970) *The Order of Things*. London: Tavistock.

Foucault, M. (1977) *Discipline and Punish*. Harmondsworth: Penguin.

Foucault, M. (1984) 'What Is Enlightenment?', in P. Rabinow (ed.), *The Foucault Reader*. Harmondsworth: Penguin.

Foucault, M. (1991) 'Nietzsche, Genealogy and History', in P. Rabinow (ed.), *The Foucault Reader*. Harmondsworth: Penguin.

Fraser, M., Kember, S. and Lury, C. (2005) 'Inventive Life: Approaches to the New Vitalism', *Theory, Culture and Society*, 22(1).

Fraser, M., Kember, S. and Lury, C. (eds) (2005) Inventive Life: Approaches to the New Vitalism', *Theory, Culture & Society* special issue, 22(1). Reprinted in the *Theory, Culture & Society* Book Series. London: Sage, 2006.

Fraser, N. (2007) 'Transnationalizing the Public Sphere: On the Legitimacy and Efficacy of Public Opinion in a Postwestphalian World', *Theory, Culture & Society*, 24(6).

Friedman, J. (1987) 'Prolegomena to the Adventures of Phallus in Blunderland: An Anti-Anti Discourse', *Culture and History*, 1(1).

Friedman, J. (1988) 'Cultural Logics of the Global System', *Theory, Culture & Society*, 5(2–3).

Frisby, D. (1981) *Sociological Impressionism: A Reassessment of Georg Simmel's Social Theory*, London: Heinemann.

Frisby, D. (1985a) 'Georg Simmel, First Sociologist of Modernity', *Theory, Culture & Society*, 2(3).

Frisby, D. (1985b) *Fragments of Modernity*. Oxford: Polity Press.

Frith, S. and Horne, H. (1987) *Art into Pop*. London: Methuen.

Gane, N. (2006) 'When We Have Never Been Human. What Is to Be Done. An Interview with Donna Haraway', *Theory, Culture & Society Annual Review*, 23(7–8).

Gaonkar, D. (1999) 'On Alternative Modernities', *Public Culture*, 11(1).

Garnham, N. (1987) 'Concepts of Culture, Public Policy and the Culture Industries', *Cultural Studies*, 1(1).

Garon, S. and MacLachlan, P.L. (2006) 'Introduction' to Garon, S. and MacLachlan, P.L. (eds), *The Ambivalent Consumer: Questioning Consumption in East Asia and the West*. Ithaca, NY: Cornell University Press.

Geertz, C. (1983) *Local Knowledge*. New York: Basic Books.

Geist, H. (1983) *Arcades: The History of a Building Type*. Boston, MA: MIT Press.

Gellner, E. (1979) 'The Social Roots of Egalitarianism', *Dialectics and Humanism*, 4.

Gershuny, J. and Jones, S. (1987) 'The Changing Work/Leisure Balance in Britain: 1961–1984', in J. Horne, D. Jary and A. Tomlinson (eds), *Sport, Leisure and Social Relations*. London: Routledge & Kegan Paul.

Gessner, V. and Schade, A. (1990) 'Conflicts of Culture in Cross-Border Legal Relations', *Theory, Culture & Society*, 7(2–3).

Giddens, A. (1973) *Capitalism and Modern Social Theory*. Cambridge: Cambridge University Press.

Giddens, A. (1981a) 'Modernism and Postmodernism', *New German Critique*, 22.

Giddens, A. (1981b) *A Contemporary Critique of Historical Materialism*. London: Macmillan.

Giddens, A. (1984) *The Constitution of Society*. Oxford: Polity Press.

Giddens, A. (1985) *The Nation State and Violence*. Cambridge: Polity Press.

Giddens, A. (1987a) 'Nine Theses on the Future of Sociology', in *Social Theory and Modern Sociology*. Cambridge: Polity Press.

Giddens, A. (1987b) 'Structuralism, Post-structuralism and the Production of Culture', in *Social Theory and Modern Sociology*. Cambridge: Polity Press.

Giddens, A. (1990) *The Consequences of Modernity*. Oxford: Polity Press

Giddens, A. (1991) *Modernity and Self-Identity*. Oxford: Polity.

Ginzburg, C. (1980) *The Worm and the Cheese*. London: Routledge & Kegan Paul.

Gluck, C. (1998) 'The Invention of Edo', in S. Vlastos (ed.), *Mirror of Modernity: Invention of Tradition in Modern Japan*. Berkeley: University of California Press.

Goffman, E. (1951) 'Systems of Class Status', *British Journal of Sociology*, 2.

Gore, A. (2006) *An Inconvenient Truth: The Planetary Emergency of Global Warming and What We Can Do About It*. London: Bloomsbury.

Goiten, S.D. (1967) *A Mediterranean Society: The Jewish Communities of the Arab World as Portrayed in the Documents of the Cairo Geniza*. Vol. 1. *Economic Foundations*. Berkeley: University of California Press.

Goody, J. (2004) *Capitalism and Modernity: the Great Debate*. Cambridge: Polity Press.

Goonatilake, S. (1998) *Towards a Global Science*. Bloomington: Indiana University Press.

Gott, R. (1986) 'The Crisis of Contemporary Culture', *Guardian*, 1 December, p. 10.

Goudsblom, J. (1987) 'On High and Low in Society and Sociology', *Sociologisch Tijdschrift*, 13(1).

Gouldner, A. (1971) *The Coming Crisis of Western Sociology*. London: Heinemann.
Gouldner, A. (1979) *The Future of the Intellectuals and the Rise of the New Class*. London: Macmillan.
Gunaratne, S. A. (2005) *The Dao of the Press: A Humanocentric Theory*. Cresskill, NJ: Hampton Press Inc.
Gunder Frank, A. (1998) *Re-ORIENT: Global Economy in the Asian Age*. Berkeley: University of California Press.
Gusfield, J.R. (1963) *Symbolic Crusade*. Urbana: University of Illinois Press.
Gusfield, J.R. and Michalowicz, J. (1984) 'Secular Symbolism', *Annual Review of Sociology*, 10.
Habermas, J. (1971) 'Technology, Science and Ideology', in *Toward a Rational Sociology*, London: Heinemann.
Habermas, J. (1975) *Legitimation Crisis*. Boston: Beacon Press.
Habermas, J. (1981a) 'Modernity versus Postmodernity', *New German Critique*, 22.
Habermas, J. (1981b) *Theorie des Kommunikativen Handelus*. Frankfurt: Suhrkamp.
Habermas, J. (1983) *The Philosophical Discourse of Modernity. Twelve Lectures*. Cambridge: Polity Press.
Habermas, J. (1984) *Theory of Communicative Action*, Vol. I. London: Heinemann..
Habermas, J. (1985a) 'Questions and Counter-questions', in R.J. Bernstein (ed.), *Habermas and Modernity*, Oxford: Polity Press.
Habermas, J. (1985b) 'Modernity: An Incomplete Project', in H. Foster (ed.), *Postmodern Culture*. London: Pluto.
Habermas, J. (1987) *Theory of Communicative Action*, Vol. II. Oxford: Polity Press.
Habermas, J. (1989) *The Structural Transformation of the Public Sphere*. Cambridge: Polity Press.
Habib, I. (1990) 'Merchant Communities in Precolonial India', in J.D. Tracy (ed.), *The Rise of Merchant Empires*. Cambridge: Cambridge University Press.
Haferkamp, H. (1987) 'Beyond the Iron Cage of Modernity: Achievement, Negotiation and Changes in the Power Structure', *Theory, Culture & Society*, 4(1).
Hall, J. (1985) *Powers and Liberties: The Causes and Consequences of the Rise of the West*. Oxford: Basil Blackwell.
Hall, S. and Gieben, B. (eds) (1991) *Formations of Modernity*. Oxford: Polity Press.
Hall, S. (1992) 'The Question of Cultural Identity', in S. Hall, D. Held and T McGrew (eds), *Modernity and Its Futures*. Oxford: Polity Press.
Hamilton, C. (2003) *Growth Fetish*. Sydney: Allen & Unwin.
Hammond, J.L. (1986) 'Yuppies', *Public Opinion Quarterly*, 50.
Hammond, P.E. (1986) 'Religion in the Modern World', in J.D. Hunter and S.C. Ainlay (eds), *Making Sense of Modern Times: P. L. Berger and the Vision of Interpretive Sociology*. London: Routledge & Kegan Paul.
Hanada, Tatsuro (2006) 'The Japanese "Public Sphere": The *Kugai*', in M. Featherstone et al. (eds), 'Problematizing Global Knowledge', *Theory, Culture & Society* special issue, 23(1–2).
Harootunian, H. (1998) 'Poetry', in S. Vlastos (ed.), *Mirror of Modernity: Invented Traditions of Modern Japan*. Berkeley: University of California Press.
Harootunian, H. (2000) *Overcome by Modernity*. Princeton, NJ: Princeton University Press.
Harvey, D. (1988) 'Voodoo Cities', *New Statesman and Society*, 30 September.
Hassan, I. (1985) 'The Culture of Postmodernism', *Theory, Culture & Society*, 2(3).
Haug, W. F. (1987) *Critique of Commodity Aesthetics*. Oxford: Polity Press.
Haug, W. F. (1987) *Commodity Aesthetics, Ideology and Culture*. New York: International General.
Hauser, A. (1982) *The Sociology of Art*. London: Routledge & Kegan Paul.
Hayashi, Kaori (2006) 'The Public in Japan', in M. Featherstone et al. (eds), 'Problematizing Global Knowledge', *Theory, Culture & Society* special issue, 23(1–2).
Hazard, P. (1964) *The European Mind 1680–1715*. Harmondsworth: Penguin.
Hebdige, D. (1983) 'In Poor Taste: Notes on Pop', *Block*, 3: 54–68.
Hebdige, D. (1988) *Hiding in the Light*. London: Routledge & Kegan Paul.
Heisig, J.W. (1996) *Philosophers of Nothingness: An Essay on the Kyoto School*. Honolulu: Hawaii University Press.
Hepworth, M. and Featherstone, M. (1982) *Surviving Middle Age*. Oxford: Basil Blackwell.

Herf, J. (1986) *Reactionary Modernism*. Cambridge: Cambridge University Press.

Hirsch, F. (1976) *The Social Limits to Growth*. Cambridge, MA: Harvard University Press.

Hirshman, A. (1982) *Shifting Involvements*. Oxford: Basil Blackwell.

Hobsbawm, E. and Ranger, T. (1983) *The Invention of Tradition*. Cambridge: Cambridge University Press.

Hobson, John M. (2004) *The Eastern Origins of Western Civilization*. Cambridge: Cambridge University Press.

Hobson, John M. (2006) 'East and West in Global History', in M. Featherstone et al. (eds), 'Problematizing Global Knowledge', *Theory, Culture & Society* special issue, 23(1–2).

Hochschild, A. (1983) *The Managed Heart*. Berkeley: California University Press.

Horkheimer, M. and Adorno, T. (1972) *Dialectic of Enlightenment*. New York: Herder & Herder.

Horne, D. (1984) *The Great Museum*. London: Pluto Press.

Hountondji, P.J. (1983) *African Philosophy: Myth and Reality*. Bloomington: Indiana University Press.

Hountondji, P.J. (2002) *The Struggle for Meaning: Reflections on Philosophy, Culture and Democracy in Africa*. Athens: Ohio University Press.

Hoy, D.C. (ed.) (1986) *Foucault: A Critical Reader*. Oxford: Basil Blackwell.

Hutcheon, L. (1984) *Narcissistic Narrative: The Metafictional Paradox*. London: Methuen.

Hutcheon, L. (1986–7) 'The Politics of Postmodernism', *Cultural Critique*, 5.

Hutcheon, L. (1987) 'Beginning to Theorize Postmodernism'. *Textual Practice*, 1(1).

Huyssen, A. (1981) 'The Search for Tradition: Avant-Garde and Postmodernism in the 1980s', *New German Critique*, 22.

Huyssen, A. (1984) 'Mapping the Postmodern', *New German Critique*, 33: 5–52.

Ikegami, E. (1995) *The Taming of the Samurai: Honorific Individualism and the Making of Modern Japan*. Cambridge, MA: Harvard University Press.

Ikegami, E. (2005) *Bonds of Civility*. Cambridge: Cambridge University Press.

Ingelhart, R. (1997) *Modernization and Postmodernization*. Princeton, NJ: Princeton University Press.

Ishihara, Shintaro (1991) *The Japan that Can Say No*. New York: Simon and Schuster.

Jackson, B. (1968) *Working Class Community*. London.

Jackson, P. (1985) 'Neighborhood Change in New York: The Loft Conversion Process', *Tijdschrift voor economische en sociale geografie*, 74(3).

Jacoby, R. (1987) The Last Intellectuals. New York: Basic Books.

Jameson, F. (1979) 'Reification and Utopia in Mass Culture', *Social Text*, 1(1).

Jameson, F. (1981) *The Political Unconscious*. Ithaca, NY: Cornell University Press.

Jameson, F. (1984a) 'Postmodernism: Or the Cultural Logic of Late Capitalism'. *New Left Review*, 146.

Jameson, F. (1984b) 'Postmodernism and the Consumer Society', in H. Foster (ed.), *Postmodern Culture*. London: Pluto Press.

Jameson, F. (1984c) 'The Politics of Theory', *New German Critique*, 33.

Jameson, F. (1984d) Foreword to J.F. Lyotard, *The Postmodern Condition*. Manchester: Manchester University Press.

Jameson, F. (1987) 'Regarding Postmodernism: A Conversation', *Social Text*, 17 (Fall).

Jameson, F. (1991) *Postmodernism or the Cultural Logic of Capitalism*. London: Verso.

Jencks, C. (1984) *The Language of Postmodern Architecture*. London: Academy.

Johnson, R. (1976) 'Barrington Moore, Perry Anderson and English Social Development', *Working Papers in Cultural Studies*, 9.

Johnson, R. (1979) 'Histories of Culture: Theories of Ideology: Notes on an Impasse', in M. Barrett, P. Corrigan, A. Kuhn and J. Wolff (eds), *Ideology and Cultural Reproduction*, London: Croom Helm.

Kalberg, S. (1987) 'The Origin and Expansion of *Kulturpessimismus*', *Sociological Theory*, 5 (Fall).

Kamata, S. (1983) *Japan in the Passing Lane*. New York: Pantheon.

Kant, I. (1790/1952) *Critique of Aesthetic Judgment*. London: Oxford University Press.

Kaplan, E.A. (1986) 'History, Spectator and Gender Address in Music Television', *Journal of Communications Inquiry*, 10(1).

Kaplan, E.A. (1987) *Rocking around the Clock: Music, Television, Postmodernism and Consumer Culture*. London: Methuen.

Kauffmann, R.L. (1986) 'Post-Criticism, or the Limits of Avant-Garde Theory', *Telos*, 67.

Kellner, D. (1983) 'Critical Theory. Commodities and the Consumer Society', *Theory, Culture & Society*, 13.

Kellner, D. (1987) 'Baudrillard, Semiurgy and Death', *Theory, Culture & Society*, 4(1).

Kellner, D. (1988) 'Postmodernism as Social Theory: Some Challenges and Problems'. *Theory. Culture & Society*, 5(2–3).

Klein, N. (2001) *No Logo*. London: Flamingo.

Kohler, M. (1977) 'Postmodernismus: Ein begriffsgeschichter Überblick', *America Studies*, 22(1).

Koselleck, R. (1993) *Futures Past: On the Semantics of Time*. New York: Columbia University Press.

Kramer, H. (1982) 'Postmodern: Art and Culture in the 1980s', *The New Criterion*, 1(1).

Kroll, Luisa and Allison Fass (eds) (2006) 'Billionaire Bacchanalia', *Forbes Magazine* 03.27.06, http://www.forbes.com/billionaires/

Kroker, A. (1985) 'Baudrillard's Marx', *Theory, Culture & Society*, 2(3).

Kroker, A. and Cook, D. (1987) *The Postmodern Scene*. New York: St Martin's Press.

Kroker, A. and Kroker, M. (1987) 'Body Digest', *Canadian Journal of Political and Social Theory*, 11(1–2).

Kuenzli, R. (1987) 'Nietzschean Strategies: Dada and Postmodernism', paper presented at the IALP Conference on Postmodernism, Lawrence. Kansas.

Kuper, A. (1988) *The Making of Primitive Society*. London: Routledge & Kegan Paul.

Ladurie, E. le Roy (1981) *Carnival in Romans*. Harmondsworth: Penguin.

Lamont, M. and Lareau, A. (1988) 'Culture Capital', *Sociological Theory*, 6(2).

Langer, B.D. (1984) 'Studies in from the Cold', in Veliz, C., Carroll, J., Goldlust. J., Pelz, W., Langer, B.D., Arnason, J., Heller, E., Mackie, F. and Brown, R., *Sociology of Culture*. Melbourne: La Trobe University.

Lasch, C. (1979) *The Culture of Narcissism*. New York: Norton.

Lasch, C. (1996) *The Revolt of the Elites*. New York: Norton.

Lash, S. (1988) 'Discourse or Figure? Postmodernism as a Regime of Signification', *Theory, Culture & Society*, 5(2–3).

Lash, S. (2005) *'Lebenssoziologie:* Georg Simmel in the Information Age,' *Theory, Culture & Society*, 22(3).

Lash, S. and Urry, J. (1987) *The End of Organised Capitalism*. Oxford: Polity Press.

Laslett, P. (1965) *The World We Have Lost*. London: Methuen.

Latour, B. (1993) *We Have Never Been Modern*, trans. C. Porter. Cambridge, MA: Harvard University Press.

Lazzaratto, M. (2007) 'Machines to Crystallize Time: Bergson', *Theory, Culture & Society*, 24(5).

Le Goff, J. (1984) *La Civilisation de l'occident médiéval*. Paris: Artaud.

Leach, W.R. (1993) *Land of Desire: Merchants, Power and the Rise of a New American Culture*. New York: Vintage.

Leal, O.F. and Oliven, R.G. (1988) 'Class Interpretations of a Soap Opera Narrative', *Theory, Culture & Society*, 5(1).

Lears, Jackson (1998) 'Reconsidering Abundance: A Plea for Ambiguity', in S. Strasser, C. McGovern and M. Judt (eds), *Getting and Spending: European and American Consumer Societies in the Twentieth Century*. Cambridge: Cambridge University Press.

Lee, R.L.M. (2006) 'Reinventing Modernity: Reflexive Modernizaion vs. Liquid Modernity vs. Multiple Modernities', *European Journal of Social Theory*, 9(3).

Lefebvre, H. (1971) *Everyday Life in the Modern World*. London: Allen Lane.

Lefebvre, H. (1978) *Einführung in die Modernität*. Frankfurt: Suhrkamp.

Leiss, W. (1978) *The Limits to Satisfaction*. London: Marion Boyars.

Leiss, W. (1983) 'The Icons of the Marketplace', *Theory, Culture & Society*, 1(3).

Leiss, W., Kline, S. and Jhally, S. (1986) *Social Communication in Advertising*. New York: Macmillan.

191

Lepenies, W. (1988) *Between Literature and Science: The Rise of Sociology*. Cambridge: Cambridge University Press.

Levathes, L. (1994) *When China Ruled the Seas*. New York: Oxford University Press.

Levine, D. (1985) *The Flight from Ambiguity*. Chicago: Chicago University press.

Levine, L. (1989) *Highbrow/Lowbrow: The Emergence of Cultural Hierarchy in America*. Cambridge, MA: Harvard University Press.

Lieberman, V. (ed.) (1999) *Beyond Binary Histories: Re-imagining Eurasia to c. 1830*. MI: Michigan University Press.

Liebersohn, H. (1988) *Fate and Utopia in German Sociology*. Cambridge, MA: MIT Press.

Linder, S.B. (1970) *The Harried Leisure Class*. New York: Columbia University Press.

Lockwood, D. (1964) 'Social Integration and System Integration', in G.K. Zollschan and W. Hirsch (eds), *Explorations in Social Change*. Boston, MA: Houghton Mifflin.

Lovelock, J. (2006) *The Revenge of Gaia: Why the Earth Is Fighting Back – and How We Can Still Save Humanity*. Harmondsworth: Allen Lane.

Lowenthal, L. (1961) *Literature, Popular Culture and Society*. Palo Alto, CA: Pacific Books.

Luckmann, B. (1971) 'The Small Life-Worlds of Modern Man', *Social Research*, 32.

Luckmann, T. (1967) *The Invisible Religion*. London: Macmillan.

Luhmann, N. (1998) *Observations on Modernity*. Stanford: Stanford University Press.

Lukács, G. (1971) *History and Class Consciousness*, trans. R. Livingstone. London: Merlin Press.

Lukes, S. (1973) *Emile Durkheim: His Life and Work*. Harmondsworth: Allen Lane.

Lunn. E. (1985) *Marxism and Modernism*. London: Verso.

Lyotard, J.F. (1971) *Discours, figure*. Paris: Klincksiek.

Lyotard, J.F. (1977) *Instructions païnnes*. Paris: Galilée.

Lyotard, J.F. (1984) *The Postmodern Condition*. Manchester: Manchester University Press.

Lyotard, J.F. (1986–7) 'Rules and Paradoxes or Svelte Appendix', *Cultural Critique*, 5.

Lyotard, J.F. (1988) 'Interview', *Theory, Culture & Society*, 5(2–3).

McClain, J., Merriman, J.M. and K. Ugawa (eds) (1994) *Edo and Paris*. Ithaca, NY: Cornell University Press.

McCracken, G. (1988) *Culture and Consumption*. Bloomington: Indiana U.P.

McGovern, C. (1998) 'Consumption and Citizenship in the United State, 1900–1940', in S. Strasser, C. McGovern and M. Judt (eds), *Getting and Spending: European and American Consumer Societies in the Twentieth Century*. Cambridge: Cambridge University Press.

McGregor, C. (1984) *Pop Goes the Culture*. London: Pluto Press.

McKendrick, N., Brewer, J. and Plumb, J.H. (1982) *The Birth of a Consumer Society*. London: Europa.

Maffesoli. M. (1988a) 'Affectual Postmodernism and the Megapolis', *Threshold IV*.1.

Maffesoli, M. (1988b) 'Jeux de Masques: Postmoderne Tribalisme', *Design Issues*, 4(1–2).

Maffesoli, M. (1991) 'The Ethic of Aesthetics', *Theory Culture & Society*, 8(1).

Malik, S. (2006) 'Global Sovereignty', in special issue on Problematizing Global Knowledge (ed. M. Featherstone, C. Venn, R. Bishop and J. Phillips), *Theory, Culture & Society*, 23(2–3).

Malraux, A. (1967) *Museum without Walls*. London.

Mandel, E. (1975) *Late Capitalism*. London: New Left Books.

Mann, M. (1986) *The Sources of Social Power*. Cambridge: Cambridge University Press.

Mannheim, K. (1956) 'The Democratization of Culture', in *Essays on the Sociology of Culture*. London: Routledge & Kegan Paul.

Marcuse, H. (1964) *One Dimensional Man*. London: Routledge & Kegan Paul.

Marcuse, H. (1969) *An Essay on Liberation*. Harmondsworth: Penguin.

Martin, B. (1981) *A Sociology of Contemporary Cultural Change*. Oxford: Basil Blackwell.

Marwick, A. (1988) *Beauty in History*. London: Thames & Hudson.

Masahide, Bito (1992) *Edo jidai towa nanika: nihonshijoo no kinsei to kindai*. Tokyo: Iwanami Shoten.

Mattelart, A. (1979) *Multinational Corporations and the Control of Culture*. Brighton: Harvester Press.

Mbembe, A. (2001) *On the Postcolony*. Berkeley: University of California Press.

Megill, A. (1985) *Prophet of Extremity*. Berkeley: University of California Press.

Mennell, S. (1989) *Norbert Elias: Civilization and the Human Self-Image*. Oxford: Blackwell.

Mercer, C. (1983) 'A Poverty of Desire: Pleasure and Popular Politics', in T. Bennett et al. (eds), *Formations of Pleasure*. London: Routledge & Kegan Paul.

Meyrowitz, J. (1985) *No Sense of Place*. Oxford: Oxford University Press.

Miller, D. (1994) *Modernity: An Ethnographic Approach*. Oxford: Berg.

Millot, B. (1988) 'Symbol, Desire and Power', *Theory, Culture & Society*, 5(4).

Mintz, S. (1995) *Sweetness and Power: The Place of Sugar in Modern History*. Harmondsworth: Penguin.

Miyoshi, M. (2003) 'Ivory Tower in Eskrow', in M. Myoshi and H. Harootunian (eds), *Learning Places: The Afterlife of Area Studies*. Durham, NC: Duke University Press.

Mullin, B. and Taylor. L. (1986) *Uninvited Guests*. London.

Murphy, R. (1989) *Social Closure: The Theory of Monopolization and Exclusion*. Oxford: Clarendon Press.

Needham, J. (1980) *Shorter Science and Civilization in China*. Vols 1–5. Cambridge: Cambridge University Press.

Nuttall, J. and Carmichael, R. (1977) *Common Factors/Vulgar Factions*. London: Routledge & Kegan Paul.

Olma, S. (2007) 'Introduction', to special section on Life's (Re)Emergences, *Theory, Culture & Society*, 24(5).

Olsen, D. (1986) *The City as a Work of Art*. New Haven, CT: Yale University Press.

O'Neill, J. (1988) 'Religion and Postmodernism: The Durkheimian Bond in Bell and Jameson', *Theory, Culture & Society*, 5(2–3).

Ong, Aihwa (2006) 'Mutations in Citizenship', in special issue on Problematizing Global Knowledge (ed. M. Featherstone, C. Venn, R. Bishop and J. Phillips), *Theory, Culture & Society*, 23(2–3).

Osiel, M.J. (1984) 'Going to the People: Popular Culture and the Intellectuals in Brazil', *European Journal of Sociology*, 25.

Pagden, A. (1993) *European Encounters with the New World*. New Haven, CT: Yale University Press.

Palmer, R.E. (1977) 'Postmodernity and Hermeneutics', *Boundary*, 2, 22.

Parenti, M. (2002) The Super Rich Are Out of Sight', *Common Dreams.org*, 27 December.

Parkin, F. (1979) *Marxism and Class Theory: A Bourgeois Critique*. London: Tavistock.

Parsons, T. (1937) *The Structure of Social Action*. New York: McGraw Hill.

Parsons, T. (1951) *The Social System*. New York: Free Press.

Parsons, T. (1961) 'Culture and the Social System: Introduction', in T. Parsons, E. Shils, K.D. Naegele and J.R. Pitts (eds), *Theories of Society*. New York: Free Press.

Patomäki, Heikki (2006) 'Global Democracy', in special issue on Problematizing Global Knowledge (ed. M. Featherstone, C. Venn, R. Bishop and J. Phillips), *Theory, Culture & Society*, 23(2–3).

Patomäki, Heikki and Teivainen, T. (2004) 'The World Social Forum: An Open Space or a Movement of Movements?', *Theory, Culture & Society*, 21(6).

Pawley, M. (1986) 'Architecture: All the History that Fits', *Guardian*, 3 December: 10.

Perdue, P. (1987) *Exhausting the Earth: State and Peasant in Hunan 1500–1850*. Cambridge, MA: Harvard University Press.

Perkins, F. (2004) *Leibniz and China*. Cambridge: Cambridge University Press.

Pieterse, J.N. (2006) 'Oriental Globalization', in M. Featherstone et al. (eds), 'Problematizing Global Knowledge', *Theory, Culture & Society* special issue, 23(1–2).

Poggioli, R. (1973) 'The Concept of the Avant-Garde', in T. Burns and E. Burns (eds), *The Sociology of Literature and Drama*. Harmondsworth: Penguin.

Pollock, G. (1985/6) 'Art, Artschool, Culture: Individualism after the Death of the Artist', *Block*, 11.

Pomeranz, K. (2000) *The Great Divergence: China, Europe and the Making of the Modern World Economy*. Princeton, NJ: Princeton University Press.

Poster, M. (1975) *Existential Marxism in Postwar France*. Princeton, NJ: Princeton University Press.

Preteceille, E. and Terrail, J.P. (1985) *Capitalism, Consumption and Needs*. Oxford: Basil Blackwell.

Rajchman, J. (1985) 'Foucault and the End of Modernism', in *Michel Foucault: The Freedom of Philosophy*. New York: Columbia University Press.

Randerson, J. (2006) 'World's richest 1% own 40% of all wealth, UN report discovers', *Guardian*, 6 December.

Raz, J. and Raz, A.E. (1996) '"America" Meets "Japan": A Journey for Real between Two Imaginaries', *Theory, Culture & Society*, 13(3).

Reay, B. (1985a) 'Introduction', in *Popular Culture in Seventeenth Century England*. London: Croom Helm.

Reay, B. (1985b) 'Popular Religion', in *Popular Culture in Seventeenth Century England*. Cambridge: Cambridge University Press.

Reddy, W.M. (1984) *The Rise of Market Culture*. Cambridge: Cambridge University Press.

Reich, R. (2006) 'The New Rich–Rich Gap', *Newsweek*.

Robbins, D. (1987) 'Sport, Hegemony and the Middle Class: The Victorian Mountaineers', *Theory, Culture & Society*, 4(4).

Roberts, D. (1988) 'Beyond Progress: The Museum and Montage', *Theory, Culture & Society*, 5(2–3).

Robertson, R. (1978) *Meaning and Change*. Oxford: Basil Blackwell.

Robertson, R. (1987) 'Globalization Theory and Civilizational Analysis', *Comparative Civilizations Review*, Fall.

Robertson, R. (1988) 'The Sociological Significance of Culture: Some General Considerations', *Theory, Culture & Society*, 5(1).

Robertson, R. (1990) 'Mapping the Global Conditions', *Theory, Culture & Society*, 7(2–3).

Rochberg-Halton, E. (1986) *Meaning and Modernity*. Chicago: Chicago University Press.

Rojek, C. (1985) *Capitalism and Leisure Theory*. London: Tavistock.

Rose, G. (1978) *The Melancholy Science: An Introduction to the Thought of Theodor W. Adorno*. London: Macmillan.

Rowe, W.T. (1984) *Hankow: Commerce and Society in China 1796–1889*. Stanford, CA: Stanford University Press.

Sahlins, M. (1974) *Stone Age Economics*. London: Tavistock.

Sahlins, M. (1976) *Culture and Practical Reason*. Chicago: Chicago University Press.

Said, E.W. (1978) *Orientalism*. London: Routledge & Kegan Paul.

Sakai, N. (1989) 'Modernity and Its Critique: The Problem of Universalism and Particularism,' in H. Harootunian and M. Myoshi (eds), *Postmodernism and Japan*. Durham, NC: Duke University Press.

Sakai, N. (1993) 'Return to the West/Return to the East: Watsuji Tetsuro's Anthropology and Discussions of Authenticity', in M. Myoshi and H.D. Harootunian (eds), *Japan in the World*. Durham, NC: Duke University Press.

Sakai, N. (1998) *Translation and Subjectivity*. Minneapolis: Minnesota University Press.

Sakai, N. (2001) 'Introduction', *Traces*, No 1.

Santos, Boaventura (2006) 'Globalizations', in special issue on Problematizing Global Knowledge (ed. M. Featherstone, C. Venn, R. Bishop and J. Phillips), *Theory, Culture & Society*, 23(2–3).

Sassatelli, R. (2006) 'Virtue, Responsibility and Consumer Choice', in J. Brewer and F. Trentman (eds), *Consuming Cultures, Global Perspectives*. Oxford: Berg.

Sayre, R. and Löwy, M. (1984) 'Figures of Romantic Anti-Capitalism', *New German Critique*, 32.

Sayyid, S. (2006) 'Islam and Knowledge', in special issue on Problematizing Global Knowledge (ed. M. Featherstone, C. Venn, R. Bishop and J. Phillips), *Theory, Culture & Society*, 23(2–3).

Schapiro, M. (1961) 'Style', in M. Phillipson (ed.), *Aesthetics Today*. London: Meridian Books.

Schifferes, S. (2006) 'The End of the American Dream?' *BBC News* website, 4 September.

Schlesinger, P. (1987) 'On National Identity: Some Conceptions and Misconceptions Criticised', *Social Science Information*, 26(2).

Schmidt, M. (1988) 'The Place of Culture in Parsons's Theory of Social Action', paper presented it the 3rd American–German Sociological Theory Conference, Bremen.

Schmidt, V.H. (2006) 'Multiple Modernities or Varieties of Modernity?', *Current Sociology*, 54(1).

Schor, J. (1999) 'The New Politics of Consumption: Why Americans want so much more than they need', *Boston Review*.

Schudson, M. (1986) *Advertising: The Uneasy Persuasion*. New York: Harper.

Schudson, M. (1987) 'The New Validation of Popular Culture', *Critical Studies in Mass Communications*, 4.

Shusterman, R. (1988) 'Postmodernist Aestheticism: A New Moral Philosophy?', *Theory, Culture & Society*, 5(2–3).

Schwartz, B. (1983) *Vertical Classification*. Chicago: Chicago University Press.

Schweder, R.A. (1984) 'Anthropology's Romantic Rebellion against the Enlightenment', in R.A. Schweder and R.A. Levine (eds), *Culture Theory*. Cambridge: Cambridge University Press.

Seigel, J. (1986) *Bohemian Paris*. New York: Viking.

Sennett, R. (1976) *The Fall of Public Man*. Cambridge: Cambridge University Press.

Sennett, R. (1999) 'Growth and Failure: The New Political Economy and Its Culture', in M. Featherstone and S. Lash (eds), *Spaces of Culture: City, Nation, World*. London: Sage.

Sennett, R. (2006) *The Culture of the New Capitalism*. New Haven, CT: Yale University Press.

Shama, S. (1987) *The Embarrassment of Riches: An Interpretation of Dutch Culture in the Golden Age*. London: Fontana.

Shields, R. (1987) 'Social Spatialization and the Built Environment: The West Edmonton Mall'. Sussex University, mimeo.

Shields, R. (1990) '"The System of Pleasure": Liminality and the Carnivalesque in Brighton', *Theory, Culture & Society*, 7(1).

Shils, E. and Young, M. (1953) 'The Meaning of the Coronation', *Sociological Review*, 1(2).

Silberman, B.A. (2002) 'The Disappearance of Modern Japan: Japan and Social Science', in H. Harootunian and M. Myoshi (eds), *Learning Places: The Afterlives of Area Studies*. Durham, NC: Duke University Press.

Silverberg, M. (1998) 'The Café Waitress Serving Modern Japan', in S. Vlastos (ed.), *Mirror of Modernity: Invented Traditions of Modern Japan*. Berkeley: University of California Press.

Silverman, D. (1986) *Selling Culture*. New York.

Simmel, G. (1978) *The Philosophy of Money*, trans. T. Bottomore and D. Frisby. London: Routledge & Kegan Paul.

Simmel, G. (1997a) 'Fashion', in D. Frisby and M. Featherstone (eds), *Simmel on Culture*. London: Sage.

Simmel, G. (1997b) 'The Metropolis and Mental Life,' in D. Frisby and M. Featherstone (eds), *Simmel on Culture*. London: Sage.

Simone, A. (2004) *For the City Yet to Come: Changing African Life in Four Cities*. Durham, NC: Duke University Press.

Simpson, C. (1981) *SoHo: The Artist in the City*. Chicago: Chicago University Press.

Slater, P. (1973) *The Origin and Significance of the Frankfurt School*. London: Routledge & Kegan Paul.

Smith, A. (1990) 'Is There a Global Culture'?', *Theory, Culture & Society*, 7(2–3).

Smith, A.D. (1998) *Nationalism and Modernism*. London: Routledge.

Smith, D. (1988) 'History, Geography and Sociology: Lessons from the Annales School', *Theory. Culture & Society*, 5(1).

Sobel, E. (1982) *Lifestyle*. New York: Academic Press.

Sontag, S. (1967) *Against Interpretation*. London: Eyre & Spottiswoode.

Sorokin, P. (1957) *Social and Cultural Dynamics*. Boston, MA: Porter Sargent.

Spanos, W. (1987) *Repetitions: The Postmodern Occasion in Literature*. Baton Rouge: Louisiana State University Press.

Spencer, L. (1985) 'Allegory in the World of the Commodity: The Importance of Central Park', *New German Critique*, 34.

Stallybrass, P. and White, A. (1986) *The Politics and Poetics of Transgression*. London: Methuen.

Stauth, G. and Turner, B.S. (1988) 'Nostalgia, Postmodernism and the Critique of Mass Culture', *Theory, Culture & Society*, 5(2–3).

Steiner, G. (1971) *In Bluebeard's Castle: Some Notes Towards the Re-definition of Culture*. London: Faber and Faber.

Stratton, J. (1989) 'Postmodernism and Popular Music', *Theory, Culture & Society*, 6(1).

Susman, W. (1979) 'Personality and the Making of Twentieth Century Culture', in J. Higham and P.K. Conkin (eds), *New Directions in American Cultural History*. Baltimore, MD: Johns Hopkins University Press.

Susman, W. (1982) *Culture and Commitment 1929–1945*. New York: Braziller.

Swingewood, A. (1977) *The Myth of Mass Culture*. London: Macmillan.

Tagg, J. (1985/6) 'Postmodernism and the Born Again Avant-Garde', *Block*, 11.

Tamari, T. (2006) 'The Rise of the Department Store and the Aestheticization of Everyday Life in Early Twentieth Century Japan', *International Journal of Japanese Sociology*, 15.

Taussig, M. (2007) 'Redeeming Indigo', *Theory, Culture & Society*, 24(5).

Taylor, C. (1999) 'Two Theories of Modernity', *Public Culture*, 11(1).

Terranova, T. (2007) 'Future Public: Hegemonic and Counter-hegemonic Tactics for Bioracist Times', *Theory, Culture & Society*, 24(2).

Thompson, K. (1986) *Beliefs and Ideology*. London: Tavistock.

Tiryakian, E.A. (1978) 'Emile Durkheim', in T.B. Bottomore and R. Nisbet (eds), *A History of Sociological Analysis*. London: Heinemann.

Todorov, T. (1992) *The Conquest of America*. New York: Harper.

Toscano, A. (2007) 'Vital Strategies: Maurizio Lazzarato and the Metaphysics of Contemporary Capitalism', *Theory, Culture & Society*, 24(5).

Touraine, A. (1985) 'An Introduction to the Study of Social Movements', *Social Research*, 52(4).

Turner, B.S. (1983) *Religion and Social Theory*. London: Heinemann.

Turner, B.S. (1986) *Equality*. London: Tavistock.

Turner, B.S. (1987) 'A Note on Nostalgia', *Theory, Culture & Society*, 4(1).

Turner, B.S. (1988) *Status*. Milton Keynes: Open University Press.

Turner, B.S. (1990) 'Introduction: Reflections on the Dominant Ideology Thesis after a Decade', in B.S. Turner (ed.), *The Dominant Ideology Debate*. London: Allen and Unwin.

Turner, B.S. (2005) 'Obituaries and the Legacy of Derrida', *Theory, Culture & Society*, 22(2).

Turner, V.W. (1969) *The Ritual Process: Structure and Anti-Structure*. London: Allen Lane.

Ugarteche, O. (2007) 'Transationalizing the Public Sphere: A Critique of Fraser', *Theory, Culture & Society*, 24(4).

Ulmer, G.L. (1984) 'The Object of Post-Criticism', in H. Foster (ed.), *Postmodern Culture*. London: Pluto Press.

Urry, J. (1988) 'Cultural Change and Contemporary Holiday-making', *Theory, Culture & Society*, 5(1).

Urry, J. (2005) 'Introduction', to special issue on Complexity, *Theory, Culture & Society*, 22(5).

van Reijen, W. (1988) '*The Dialectic of Enlightenment* Read as Allegory', *Theory, Culture & Society*, 5(2–3).

Vattimo, G. (1985) *La fine della modernita*. Milan: Aldo Garzanti Editore.

Vaughan, M. (1986) 'Intellectual Power and the Powerlessness of Intellectuals', *Theory, Culture & Society*, 3(3).

Venn, C. (2005) 'Appreciations: Jacques Derrida 1930–2004', *Theory, Culture & Society*, 22(2).

Venn, C. (2006) *The Postcolonial Challenge*. London: Sage.

Venn, C. (2007) 'Averroes and Medicine', *New Encyclopaedia Project*. Unpublished note.

Venn, C. and Featherstone, M. (2006) 'Modernity', in special issue on Problematizing Global Knowledge (ed. M. Featherstone, C. Venn, R. Bishop and J. Phillips), *Theory, Culture & Society*, 23(2–3).

Venturi, R., Scott Brown, D. and Izenour, D. (1977) *Learning from Las Vegas: The Forgotten Symbolism of Architecture Form*. Cambridge: MA: MIT Press.

Wall, D. (1987) 'Oppenheim under the Sign of the Mirror', paper presented to the IALP Conference on Postmodernism, Kansas.

Wallerstein, I. (1974) *The Modern World-System I*. New York: Academic Press.

Wallerstein, I. (1980) *The Modern World-System II*. New York: Academic Press.

Walvin, J. (1978) *Beside the Seaside: A Social History of the Popular Seaside Holiday*. London: Allen Lane.

Weber, M. (1930) *The Protestant Ethic and The Spirit of Capitalism*. London: Allen and Unwin.
Weber, M. (1949) '"Objectivity" in Social Science and Social Policy', in *The Methodology of the Social Sciences*. Glencoe, IL: Free Press.
Weber, M. (1968) *Economy and Society*. 3 vols. Bedminster Press.
Weiss, J. (1986) 'Wiederverzauberung der Welt', *Kölner Zeitschrift für Soziologie und Sozialpsychologie*, 27.
White, H. (1973) *Metahistory*. Baltimore, MD: Johns Hopkins University Press.
Whyte, W.H. (1956) *The Organization Man*. New York: Simon & Schuster.
Wiener, M. (1981) *English Culture and the Decline of the Industrial Spirit*. Cambridge: Cambridge University Press.
Williams, R. (1958) *Culture and Society 1780–1950*. Harmondsworth: Penguin.
Williams, R. (1961) *The Long Revolution*. Harmondsworth: Penguin.
Williams, R. (1976) *Keywords*. London: Fontana.
Williams, R. (1979) *Politics and Letters*. London: New Left Books.
Williams, R. (1983) *Towards 2000*. London: Chatto & Windus.
Williams, R. (1989) 'Common Culture' and 'Culture is Ordinary', both in *Resources of Hope*. London: New Left Books.
Williams, R.H. (1982) *Dream Worlds: Mass Consumption in Late Nineteenth Century France*. Berkeley: California University Press.
Williamson, J. (1986) *Consuming Passions*. London: Marion Boyars.
Willis, P. (1978) *Profane Culture*. London: Routledge & Kegan Paul.
Wilson, E. (1985) 'Women, Knitting and Art', *Marxism Today*.
Winship, J. (1983) '*Options* – For the Way You Want to Live Now, or a Magazine for Superwoman', *Theory, Culture & Society*, 1(3).
Wolf, E.R. (1982) *Europe and the People without History*. Berkeley: California University Press.
Wolff, J. (1983) *Aesthetics and the Sociology of Art*. London: Allen & Unwin.
Wolff, J. (1985) 'The Invisible *Flâneuse*', *Theory, Culture & Society*, 2(3).
Wolin, R. (1982) *Walter Benjamin: An Aesthetic of* Redemption. New York: Columbia University Press.
Wolin, R. (1986) 'Foucault's Aesthetic Decisionism', *Telos*, 67.
Wouters, C. (1979) 'Negotiating with de Swaan'. Amsterdam, mimeo.
Wouters, C. (1986) 'Formalization and Informalization: Changing Tension Balances in Civilizing Processes', *Theory, Culture & Society*, 3(2).
Wouters, C. (1987) 'Developments in the Behavioural Codes between the Sexes: The Formalization of Informalization in the Netherlands 1930–1985', *Theory, Culture & Society*, 4(2–3).
Wouters, C. (1989) 'The Sociology of Emotions and Flight Attendants: Hochschild's *Managed Heart*', *Theory, Culture and Society*, 6(2).
Zafrani, H, (1996) *Juifs de'Andalousie e du Maghreb*. Paris: Maisonneuve & Larose.
Zolberg, V. (1984) 'American Art Museums: Sanctuary or Free-For-All?', *Social Forces*, 63 (December).
Zukin, S. (1982a) 'Art in the Arms of Power', *Theory and Society*, 11.
Zukin, S. (1982b) *Loft Living*. Baltimore, MD: Johns Hopkins University Press.
Zukin, S. (1987) 'Gentrification', *Annual Review of Sociology*.
Zukin, S. (1988a) 'The Postmodern Debate over Urban Form', *Theory, Culture & Society*, 5(2–3).
Zukin, S. (1988b) *Loft Living*, 2nd edn. London: Hutchinson/Radius.

Index